WORLD HISTORY AND THE MYSTERIES

IN THE LIGHT OF ANTHROPOSOPHY

WORLD HISTORY AND THE MYSTERIES

IN THE LIGHT OF ANTHROPOSOPHY

Nine lectures given in Dornach between 23 December and 1 January 1924 during the Foundation Meeting of the General Anthroposophical Society

TRANSLATED BY GEORGE AND MARY ADAMS, FREDERICK AMRINE AND DOROTHY OSMOND

EDITED BY FREDERICK AMRINE

INTRODUCTION BY FREDERICK AMRINE

RUDOLF STEINER

RUDOLF STEINER PRESS

CW 233

Rudolf Steiner Press
Hillside House, The Square
Forest Row, RH18 5ES

www.rudolfsteinerpress.com

Published by Rudolf Steiner Press 2021

Originally published in German under the title *Die Weltgeschichte in anthroposophischer Beleuchtung und als Grundlage der Erkenntnis des Menschengeistes* (volume 233 in the *Rudolf Steiner Gesamtausgabe* or Collected Works) by Rudolf Steiner Verlag, Dornach. Based on shorthand notes that were not reviewed or revised by the speaker. This authorized translation is based on the fifth German edition (1991), edited by Caroline Wispler

Published by permission of the Rudolf Steiner Nachlassverwaltung, Dornach

A catalogue record for this book is available from the British Library

ISBN 978 1 85584 588 6

Cover by Morgan Creative
Typeset by Symbiosys Technologies, Vishakapatnam, India
Printed and bound by 4Edge Ltd., Essex

CONTENTS

Publisher's Note

These lectures on world history in the light of anthroposophy were presented to members of the Anthroposophical Society in the evenings during the Christmas Foundation Conference, when Rudolf Steiner refounded the Anthroposophical Society. Rudolf Steiner's reasons for doing this, the resolutions, speeches, discussion and the Articles of Incorporation and the complete proceedings of the Christmas Conference can be found in GA 260, published in English under the title *The Christmas Conference for the Foundation of the General Anthroposophical Society 1923-1924* (Anthroposophic Press, 1990).

Introduction

The cycle *World History and the Mysteries In the Light of Anthroposophy* was given on the evenings of the Christmas Conference. Indeed, the last two lectures in the cycle are also included in the separate volume that records that Conference. Thus, it is safe to assume that the two events were all of one piece, and that the separation into two volumes is quite arbitrary. In order to do justice to *World History*, we have to view it as integral to the Christmas Conference. Therefore, let us reconstruct the entire event. This will give us a much fuller picture of what is actually going on in the cycle.

*

24 December, 1923

Morning: A separate Society for the young? Treatment of the lecture cycles, 'a tragic chapter in the development of our Anthroposophical Society.'[1] Reading of the Statutes of the Society.

Rudolf Steiner proposes to adopt the presidency of the new Society:

> Out of all this, my dear friends, two alternative questions arose. In 1912, 1913 I said for good reasons that the Anthroposophical Society would now have to run itself, that it would have to manage its own affairs, and that I would have to withdraw into a position of an adviser who did not participate directly in any actions. Since then things have changed. After grave efforts in the past weeks to overcome my inner resistance I have now reached the realization that it would become impossible for me to continue to lead the Anthroposophical Movement within the Anthroposophical Society if this Christmas Conference were not to agree that I should once more take on in every way the leadership, that is the presidency, of the Anthroposophical Society to be founded here in Dornach at the Goetheanum. [49]

---

1 *The Christmas Conference For the Foundation of the General Anthroposophical Society 1923/1924*. Hudson, New York: Anthroposophic Press, 1990, p. 53.

Evening: GA 233, Lecture One. Three kinds of memory: localized, rhythmic, temporal.

25 December, 1923

Morning: The first reading of the Foundation Stone meditation. General Secretaries from various countries report.

Afternoon: Questions and answers on the Statutes.

Evening: GA 233, Lecture Two. The dreamlike Asiatic experience of the world. Conquest and enslavement: Asian consciousness of life versus Greek fear of death.

26 December, 1923

Morning: Interpretation of the Foundation Stone meditation. Reports and discussions.

Evening: GA 233, Lecture Three. The reality underlying the Epic of Gilgamesh. Biographical hints: Eabani reincarnates as Aristotle and Gilgamesh as Alexander the Great.

27 December, 1923

Morning: Interpretation of the Foundation Stone meditation. Discussion of the Statutes.

Evening: GA 233, Lecture Four. The Hibernian and Ephesian Mysteries. The tragic destinies of Aristotle and Alexander the Great. The medieval *Song of Alexander*. Aristotle teaches Alexander the doctrine of the four elements.

28 December, 1923

Morning: Interpretation of the Foundation Stone meditation. Further discussion of the Statutes.

Evening: GA 233, Lecture Five. The decline of the Ephesian Mysteries. The shadowy but still divine consciousness of Greek culture. The torching of the Temple of Ephesus on the day of Alexander's birth.

29 December, 1923

Morning: Meeting of the General Secretaries. Interpretation of the Foundation Stone meditation.

Evening: GA 233, Lecture Six. Further descent into Roman civilization. Julian the Apostate is the exception that proves the rule. Human thinking becomes abstract. Exclusion of the spirit. Aristotle's works, saved in the East, returned to Europe with Scholasticism. The centrality of Aristotle as a spiritual guide.

30 December, 1923

Morning: Interpretation of the Foundation Stone meditation. Discussion of practicalities.

Evening: GA 233, Lecture Seven. The rise of the consciousness soul, 'an unfruitful period in the evolution of the human spirit'. [109] The actual forces at work in human beings.

31 December, 1923

Morning: Interpretation of the Foundation Stone meditation. Lecture: The Idea of the Future Building in Dornach.

Afternoon: Meeting of the Swiss Delegation, discussion of practicalities.

Evening: GA 233, Lecture Eight. The solemn oath.

> But there is a *word* – a word that has come down to us in history and that can speak powerfully to the human heart even in external historical tradition, but that speaks with peculiar force and earnestness when we see it shape itself out of strange and unparalleled events, when we see it written with external letters in the history of

humanity, though the writing be only visible for a moment in the spirit. I declare to you that, wherever the eye of the spirit is turned to the deed of Herostratus, to the burning of Ephesus, then, in those flames of fire may be read the ancient words: The jealousy of the gods. [116]

And so in a certain sense we may say that in the Goetheanum we had something that could awaken in an altogether new form of memory of the old. [123]

Whoever looked upon this Goetheanum with feeling and understanding could find in it a memory of the Temple of Ephesus.

The memory, however, grew to be terribly painful. For in a manner not at all unlike what befell Ephesus in earlier time, exactly at the moment in its evolution when the Goetheanum was ready to become the bearer of the renewal of spiritual life, in that very moment there was flung into it a burning brand. [124]

1 January, 1924

Morning: Interpretation of the Foundation Stone meditation. Lecture: The Rebuilding of the Goetheanum.
Evening: GA 233, Lecture Nine. The Guardian of the Threshold.

The fact of the matter is this: the impulse that must be working in what is now to go out from Dornach must – as I emphasized from every possible point of view during the Conference itself – be an impulse originating in the spiritual world, not on the Earth. Our striving here is to develop the strength to follow impulses from the spiritual world. That is why, in the evening lectures during this Christmas Conference, I spoke of manifold impulses at work in the course of historical evolution in order that hearts could be opened for the reception of the spiritual impulses which have yet to stream into the earthly world, which are not derived from that world itself. Everything from which the earthly world hitherto has rightly been the vehicle, proceeded from the spiritual world. And if we are to achieve anything fruitful for the earthly world, the impulses for it must be brought from the spiritual world. [129]

We must leave this Conference which has led to the founding of the General Anthroposophical Society, not with trifling, but with solemn thoughts. But I think that nobody need have experienced any pessimism as a result of what took place here at Christmas. We had, it is true, to pass the tragic ruins of the Goetheanum every day, but I think that those who climbed the hill and pass the ruins during the Conference have become aware of what our friends have understood in their hearts and that the following thought will have become a reality to them: Spiritual flames of fire will go forth from the new Goetheanum that will come into being through our activity and devotion. And the greater the courage with which to

> conduct the affairs of anthroposophy that we take with us from this Conference, the more effectively we have grasped the spiritual impulse of hope that pervaded the Conference. [135-136]

*

On studying the progress of the Christmas Conference, we can see that there are three tremendous climaxes: Steiner's assumption of the leadership of the Anthroposophical Society, the speaking of the Foundation Stone on Christmas morning, and the solemn oath that he asks the assembled members to take on New Year's Eve.

Steiner barely divulged it to the membership, but assuming leadership of the Society was actually enormously daring. Heretofore, Rudolf Steiner had strenuously separated himself from the Anthroposophical Society. He had served only as a spiritual advisor, and had not even joined as a member. He was unsure whether the spiritual world wanted him to unite his personal karma with the karma of the Society. The spiritual world does not respond in principle to such a question in advance: the spiritual researcher must act freely, and then await the response. Rudolf Steiner presented his decision to the members with unqualified assurance, but it was actually a question posed to the spiritual world. How would it respond? He did not know. The stakes were the highest imaginable: the spiritual world might respond favorably, increasing his esoteric insight, but it might also respond unfavorably, putting his entire clairvoyant faculty in jeopardy.

The reading of the Foundation Stone culminated in the following words:

> Let us ever remain aware of this Foundation Stone for the Anthroposophical Society, formed today. In all that we shall do, in the outer world and here, to further, to develop and to fully unfold the Anthroposophical Society, let us preserve the remembrance of the Foundation Stone which we have today lowered into the soil of our hearts. Let us seek in the threefold being of man, which teaches us to love, which teaches us the universal Imagination, which teaches us the universal thoughts; let us seek, in this threefold being, the substance of universal love

> which we lay as the foundation, let us seek in this threefold being the archetype of the Imagination according to which we shape the universal love within our hearts, let us seek the power of thoughts from the heights which enable us to let shine forth in fitting manner this dodecahedral Imagination which has received its form through love! Then shall we carry away with us from here what we need. Then shall the Foundation Stone which has received its substance from universal love and human love, its picture image, its form, from universal Imagination and human Imagination, and its brilliant radiance from universal thoughts and human thoughts, its brilliant radiance which whenever we recollect this moment can shine towards us with warm light, with light that spurs on our deeds, our thinking, our feeling and our willing. [72-73]

It is perhaps significant that the oath did not fall within the morning's proceedings, but rather during the evening lectures. Here are the key moments:

> Our pain and grief cling to the old Goetheanum. But we shall only show ourselves worthy of having been permitted to build this Goetheanum if we fulfill the task that yet remains to us, if we take today a solemn pledge, each one of us before the highest, the divine, that we bear within our soul, a pledge to hold faithfully in remembrance the spiritual impulses that have had their outward expression in the Goetheanum that is gone. [126]
>
> My dear friends, you receive me by rising in memory of the old Goetheanum. Let us now rise in token that we pledge ourselves to continue working in the spirit of the Goetheanum with the best and highest forces that we have within us. So be it. Amen. [127]

*

Moreover, something enormously consequential happened that was not on the schedule. In the afternoon of 1 January, Rudolf Steiner became extremely ill at a social event. Somehow he managed to summon the strength to finish his ninth and last lecture. However, Steiner never fully recovered. This mysterious illness plagued him until finally he had to cease lecturing on 28 September, 1924. He was confined thereafter to what would become his deathbed on 30 March, 1925.

We can only speculate about the origin of this mysterious illness. On the one hand, the spiritual world responded affirmatively to Steiner's decision to assume leadership of the Society. He spoke of floodgates of insight opening to him, and his supra-human productivity in the year 1924 confirms this. But the illness may also have been a consequence of his assuming leadership of the Society. It may be that both developments happened simultaneously: physical decline, accompanied by a tremendously heightened spiritual activity. In that case, Steiner was granted a unique form of grace for a relatively short period, but then he had to die.

*

Taking this all together, one sees a single overarching theme in the events of the conference, and that is *tragedy*. By tragedy, I mean spiritual progress purchased at an unspeakably high price. In order for the Foundation Stone and the Spiritual Goetheanum to be laid in the hearts of the members, the physical Goetheanum had to go up in flames. In order for Steiner to achieve a breakthrough, in order for him to give the First Class and to fulfill the mission of his incarnation by teaching karma, he had to perish. On a larger scale, the wisdom of the Mysteries had to die out completely in the outer world so that it could be renewed within. That is what lies at the heart of this cycle of lectures on *World History*. Progress, but at a nearly unbearable cost.

Tragedy.

Frederick Amrine
April 2021

Lecture 1

DORNACH, 24 DECEMBER 1923

In the evening hours of our Christmas Conference,[1] I should like to give you a kind of survey of human evolution on Earth that may help us to become more intimately conscious of the nature of present-day humanity. At this time in human history, when we can see already in preparation events of extraordinary importance for the whole civilization of humanity, every thinker must be inclined to ask: 'How has the present configuration, the present make-up of the human soul arisen? How has it come about through the long course of evolution?' For it cannot be denied that the present only becomes comprehensible as we try to understand its origin in the past.

The present age is however one that is peculiarly prejudiced in its thought about the evolution of humanity. It is commonly believed that, as regards his life of soul and spirit, we have always been essentially the same as we are today throughout the whole of the time that we call history. True, in respect of knowledge, it is imagined that in ancient times human beings were childlike, that they believed in all kinds of fancies, and that we have really only become clever in the scientific sense in modern times. But if we look away from the actual sphere of knowledge, it is generally held that the constitution of soul which humans have today was also possessed by the ancient Greek and by the ancient Oriental. Even though it is admitted that modifications may have occured in detail, on the whole it is supposed that throughout the historical period, everything in the life of the soul has been as it is today. We go on to assume a human prehistoric life, and say that nothing is really known of this. Going still further back, we picture the human being in a kind of animal form. Thus, in the first place, as we trace back in historical time, we see a life of soul undergoing comparatively little change. Then the picture disappears in a kind of cloud, and before that again we see ourselves in our animal imperfection as a kind of higher ape. Such is approximately the usual conception of today.

Now all this rests on an extraordinary prejudice, for in forming such a conception, we do not take the trouble to observe the important differences that exist in the human constitution of the present time, as compared even with that of a relatively not very far distant past—say, of the eleventh, tenth, and ninth centuries CE. The difference goes deeper when we compare the psychic constitution in the human being of today and in contemporaries of the Mystery of Golgotha,[2] or in a Greek. And if we go over to the ancient Oriental world of which the Greek civilization was, in a sense, a kind of colony, a late colony, we find there a disposition of soul utterly different from that of the humanity of today. I should like to show you from real instances how humans lived in the East, let us say, ten thousand, or fifteen thousand years ago, and how different they were in nature from the Greek, and how still more different from what we ourselves are.[3]

Let us first call to mind our own lives of soul. I will take an example from it. We have a certain experience; and of this experience, in which we take part through our senses, or through our personality in some other way, we form an idea, a representation,[4] and we retain this representation in our thought. After a certain time the idea may arise again out of our thought into our conscious life of soul as memory. You have perhaps today an experience of memory that leads you back to experiences in perception of some ten years ago. Now try to understand exactly what that really means. Ten years ago you experienced something. Ten years ago you may have visited a gathering of men and women. You formed a representation of each one of these persons, of their appearance and so on. You experienced what they said to you, and what you did in common with them. All that, in the form of pictures, may arise before you today. It is an inner psychic image that is present within you, connected with the event which occurred ten years ago. Now not only according to science, but according to a general feeling—which is, of course, experienced by us today in an extremely weak form, but which nevertheless *is* experienced—according to this general feeling, we localize such a representational memory which brings back a past experience in our heads. We say: 'What lives as the memory of an experience is present in my head.'

Now let us jump a long way back in human evolution, and consider the early population of the Orient, of which the Chinese and Indians as we know them in history were only the late descendants; that is, let us really go back thousands of years. Then, if we contemplate humans of that ancient epoch, we find that they did not live in such a way as to say: 'I have in my head the memory of something I have experienced, something I have undergone, in external life.' We had no such inner feeling or experience; it simply did not exist for us. Our heads were not filled with thoughts and ideas. Present-day humanity thinks in its superficial way that as we today have ideas, thoughts, and concepts, so human beings always possessed these, as far back as history records; but that is not the case. If with spiritual insight we go back far enough, we meet with human beings who did not have ideas, concepts, thoughts all in their head, who did not experience any such abstract content of the head, but, strange as it may seem, experienced the whole head; they perceived and felt their whole head. These people did not give themselves up to abstractions as we do. To experience ideas in the head was something quite foreign to them, but they knew how to experience their own head. And as you, when you have a representation of memory, refer the representation of memory to an experience, as a relationship exists between your representation of memory and the experience, similarly these individuals related the experience of their head to the Earth, to the whole Earth. They said: 'There exists in the cosmos the Earth. And there exists in the cosmos I myself, and as a part of me, my head; and the head which I carry on my shoulders, is the cosmic memory of the Earth. The Earth existed earlier; my head later. That I have a head is due to the memory, the cosmic memory of earthly existence. The earthly existence is always there. But the whole configuration, the whole shape of the human head, is in relation to the whole Earth.' Thus an ancient Oriental felt in his own head the being of the planet Earth itself. He said: 'Out of the whole great cosmic existence the Gods have created, have generated the Earth with its kingdoms of nature, the Earth with its rivers and mountains. I carry on my shoulders my head; and this head of mine is a true picture of the Earth. This head, with the blood flowing in it, is a true picture of the Earth with the land and water coursing over it. The configuration of mountains on the Earth repeats itself in my head in the configurations of my brain; I carry on my shoulders an image belonging to me of the earthly planet.' Exactly as we moderns refer our representation of memory to our experience, so did humans of old refer their entire head to the planet Earth. A considerable difference of inner intuition!

Further, when we consider the periphery of the Earth, and fit it, as it were, into our vision of things, we feel this air surrounding the Earth as air permeated by the Sun's warmth and light; and in a certain sense, we can say: 'The Sun lives in the atmosphere of the Earth.' The Earth opens herself to the cosmic universe; the activities that come forth from herself she yields up to the encircling atmosphere, and opens herself to receive the activities of the Sun. Now each of us, in those ancient times, experienced the region of the Earth on which we lived as of peculiar importance. Ancient Orientals would feel some portion of the surface of the Earth as their own; beneath them the Earth, and above them the encircling atmosphere turned towards the Sun. The rest of the Earth that lay to the left and right, in front and behind—all the rest of the Earth merged into a general whole [See Plate 1, left].

Thus if ancient Orientals lived, for example, on Indian soil, they experienced the Indian soil as especially important for them; but everything else on the Earth, East, West, South of them, disappeared into the universal. They did not concern themselves much with the way in which the Earth in these other parts was bounded by the rest of cosmic space; while on the other hand, not only was the soil on which they lived something important [see Plate 1, left, red], but the extension of the Earth into cosmic space in this region became a matter of great moment to them. The way in which they were able to breathe on this particular soil was felt by them as an experience of special importance.

Today, we are not in the habit of asking, how does one breathe in this or that place? We are of course still subject to favourable or

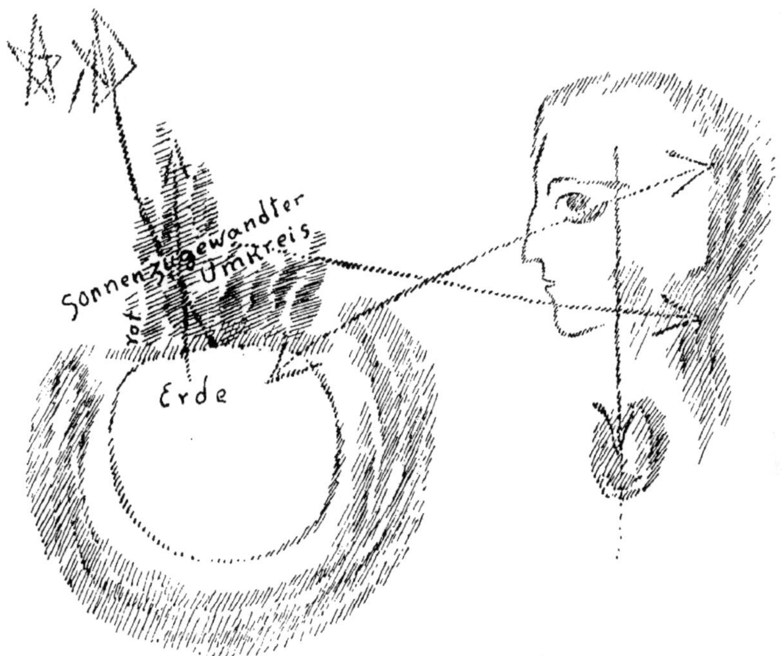

[Sonnenzugewandter = circle facing the sun; rot = red; erde = earth]
[See also Plate 1]

unfavourable conditions for breathing, but we are no longer so conscious of the fact. For an ancient Oriental this was different. The way that they were able to breathe was for them a very deep experience, and so also were many other things that depend on the character of the Earth's relation and contact with cosmic space. All that goes to make up the Earth, the whole Earth, was felt by humans of those early times as that which lived in their heads.

Now the head is enclosed by the hard, firm bones of the skull. Thus it is closed above, on two sides and behind. But it has certain exits; it has a free opening downwards towards the chest. And it was of special importance for humans of olden time to feel how the head opens with relative freedom in the direction of the chest [see Plate 1, right]. And as we had to feel the inner configuration of the head as an image of the Earth, so we had to bring the environment of the Earth, all that is above and around the Earth, into connection with the opening downwards, the turning towards the heart. In this they saw an image of how Earth opens to the cosmos. It was a mighty experience for humans of those ancient times when they said: 'In my head I feel the whole Earth. But this Earth opens to my chest which carries within it my heart. And what takes place between head, chest, and heart is an image of what is borne out from my life into the cosmos, borne out to the surrounding atmosphere that is open to the Sun.'

It was a great experience for them, a fundamental one, when they were able to say: 'Here in my head lives the Earth. When I go deeper, there the Earth is turning towards the Sun; my heart is the image of the Sun' [see arrow]. The people of olden times attained in this way what corresponds to our life of feeling.

We still have the abstract life of feeling. But who of us knows anything directly about out hearts? Through anatomy and physiology, we think we know something, but it is about as much as we know of some papier-mâché model of the heart that we may have before us. On the other hand, what we have as an experience of the world in feeling is something that the people of olden times did not have. In place of it, we had the experience of our hearts. Just as we relate our feeling to the world in which we live, just as we feel whether we love someone or meet them with antipathy, whether we like this or that flower, whether we incline towards this or that, just as we relate our feelings to the world—but to a world torn out, as it were, in airy abstraction, from the solid, firm cosmos—in the same way did the ancient Orientals relate their hearts to the cosmos, that is, to what goes away from the Earth in the direction of the Sun.

Again, we say today: I will walk. We know that our will lives in our limbs. The ancient peoples of the East had an essentially different experience. What we call 'will' was quite unknown to them. It is pure prejudice when we believe that what we call thinking, feeling, and willing were present among the ancient Eastern cultures. This was not at all the case. They had head experiences, which were earthly experiences. They had experiences of the chest or heart, which were experiences of the environment of the Earth as far out as the Sun. The Sun corresponds to the heart experience. Then they had a further experience, a feeling of expanding and stretching out into their limbs. They became conscious and aware of their own humanity in the movement of their legs and feet, or of their arms and hands. They themselves were within the movements. And in this expansion on the inner being into the limbs, they felt a direct picture of their connection with the starry worlds [see Plate 1]. 'In my head I have a picture of the Earth. Where my head opens freely downwards into the chest and reaches down to my heart, I have a picture of what lives in the Earth's environment. In what I experience as the forces of my arms and hands, of my feet and legs, I have something which represents the relation the Earth bears to the stars that live far out there in cosmic space.'

When therefore they wanted to express the experience they had as a 'willing' human being—to use the language of today—they did not say: I walk. We can see that from the very words that they used. Nor did they say: I sit down. If we investigate the ancient languages in respect of their finer content, we find everywhere that for the action which we described by saying: I walk, the ancient Oriental would have said: Mars impels me, Mars is active in me. Going forward was felt as a Mars-impulse in the legs.

Grasping hold of something, feeling and touching with the hands, was expressed by saying: Venus works in me. Pointing out something to another person was expressed by saying: Mercury works in me. Even when a rude person attracted someone's attention by giving them a push or a kick, the action would be described by saying: Mercury was working in that person. Sitting down was a Jupiter activity, and lying down, whether for rest or from sheer laziness, was expressed by saying: I give myself over to the impulses of Saturn. Thus they felt in their limbs the wide spaces of cosmos out beyond. They knew that when they went away from the Earth out into cosmic space, they came into the Earth's environment and then into the starry spheres. If they went downwards from their heads, they passed through the very same experience, only this time within their own being. In their heads they were in the Earth, in their chest and heart they were in the environment of the Earth, in their limbs they were in the starry cosmos beyond.

From a certain point of view, such an experience is perfectly possible for us. Alas for us, poor people of today, who can experience only abstract thoughts! What are these really, for the most part? We are very proud of them, but we utterly forget what is far beyond the cleverest of them—our head; our head is much richer in content than the very cleverest of our abstract thoughts. Anatomy and physiology know little of the marvel and mystery of the convolutions of the brain, but one single convolution of the brain is more majestic and more powerful than the abstract knowledge of the greatest genius. There was once a time on the Earth when humans were not merely conscious as we are of our paltry thoughts, so to speak, but were conscious of their own heads; they felt the head to be the image of the Earth, and they felt this or that part of the head—let us say, the *optic thalamus* or the *corpora quadrigemina*[5] to be the image of a certain physical, mountainous configuration of the Earth. They did not then merely relate their hearts to the Sun in accordance with some abstract theory. Rather, they felt: 'My head stands in the same relation to my chest, to my heart, as the Earth does to the Sun.' That was the time when they had grown together, in their whole life, with the cosmic universe; they had become one with the cosmos. And this found expression in their whole life.

Because we today put our puny thinking in the place of our head, through this very fact we are able to have a conceptual memory; we are able to remember things in thought. We form pictures in thought of what we have experienced as abstract memories in our head. That could not be done by individuals of olden times who did not have thoughts, but still had their head. They could not form memory pictures. And so, in those regions of the Ancient East where people were still conscious of their heads, but had as yet no thoughts and hence no memories, we find developed to a remarkable degree something of which people are again beginning to feel the need today. For a long time such a thing has not been necessary, and if today the need for it is returning, it is due to what I can only call slovenliness of soul.

If in that time of which I have spoken, if we were to enter the region inhabited by people who were still conscious of their head, chest, heart and limbs, we would see on every hand small pegs placed in the earth and marked with some sign. Or here and there a sign made upon a wall. Such memorials were to be found scattered over all inhabited regions. Wherever anything happened, someone would set up some kind of memorial, and when they came back to the place, they lived through the event over again in the memorial they had made. They had grown together with the Earth; they had become one with it in their heads. Today, we merely make a note of some event in our heads. As I have pointed out already, we are beginning once more to find it necessary to make notes not only in our heads, but also in a notebook; this is due, as I said, to slovenliness of soul, but nevertheless we shall need to do it more and more. At that time, however, there was no such thing as marking notes even in one's head, because thoughts and ideas were simply non-existent. Instead, the land was dotted over with signs. And from this habit, so naturally acquired by people in olden times, has arisen the whole custom of making monuments and memorials.

Everything that has happened in the historical evolution of humanity has its origin and cause in our inner being. If we were but honest, we would have to admit that we moderns do not have the faintest knowledge of the deeper basis of this custom of erecting memorials. We set them up from habit. They are however the relics of the ancient monuments and signs put up by humanity in a time when we had no memory such as we have today, but were taught, in any place where we had some experience, there to set up a memorial, so that when we came that way again we might re-experience the event in our heads. For the head can call up again everything that has connection with the Earth. 'We give over to the earth what our head has experienced.' This was a principle of olden times.

And so we have to point to a very early time in the ancient East, the epoch of *localized memory,* when everything of the nature of memory was connected with the setting up of signs and memorials on the Earth. Memory was not within, but without. Everywhere were memorial tablets and memorial stones. It was localized memory, a remembering connected with place.

Even today it is still of no small value for a humanity's spiritual evolution that we should sometimes make use of our capacity for this kind of memory, for a memory that is not within us, but is unfolded in connection with the outer world. It is good sometimes to say: I will *remember* this or that, but I will set here or there a *sign*, or token; or, I will let my soul unfold an experience about certain things, only in connection with signs or tokens. I will, for instance, hang a picture of the Madonna in a corner of my room, and when the picture is before me, I will experience in my soul all that I can experience by turning with my whole soul to the Madonna. For there is a subtle relation to a thing belonging so intimately to the home as does the picture of the Madonna that we meet with in the homes of the people, when we go a little way eastwards in Europe; we have not even to go as far as Russia, we find them everywhere in Central Europe. All experience of this nature is in reality a relic of the epoch of localized memory. The memory is outside, it attaches to the place.

A second stage is reached when we pass from localized to *rhythmic* memory. Thus we have first, localized memory; and second, rhythmic memory.

We have now come to the time when, not from any conscious, subtle finesse, but right out of our own inner being, we had developed the need of living in rhythm. We felt a need so to reproduce, within ourselves, what we heard so that a rhythm was formed. If their experience of a cow, for instance, suggested 'moo', they did not simply call her 'moo', but 'moo-moo',—perhaps, in very ancient times, 'moo-moo-moo'. That is to say, the perception was, as it were, piled up in repetition, so as to produce rhythm. You can follow the same process in the formation of many words today, such as 'cuckoo'. And you can observe how little children still feel the need of these repetitions, even when the words are not immediately following one another. We have here again a heritage that has come down from the time when rhythmic memory prevailed, the time when we had no memory at all of what we had merely experienced, but only of what we experienced in rhythmic form—in repetitions, in rhythmic repetition. There had to be at any rate some similarity between a sequence of words. 'Might and main', 'stock and stone'—such a setting of experience in rhythmic sequence is a last relic of an extreme longing to bring everything into rhythm. For in this second epoch, that followed the epoch of localized memory, what was not set into rhythm, was not retained. It is from this rhythmic memory that the whole ancient art of verse developed—indeed all metrical poetry.

Only in the third stage does that develop which we still know today—*temporal memory*. We no longer have a point in space to which memory attaches, nor are we any longer dependent on rhythm. Instead, what is inserted into the course of time can be evoked again later. This very abstract form or recollection is the third stage in the evolution of memory.

Let us now call to mind the point of time in human evolution when rhythmic memory passes over into temporal memory, when that form of memory first made its appearance which we, with lamentable abstractness of thought, take entirely as a matter of course. It is the memory whereby we evoke something in pictorial form, no longer needing to make use of semi-conscious or unconscious rhythmic repetitions in order to call it up again.

The epoch of the transition from rhythmic memory to temporal memory is the time when the ancient East was sending colonies to Greece, the beginning of the colonies planted from Asia in Europe. When the Greeks relate stories of the heroes who came over from Asia and Egypt to settle on Greek soil, they are really relating how the great heroes went forth from the land of rhythmic memory to seek a climate where rhythmic memory could pass over into temporal memory, into a remembering in time.

We are thus able to define very precisely the time of the rise of Greece. For what may be called the motherland and ancestral seat of Greece was the home of a people with strongly developed rhythmic memory. There rhythm lived. The ancient East is indeed only rightly understood when we see it as the land of rhythm. And if we place Paradise only so far back as the Bible places it, if we lay the scene of Paradise in Asia, then we have to see it as a land where purest rhythms resounded through the cosmos and enkindled again in humans as rhythmic memory, a land where we lived not only as experiencing rhythm in a cosmos, but as ourselves a creator of rhythm.

Listen to the *Bhagavad Gita*[6] and you will catch the after-echo of that mighty rhythm that once lived in human experience. You will hear its echo also in the Vedas,[7] and you will even hear it in the poetry and literature—to use a modern word—of Western Asia. In all these live the echoes of that rhythm which once filled the whole of Asia with majestic content and, bearing with it the mysteries of the environment of the Earth, made these resound again in the human breast, in the beat of the human heart. Then we come to a still more ancient time, when rhythmic memory leads back into localized memory, when we did not even have rhythmic memories, but instead were taught, in the place where we experienced something, to erect a memorial. When they were away from the place, they needed no memorial; but when they came thither again, they had to recall the experience. Yet it was not they who recalled it to themselves; the memorial, the very Earth, recalled it to them. As the head is the image of the Earth, so for the human with localized memory the memorial in the Earth evoked its own image in the head. They lived completely with the Earth; in their connection with the Earth, they had their memory.

The Gospels contain a passage that recalls this kind of memory, where we are told that Christ wrote something in the Earth.[8] The period we have thus defined as the transition from localized memory to rhythmic memory is the time when ancient Atlantis[9] was declining and the primordial post-Atlantean[10] peoples were wandering eastward in the direction of Asia. For we have first the wanderings from ancient Atlantis—the continent that today forms the bed of the Atlantic Ocean—right across Europe into Asia [see Plate 2],

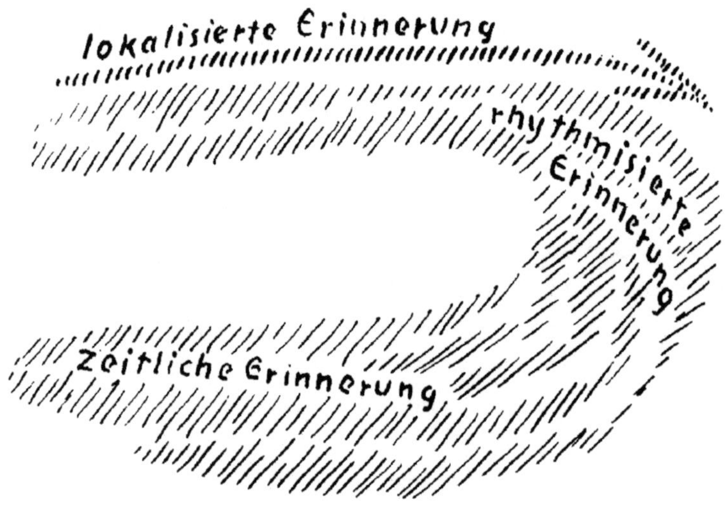

[lokalisierte Erinnerung = localized memory; rhythmisierte Erinnerung = rhythmic memory; zeitliche Erinnerung = temporal memory]

[See Plate 2]

and later the wanderings back again from Asia into Europe. The migration of the Atlantean peoples to Asia marks the transition from localized memory to rhythmic memory, which latter finds its completion in the spiritual life of Asia. The colonization of Greece marks the transition from rhythmic memory to temporal memory, the memory that we still carry within us today. And within this evolution of memory lies the whole development of civilization between the Atlantean catastrophe and the rise of Greece, all that resounds to us from ancient Asia, coming to us in the form of legend and saga rather than as history. We shall not arrive at an understanding of the evolution of humanity on the Earth by looking principally to the external phenomena, by investigating the external documents. Rather, we need to fix our attention on the evolution of what is within us. We must consider how such a thing as the faculty of memory has developed, passing in its development from without into our inner human being.

You know how much the power of memory means for us today. You will have heard of persons who through some condition of illness suddenly find that a portion of their past life, which they ought to remember quite easily, has been completely wiped out. A terrible destiny of this kind befell a friend of mine before his death. One day he left his home, bought a ticket at the railway station for a certain place, alighted there, and bought another ticket. He did all this, having lost for the time the memory of his life up to the moment of buying the ticket. He carried everything out quite sensibly. His reason was sound. But his memory was blotted out. And he found himself, when his memory came back, in an asylum for the homeless in Berlin. It was afterwards proved that in the interval he had wandered over half of Europe, without being able to connect the experience with the earlier experiences of his life. Memory did not re-awaken in him until he had found his way—he himself did not know how—into an asylum for the homeless in Berlin. This is only one of countless cases which we meet in life that show us how the human life of soul today is not intact unless the threads of memory are able to reach back unbroken to a certain period after birth.

With the people of olden time who had developed a localized memory, this was not the case. They knew nothing of these threads of memory. They, on the other hand, would have been unhappy in their life of soul, they would have felt as we feel when something robs us of ourselves, if they had not been surrounded by memorials which recalled to them what they had experienced; and not alone by memorials which they themselves had set up, but also memorials erected by their forefathers, or by their brothers and sisters, similar in configuration to their own and bringing them into contact with their own kinsmen. Whereas we are conscious of something inward as the condition for keeping our self intact, for these people of bygone times the condition was to be sought outside themselves—in the world without.

We have to let the whole picture of this change in the human soul pass before our eyes in order to realize its significance in the history of human evolution. It is by observing such things as these that we begin to cast light upon history. Today I wanted to show, by a special example, how the human mind and soul have evolved in respect of one faculty—the faculty of memory. We shall go on to see in the course of the succeeding lectures how the events of history begin to reveal themselves in their true shape when we can thus illuminate them with light that derives from knowledge of the human soul.

Lecture 2

DORNACH, 25 DECEMBER 1923

FROM the foregoing lecture it will be clear to you that it is only possible to gain a correct view of the historical evolution of humanity when we take into consideration the totally different conditions of mind and soul that prevailed during the various epochs. In the first part of my lecture, I attempted to define the Asiatic period of evolution, the genuine ancient East, and we saw that we have to look back to the time when the descendants of the cultures of Atlantis were finding their way eastwards after the Atlantean catastrophe, moving from west to east, and gradually peopling Europe and Asia. All that took place in ancient Asia in connection with these peoples was under the influence of a condition of soul accustomed and attuned to rhythm. At the beginning of the Asiatic period, we still have a distant echo of what was present in all its fullness in Atlantis—the localized memory. During the oriental evolution, this localized memory passed over into rhythmic memory, and I showed how with Greek evolution, that great change came about which brought in a new kind of memory, the temporal memory.

This means that the Asiatic period of evolution (we are now speaking of what may rightly be called the Asiatic period, for what history refers to is in reality a later and decadent period) was an age altogether differently constituted from later times. And the external events of history were in those days much more dependent than in later times on the character and constitution of our inner life. What lived in our mind and soul also lived in our entire being. A separated life of thought and feeling, such as we have today, was unknown. Thinking that does not feel itself to be connected with the inner processes of the human head was unknown. So too was the abstract feeling that knows no connection with the circulation of the blood. We had in those times a thinking that was inwardly experienced as a 'happening' in the head, a feeling that was experienced in the rhythm of the breath, in the circulation of blood, and so on. We experienced our whole being in undivided unity.

All this was closely connected with the altogether different experience we had of our relation to the world about us, to the cosmos, to the spiritual, and the physical and the cosmic whole. We of the present day live, let us say, in town or in the country, and our experience varies accordingly. We are surrounded by woods, rivers, and mountains; or, if we live in town, bricks and mortar meet our gaze on every hand. When we speak of the cosmic and supra-sensible, where do we think it is? We can point to no sphere within which we can conceive of what is cosmic and supra-sensible as having place. It is nowhere to be laid hold of; we cannot grasp it. Even spiritually, we cannot grasp it.

But this was not so in that oriental stream of evolution. To Orientals, the world around them which we today call our physical environment was the lowest portion of the cosmos conceived as a unity. We had around us what is contained in the three kingdoms of nature. We had around us the rivers, mountains, and so forth. But for us, this environment was permeated through and through with spirit, interpenetrated and interwoven with spirit. The Oriental of ancient times would say: I live with the mountains, I live with the rivers; but I also live with the elemental beings of the mountains and of the rivers. I live in the physical realm, but this physical realm is the body of the spiritual realm. Around me is the spiritual world, the lowest spiritual world.

There below was this realm that for us has become the earthly realm. We lived in it. [See Plate 3.] But we pictured to ourselves that where this realm ends [bright], another round begins above [yellow -red], then again above that another [blue]; and finally the highest realm that it is possible to reach [orange]. And if we were to name these realms in accordance with the language that has become current with us in anthroposophical knowledge—the ancient Orientals

[hell = bright; gelb-rot = yellow-red; blau = blue]

[See Plate 3]

had other names for them, but that does not matter; we will name them as they are for us—then we should have above, for the highest realm, the First Hierarchy: Seraphim, Cherubim, Thrones; then the Second Hierarchy: Kyriotetes, Dynamis, Exusiai; and the Third Hierarchy: Archai, Archangels, Angels.[11]

And now there came the fourth realm where human beings live, the realm where, according to our method of cognition, we place today only the natural objects and processes of nature, where the ancient Oriental felt the whole of nature penetrated with the elemental spirits of water and of earth. This was Asia. [See Plate 3.]

Asia meant the lowest spiritual realm, in which human beings lived. You must remember that our present-day conception of things and our ordinary consciousness were unknown to the individual of the ancient Orient. It would be complete nonsense to suppose that it were in any way possible for him to imagine such a thing as matter devoid of spirit. To speak as we do, of oxygen and nitrogen, would have been a sheer impossibility for the ancient Orientals. To them, oxygen was spirit; it was that spiritual thing which worked as a stimulating and quickening agent on what already possessed life, accelerating the life-processes in a living organism. Nitrogen, which we think of today as contained in the atmosphere together with oxygen, was also spiritual; it was what weaves throughout the cosmos, working upon what is living and organic in such a way as to prepare it to receive a psychic nature. Only this was the knowledge the Orientals of old had, for example, of oxygen and nitrogen. And they knew all the processes of nature in this way, in a connection with spirit; for the present-day conceptions were unknown to them. There were a few individuals who knew them, and they were the initiates. The rest of humanity had as their ordinary, everyday consciousness, something very similar to a waking dream; it was a dream condition that with us only occurs in abnormal experiences.

The ancient Oriental went about with these dreams. He looked on the mountains, rivers, and clouds, and saw everything in the way that things can be seen and heard in this dream condition. Picture to yourself what may happen to the people of today in a dream. They are asleep. Suddenly there appears before them a dream image of a fiery oven. They hear the call of 'Fire!'. Outside in the street, a fire engine is passing, to put out a fire somewhere or other. But what a difference between the conception of the work of the fire-brigade that can be formed by the human intellect and its matter-of-fact way with the aid of ordinary sensory perception, and the images that a dream can conjure up! For the ancient Orientals, however, all their experiences manifested themselves in such dream images. Everything outside in the kingdoms of nature was transformed in their souls into images.

In these dream images, we experienced the elemental spirits of water, earth, air, and fire. And sleep brought us also other experiences. Sleep was not that deep, heavy sleep we have when we lie, as we say, 'like a log', and know nothing of ourselves. I believe there are people today who sleep like this, are there not? But then there was no such thing: even in sleep, we had still a dull form of consciousness. While on the one hand we were, as we now say, resting our bodies, the spirit was weaving within us in a spiritual activity of the external world. And in this weaving, we perceive the Beings of the Third Hierarchy. Asia they perceived in their ordinary waking-dream condition, that is to say in what was the everyday consciousness of that time. At night, in sleep, they perceived the Third Hierarchy. And from time to time there entered into their sleep a still dim and dark consciousness, but a consciousness that engraved its experiences deeply into their thought and feeling. Thus these Eastern peoples had their everyday consciousness, in which everything was changed into Imaginations and pictures. The pictures were not so real as those of still older times, for example the time of Atlantis or Lemuria, or of the Moon epoch.[12] Nevertheless they were still there, even during this Asiatic evolution. By day, then, we had these pictures. And in sleep they had an experience which they might have clothed in the following words: We 'sleep away' the ordinary earthly existence, we enter the realm of the Angels, Archangels, and Archai, and live among them. The soul sets itself free from the organism and lives among the Beings of the higher Hierarchies.

We knew at the same time that whereas we lived in Asia with gnomes, undines, sylphs, and salamanders—that is, with the elemental spirits of earth, water, air, and fire—in sleep, while the body rested, they experienced the Beings of the Third Hierarchy, but at the same time they experienced the planetary existence, which lives in the planetary system that belongs to the Earth. But then there often entered into sleeping consciousness, in which they perceived the Third Hierarchy, an extraordinary state, in which the sleeper felt: An utterly alien realm is approaching me. It takes me into itself; it causes me to withdraw somewhat from earthly consciousness. They did not yet experience being transported into the Third Hierarchy, but they felt it in this deeper state of sleep. Actually, there never was present a clear consciousness of what occurred during this state of sleep of the third kind. There bored deeply, deeply into human existence what was experienced from the Second Hierarchy. And upon waking, they had it in their souls and said: I have been graciously blessed by higher Spirits, whose life is beyond the planetary existence. Thus did these ancient peoples speak of that Hierarchy which embraces the Kyriotetes, the Dynamis, and the Exousiai. What we are now describing are the ordinary states of consciousness of this ancient Asiatic period. The first two states of consciousness—the waking-sleeping, sleeping-waking, and sleep, into which the Third Hierarchy towered—were experienced from the beginning by everyone. And many, through a special endowment of nature, experienced also the intervention of a deeper sleep, during which the Second Hierarchy played into human consciousness.

And the initiates in the Mysteries[13] received a still further degree of consciousness. Of what nature was this? The answer is astonishing; for the fact is, the initiate of the ancient East acquired the same consciousness that you have now by day! You develop it in a perfectly natural way in your second or third year of life. No ancient Orientals ever attained the state of consciousness in a natural way; they had to develop it artificially in themselves. They had to develop it out of the waking-dreaming, dreaming-waking. As long as they went about with this waking-dreaming, dreaming-waking, they saw everywhere pictures, rendering only in more or less symbolic fashion what we see today in clear, sharp outlines. The initiates, however, attained to see things as we see them today in our ordinary consciousness. The initiates, by means of their developed consciousness, attained what every boy and girl learns at school today. The difference between their consciousness and a normal consciousness of today is not that the content was different. Of course, the abstract forms of letters that we have today were unknown then; their script was in more intimate connection with the things and processes of the cosmos. The initiates nevertheless learned reading and writing in those days; although of course by them alone, for reading and writing can only be learned with that clear, intellectual consciousness which is natural for the person of today.

Supposing that somewhere or other this world of the ancient East were to reappear, inhabited by human beings having the kind of consciousness they had in those olden times, and you were to come among them with your consciousness of the present day. Then, for them, you would all be initiates. The difference does not lie in the content of consciousness. You would be initiates.

However, the moment the people recognized you as initiates, they would immediately drive you out of the land by every means in their power, for it would be very clear to them that an initiated person ought not to know things in the way we know them today. We ought not, for example, to be able to write as we are able to write today. If I were to transport myself into the soul of someone of that time, and were to meet such as pseudo-initiate, that is to say, an ordinary clever individual of the present day, I should find myself saying of them: They can write; they make signs on paper that mean something, and yet they have no idea how devilish it is to do such a thing without bearing the consciousness that it may only be done in the service of divine, cosmic consciousness. They do not know that someone may only make such signs on paper when they can feel how God works in their hand, in their very fingers, works in their soul, enabling it to express itself through these letters. Therein lies the whole difference between initiates of olden times and the ordinary individual of the present day. It is not a difference in the content of consciousness, but in the way of comprehending and understanding things. Read my book *Christianity as a Mystical Fact*,[14] of which the new edition has recently appeared, and you will find right at the beginning the same indication as to the essential nature of the initiate in olden times. It is in point of fact always so in the course of the world's evolution. What develops in humanity at a later period in a natural way had in former epochs to be won through initiation.

Through such a thing as I have brought to your notice, you will be able to detect the radical difference between the condition of mind and soul prevalent among the Eastern peoples of prehistoric times and that of a later civilization. It was another humanity altogether that could call Asia the last or lowest heaven and understand by that their own land, the nature that was roundabout them. They knew where the lowest heaven was.

Compare this with the conception we have today. How far is the individual of the present time from regarding all he sees as the lowest heaven! Most people cannot think of it as the 'lowest' heaven for the simple reason that they have no knowledge of any heaven at all!

Thus we see how in that ancient Eastern time, the spiritual towers into natural existence. But nevertheless we find also among these peoples something which to most of us in the present day may easily appear extremely barbarous. To someone of that time it would have appeared terribly barbarous if someone had been able to write with the feeling and attitude of mind we have today; it would have seemed positively devilish to them. But when we today, on the other hand, see how it was accepted in those times as something quite natural and as a matter of course that people should migrate from West to East, should conquer—often with great cruelty—another people who had already settled and make slaves of them, then such a thing is bound to appear barbarous to very many of us.

This is, however, broadly speaking, the substance of oriental history over the whole of Asia. While humans had, as I described, a high spiritual conception of things, their external history ran its course in a series of conquests and enslavements. Undoubtedly that appears to many people as extremely barbarous. Today, although wars of aggression do still sometimes occur, we have an uneasy conscience about them. And this is true even of those who support and defend such wars; they are not entirely easy in their conscience.

In those times, however, people had a perfectly clear conscience as regards these wars of aggression; they felt that such conquest was willed by the gods. The longing for peace, the love of peace, that arose later and spread over a large part of Asia, is really the product of a much later civilization. The acquisition of land by conquest and enslavement of its population is a salient feature of the early civilization of Asia. The farther we go back into prehistoric times, the more do we find this kind of conquest going on. The conquests of Xerxes[15] and others of his time were in truth but faint shadows of what went on in earlier ages.

Now there is quite a definite principle underlying these conquests. As a result of the states of consciousness which I have described to you, people stood in an altogether different relation to their fellows and also to the world around them. Certain differences between various parts of the inhabited earth have today lost their essential meaning. At that time, these differences were present in an entirely

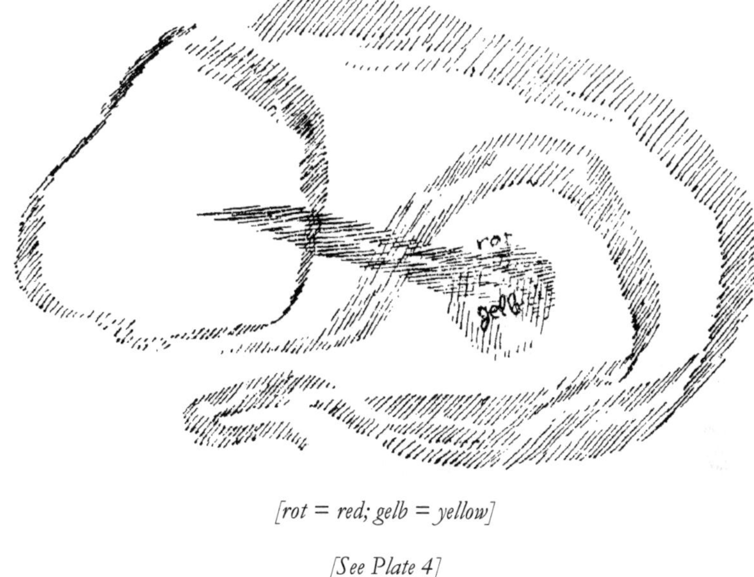

[rot = red; gelb = yellow]

[See Plate 4]

different way. Let me put before you, as an example, something which frequently occurred.

Suppose we had here on the left [see Plate 4] the European realm, and here on the right the Asiatic realm. A conquering people [red] could come over—also out of the North of Asia—and could extend itself over Asia, enslaving the population.

What has really happened? In characteristic instances that are a true expression of the trend of historical evolution, we find that the aggressors were—as a people or as a culture—young, full of youthful forces. Now what does it mean today to be young? What does it mean in our present epoch of evolution? It means to bear within at every moment of life sufficient forces of death to provide for those psychic forces that need the human dying processes. For, as you know, we have within us, the sprouting, germinating forces of life, but these life-forces are not the forces that make us reflective, thoughtful beings. On the contrary, they make us weak, unconscious. The death forces, the forces of destruction, which are also continually active within us—and are overcome again and again during sleep by the life-forces, so that we gather together all the death forces in us at the end of life in the one, final event of death—these forces are those which induce reflection, self-consciousness. This is how it is with humanity at present. Now a young culture, the young people such as I have described, suffered from its own excessively strong forces of life, and continually had the feeling: I feel my blood beating perpetually against the walls of my body. I cannot endure it. My consciousness will not become reflective. Because of my very youthfulness, I cannot develop my full humanity.

An ordinary individual would not have spoken thus, but the initiate spoke in this way in the Mysteries, and it was the initiates who guided and directed the whole course of history.

Here was then a people who had too much youth, too much of the life-forces, too little in them of what could bring about reflection and thought. They left their land and conquered the region where an older people lived, a people which had in some way or other taken into itself the forces of death, because it had already become decadent. The younger nation took up arms against the older and brought it into subjection. It was not necessary that a bond of blood should be established between conquerors and enslaved. What worked unconsciously in the soul between them had a rejuvenating effect; it worked on the reflective faculties. What the conquerors required from the slaves whom they now had in their court was influence upon their consciousness. They had only to turn their attention to those slaves and the longing for unconsciousness was quenched in their souls. Reflective consciousness began to dawn.

What we have to attain today as individuals was attained at that time by living together with others. A people who face the world as conquerors and lords; a young people, not possessing the full powers of reflection, needed around it a people that experienced more the forces of death. In overcoming another people, it won through to what is needed for its own evolution.

And so we find that these oriental conflicts, often so terrible in presenting to us such a barbarous aspect, are in reality nothing else than the impulses of human evolution. They had to take place. Humanity would not have been able to develop on the Earth had it not been for these terrible wars and struggles that seem to us so barbarous.

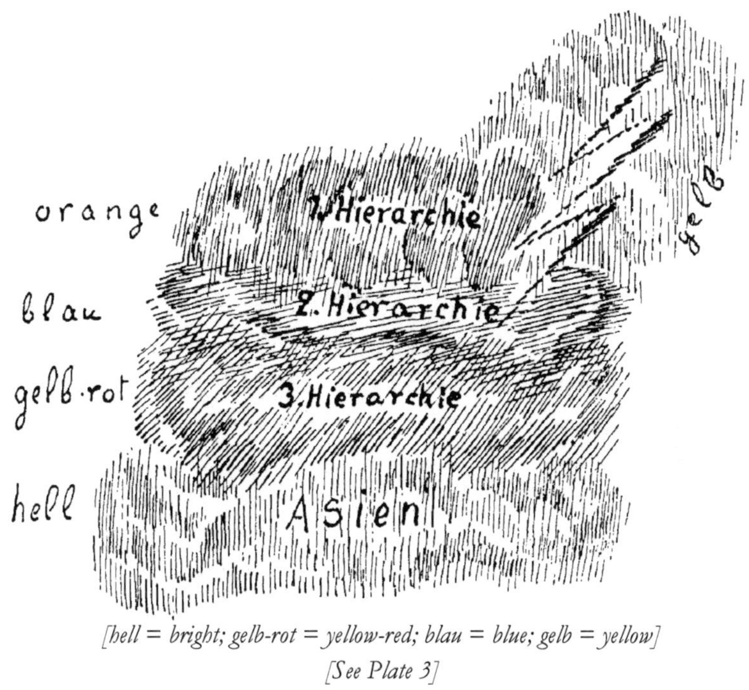

[hell = bright; gelb-rot = yellow-red; blau = blue; gelb = yellow]
[See Plate 3]

Already in those olden times, the initiates of the Mysteries saw the world as it is seen today. Only they united with this perception a different attitude of mind and soul. For them, all that they experienced in clear, sharp outlines—even as we today experience external objects in sharp outlines, when we perceive with our senses—was something that came from the gods, that came even for human consciousness from the gods. For how did external objects present themselves to an initiate of those times? There was perhaps a flash of lightning (to take a simple and obvious illustration). You know very well what a flash of lightning looks like to someone today. [See Plate 3.] The people of olden times did not see it thus. They saw in it a host of spirits moving through the sky [*gelb* = yellow], and the sharp line of the flash disappeared completely. They saw a host, a procession of spiritual Beings hurrying forward in cosmic space. The lightning as such they did not see. They saw a host of spirits hovering and moving through cosmic space.

The initiate also saw, with the rest, this spiritual host, but he had developed within him the perception that we have today, and so for him, the picture began to grow dim and the heavenly host gradually disappeared from view, and then the flash of lightning could become manifest.

The whole of nature, in the form in which we see it today, could only be attained in ancient times through initiation. But how did we feel towards such knowledge? We did not by any means look on the knowledge thus attained in the indifferent way knowledge and truth are regarded today. There was a strong moral element in the human experience of knowledge. If we turn our gaze to what happened with the neophytes of the Mysteries, we find we have to describe it in the following way. When a few individuals, after undergoing severe inner tests and trials, had been initiated into the view of nature that is today accessible to all, they had quite naturally this feeling: Consider the individuals with ordinary consciousness. They see the host of elementary beings riding through the air. But precisely because they have such a perception, they are devoid of free will. They are entirely given over to the divine, spiritual world. For in this waking-dreaming, dreaming-waking, the will does not move in freedom; rather, it is something that streams into us as divine will. And the initiate, who saw the lightning come forth out of these Imaginations, learned to say: I must be one who is free to move in the world *without* the gods, one for whom the gods cast out the content of the world into the void.

Now you must understand, this condition would have been unbearable for the initiate had there not been moments that compensated for it. Such moments they did have. For while on the one hand the initiate learned to experience Asia as God-forsaken, spirit-forsaken, he also learned to know a still deeper state of consciousness than what reached up to the Second Hierarchy. Knowing the world bereft of God, they also learned to know the world of the Seraphim, Cherubim, and Thrones.

At a certain time in the epoch of Asiatic evolution, approximately in the middle—later on we will speak more exactly of the dates—the condition of consciousness of the initiates was such that they went about on Earth with very nearly the perception of the kingdoms of the Earth which is possessed by modern humanity. They felt it, however, in their limbs. They felt their limbs set free from the gods in a God-bereft, earthly substance.

In compensation for this, however, they met in this godless land the high gods of the Seraphim, Cherubim, and Thrones. As initiates they learned to know, no longer merely the grey-green images of the forests, of the trees; they learned as initiates to know the forest devoid of spirit. There, however, was the compensation of meeting in the forest Beings of the First Hierarchy. There they would meet some Being from the kingdom of the Seraphim, Cherubim, and Thrones.

All this, understood as giving form to the social life of humanity, is the essential feature in the historical evolution of the ancient East. And the driving force for further evolution lies in the search for an adjustment between young cultures and old cultures, so that the young cultures may mature through association with the old, with the souls of those who may have been brought into subjection. However far back we look into Asia, everywhere we find how the young cultures cannot of themselves develop the reflective faculties, set out to find these in wars of aggression.

When, however, we turn our gaze away from Asia to the land of Greece, we find a somewhat different development. Over in Greece, in the time of the full flower of Greek culture, we find the people who did indeed know how to grow old, but were unable to permeate the growing old with full spirituality. I have many times had to draw attention to the characteristic Greek utterance: Better a beggar in the world of the living than a king in the realm of the shades. The Greeks could adapt neither to death outside in nature, nor to human death. They could not find their true relationship to death. On the other hand, however, they had this death within them. And so in the Greeks we find, not a longing for reflective consciousness, but apprehension and fear of death.

Such a fear of death was not felt by the young Eastern cultures; *they* went out to make conquests when, as cultures, they found themselves unable to experience death in the right way. The inner conflict, however, which the Greeks experienced with death, became in its turn an inward impulse compelling humanity, and led to what we know as the Trojan War. The Greeks had no need to seek death at the hands of a foreign culture in order to acquire the power of reflection. The Greeks needed to come into a right relationship with what they felt and experienced of death; they needed to find the inner, living mystery of death. And this led to that great conflict between the Greeks and the people in Asia from whom they had originated. The Trojan War is a war of sorrow, a war of apprehension and fear. We see facing one another the representatives of the priestly culture of Asia minor and the Greeks, who felt death within them but did not know, as it were, what to do with it, and the oriental cultures bent on conquest, who wanted death, but did not have it. The Greeks had death, but were at a loss what to do with it. They needed the infusion of another element before they could discover its secret. Achilles, Agamemnon—all these men bore death within them, but did not know what to do with it. They look across to Asia. There in Asia they see a people who are in the reverse position, who are suffering under the direct influence of the opposite condition. Over there are individuals who do not feel death in the intense way it is felt by the Greeks themselves; over there are individuals to whom death is something abounding in life.

All this has been brought to expression in a wonderful way by Homer. Wherever he sets the Trojans over against the Greeks, everywhere he lets us see this contrast. You may see it, for instance, in the characteristic figures of Hector and Achilles. And in this contrast is expressed what is taking place on the frontier of Asia and Europe. Asia, in those olden times, had, as it were, a supra-abundance of life over death; they yearned for death. Europe had, on the Greek soil, a supra-abundance of death, and the Greeks were at a loss to find their true relationship to it. Thus from a second point of view we see Europe and Asia set over against one another.

In the first place, we had the transition from rhythmic memory to temporal memory; now we have these two quite different experiences in respect of death in the human organization. Tomorrow we will consider more in detail the contrast, which I have only been able to indicate at the close of today's lecture, and so approach a fuller understanding of the transitions that lead over from Asia to Europe. For these had a deep and powerful influence on human evolution, and without understanding them we really cannot arrive at any understanding of the evolution we are passing through in the present day.

Lecture 3

DORNACH, 26 DECEMBER 1923

THIRTEEN years ago, almost to the day, in a course of lectures that I gave in Stuttgart between Christmas and New Year, I spoke of the same events that we will cover in the present course of lectures. Only we will have to alter the standpoint somewhat. In the first two introductory lectures we have been at pains to acquire an understanding for the radical change in the life of thought and feeling that has come about in the course of human evolution, prehistoric as well as historic. In today's lecture, at any rate to begin with, we shall not need to go back more than a few thousand years.

You know that from the standpoint of anthroposophy, we have to regard as of paramount importance in its consequences for human evolution the so-called Atlantean catastrophe that befell the Earth in the time commonly known as the later Ice Age. It was the last act in the downfall of the Atlantean continent, which forms today the floor of the Atlantic Ocean; and following it we have as we have often described, five great successive epochs of civilization, and leading up to our own time. The two earliest of these have no trace in historical tradition, for the literature remaining in the East, even all that is contained in the magnificent Vedas, in the profound Vedantic philosophy, is but an echo of what we should have to describe, if we wanted to recall these ancient epochs. In my book *The Secret Science*,[16] I have always spoken of them as the Ancient Indian and the Ancient Persian Epochs.

Today we shall not have to go as far back as this; we will direct our thoughts to the period which I have often designated as the Egypto-Chaldean, the period preceding the Greco-Latin. We have already had to draw attention to the fact that during the time between the

Atlantean catastrophe and the Greek period, great changes took place in regard to the human power of memory such as we have today. The temporal memory, by means of which we can take ourselves back in time was not in existence in this third post-Atlantean period; humans then had, as we have described in an earlier lecture, a memory that was linked to rhythmic experience. And we have seen how this rhythmic memory proceeded from a still earlier memory that was particularly strong in the Atlantean period, namely, localized memory, where we bore within ourselves only a consciousness of the present, but used all manner of things which we found in the external world or which we ourselves set there, as signs by means of which we put ourselves into relationship with the past; and not only with our own, personal past, but with the past of humanity in general.

In this connection, we have not only to think of signs that were on the Earth; in those ancient times the planetary constellations in the heavens served us as signs, especially in their recurrences and in the variations of these recurrences. From the constellations, humans perceived how things were in earlier times. Thus heaven and earth worked together to build the localized memory for ancient humanity.

Now humans of long past times were different in the whole constitution of their being from humans of a later time, and still more so from the people of our own time. We today, in our waking condition, bear the ego and astral body within us unnoticed, as it were; most people do not notice how the physical bears within it, along with the etheric body, a much more important organism than itself, namely, the astral body and the organization of the ego.[17] You, of course, are familiar with these connections. But ancient humanity felt this fact of their own nature quite differently.

And it is to such a humanity that we must return when we go back to the third epoch of post-Atlantean civilization, the Egypto-Chaldean. At that time we still experienced ourselves as spirit and soul to a great extent outside our physical and etheric bodies, even when awake. We knew how to distinguish: This I have as my spirit and soul—we, of course, call it the ego and the astral body—and it is linked with my physical body and my etheric body. We went through the world in this experience of twofoldness. We did not call our physical and our etheric bodies 'I'. We called 'I' only our soul and spirit, what was spiritual and was in a manner connected downward with our physical and etheric bodies, had a connection with them that we could observe and feel. And in this spirit and soul, in this ego and astral body, we were made aware of the entry of the divine and spiritual Hierarchies, even as today we feel the entry of natural substances into our physical bodies.

Today our experience in the physical body is of the following nature: We know that with the process of nourishment, with the process of breathing, we receive the substances of the external kingdoms of nature. Before that, they are outside; then they are within us. They enter us, penetrate us, and become part of us. In that earlier age, when we experienced a certain separation of our psychic and spiritual natures from our physical and etheric natures, we knew that Angels, Archangels, and other entities up to the highest Hierarchies are themselves spiritual substances that penetrate our soul and spirit and become—if I may put it so—part of us. So that at every moment of life we were able to say: In me live the gods. And we looked upon our ego, not as built up from below by means of physical and etheric substances, but as bestowed on us through grace from above, as coming from the Hierarchies. And as a burden, or rather as a vehicle, in which we feel ourselves borne forward in the physical world as in a vehicle of life—so did we conceive of our physical and etheric nature. Until this is clearly grasped, we will not understand the course of events in the evolution of humanity.

We could trace this course of events by reference to many different examples. Today we will follow one thread, the same that I touched upon 13 years ago, when I spoke of that historic document which represents the most ancient phase of the evolution we have now to consider—I mean the Epic of Gilgamesh.[18] The Epic of Gilgamesh has in part the character of a saga, and so today I will set before you the events that I described 13 years ago, as they manifest themselves directly to spiritual vision.

In a certain town in Asia Minor—it is called Uruk in the Epic—there lived a man who belonged to the conquering type of which we spoke in the last lecture, the type that sprang so truly and naturally out of the whole mental and social conditions of the time. The Epic calls him Gilgamesh. We have then to do with a personality who has preserved many characteristics of the humanity of earlier times. Clear though it is, however, to this personality that he has, as it were, a dual nature—that he has on the one hand the spiritual and psychic nature into which the gods descend, and on the other hand, the physical and etheric elements into which the substances of the Earth and the cosmos, physical and etheric substances, enter—it is nonetheless a fact that the representative people of his time are already passing through a transition that consisted in this: The ego-consciousness, which a comparatively short time previously was above in the sphere of spirit and soul, had now, if I may so express it, sunk down into the physical and etheric. Gilgamesh was one of those who began no longer to say 'I' to the spiritual and psychic part of their nature, in which they felt the presence of the gods, but rather to say 'I' to that which was earthly and etheric in them. Such was the stage of development of the human psyche of that time.

But along with this condition of soul, where the ego has descended from the spirit and soul and entered as conscious ego into the bodily and etheric, this personality had still left within habits belonging to the past, and especially the habit of experiencing memory solely in connection with rhythm. He still retained also that inward feeling that we must learn to know the forces of death, because only the forces of death can give to us what brings us to powers of reflection.

Now owing to the fact that in the personality of Gilgamesh we have to do with a soul who had already gone through many incarnations on Earth, and had now entered into the new form of human existence which I have just described, we find him at this point in a physical existence that bore in it a strain of uncertainty. The justification, as it were, of the habits of conquest; the justification, too, of the rhythmic memory, were beginning to lose their validity for the Earth. And so the experiences of Gilgamesh were thoroughly those of an age of transition.

Hence it came about that when this personality, in accordance with the old custom, conquered and seized the city that in the Epic is called Uruk, dissensions arose in the city. At first he was not liked.

He was regarded as a foreigner and indeed would never have been able alone to meet all the difficulties that presented themselves in consequence of his capture of the city.

Then, because destiny had led him thither, another personality appeared—the Epic of Gilgamesh calls him Eabani*—a personality who had descended relatively late to the Earth from that planetary existence which humanity led for a period, as you will find described in my *Secret Science*. You know how during the Atlantean epoch souls descended, some earlier, some later, from the different planets, having withdrawn thither from the Earth at a very early stage of Earth evolution.

In Gilgamesh, on the other hand, we have to do with an individuality who returned comparatively early to the Earth. Thus at the time of which we are speaking he had already experienced many earthly incarnations. In the other individuality who had now also come to that city we have to do with one who had remained comparatively long in planetary existence and only later found his way back to Earth. You may read this from a somewhat different point of view in my Stuttgart lectures of 13 years ago.[19]

Now this second individuality formed an intimate friendship with Gilgamesh, and together they were able to place the social life of the city on a permanent footing. This was possible because there remained for this second personality a great deal of the knowledge that came from that sojourn in the cosmos beyond the Earth, and that was preserved for a few incarnations after the return to Earth. He had, as I said in Stuttgart, a kind of enlightened cognition; clairvoyance, clairaudience and what we may call 'clair-cognition'. Thus we have in Gilgamesh what remained of the old habits of conquest and of the rhythmically-directed memory, and in Eabani what remained to him from vision and penetration into the secret mysteries of the cosmos. And from the flowing together of these two things, there grew up, as was indeed generally the case in those olden times, the whole social structure of that city in Asia Minor. Peace and happiness descended upon the city and its inhabitants, and everything would have been in order, had not a certain event taken place that set the whole course of affairs in another direction.

---

*Also known as Enkidu.

There was in that city a Mystery, the Mystery of a Goddess, and this Mystery preserved very many secrets relating to the cosmos. It was, however what I might call, in keeping with those times, a kind of synthetic Mystery. That is to say, in this Mystery revelations were collected together from various Mysteries of Asia. And the contents of these Mysteries were cultivated and taught there in diverse ways at different times. Now this was not initially understood by the personality who bears the name of Gilgamesh in the Epic, and he made complaint against the Mystery that its teachings were contradictory. And seeing that the two personalities of whom we are speaking were those who really held the whole ordering of the city in their hands, and that complaints against the Mystery came from so important a quarter, trouble ensued. At length things became so difficult that the priests of the Mysteries appealed to those powers who in former times were accessible to humans in the Mysteries. It will not surprise you to hear that in the ancient Mysteries they could actually address themselves to the spiritual Beings of the higher Hierarchies. For, as I told you yesterday, to the ancient Oriental, Asia was nothing other than the lowest heaven, and in this lowest heaven we are aware of the presence of spiritual Beings and had intercourse with them. Such intercourse was especially cultivated in the Mysteries. And so the priests of the Ishtar[20] Mysteries turned to those spiritual powers to whom they always turned when they sought enlightenment, and it came about that these spiritual powers inflicted a certain punishment upon the city.

What happened was expressed at the time in the following way: Something that was really a higher spiritual force was working in Uruk as an animal power, as a spectral, animal power. Trouble of all kinds befell the inhabitants, physical illnesses and more especially psychic diseases and disturbances. The consequence was that the personality who had attached himself to Gilgamesh and who is called Eabani in the Epic, dies; but in order that the mission of the other personality might be continued on Earth, Eabani remained with this personality spiritually, even after death. Thus when we consider the later life and development of the personality who in the Epic bears the name of Gilgamesh, we have still to see in it the working together in the two personalities, but now in such a way that in the subsequent years of Gilgamesh's life he receives intuitions and enlightenment from Eabani, and so continues to act, although alone, not simply out of his own will, but out of the will of both, from the flowing together of the will of both.

What I have here placed before you is something that was fully possible in those olden times. Our life of thought and feeling was not then so single and united as it is today. Hence we could not have the experience of freedom, in the sense in which we know it today. It was quite possible, either for a spiritual Being who had never incarnated on Earth to work through the will of an earthly personality, or, as was the case here, for a human personality who had passed through death and was living a posthumous existence, to speak and act through the will of a personality on Earth. So it was with Gilgamesh. And from what resulted in this way through the flowing together of the two wills, Gilgamesh was able to recognize with considerable clearness at what point he himself stood in the history of humanity. Through the influence of the spirit that inspired him, he began to know that the ego had sunk down into the physical body and etheric body, which are mortal; and from that moment, the problem of immortality began to play an intensely strong part in his life. His whole longing was set on finding his way by some means or other into the very heart of this problem. The Mysteries, wherein was preserved what there was to say on Earth in those days concerning immortality, did not readily reveal their secrets to Gilgamesh. The Mysteries had still their traditions, and in their traditions was preserved also in great measure the living knowledge that was present on Earth in Atlantean times, when the ancient original wisdom ruled among us.

The bearers of this original wisdom, however, who once went about on Earth as spiritual Beings, had long ago withdrawn and founded the cosmic colony on the Moon. For it is pure childishness to suppose that the Moon is the dead, frozen body that modern physics describes. The Moon is, above all, the cosmic world of those spiritual Beings who were the first great teachers of earthly humanity, the Beings who once brought us the primeval wisdom and who, when the Moon had left the Earth and sought a place for itself in the planetary system, withdrew also and took up their abode on this Moon.

Whoever today is able to attain through Imaginative cognition a true knowledge of the Moon, gains knowledge also of the spiritual Beings in this cosmic colony, who were once the teachers of the ancient wisdom to humanity on Earth. What they had taught was preserved in the Mysteries, and also the impulses whereby we ourselves are able to come into a certain relationship with this ancient wisdom.

The personality who is called Gilgamesh in the Epic had, however, no living connections with these Mysteries of Asia Minor. But through the supersensible influence of the friend who was still united with him in post-mortem existence, there arose in Gilgamesh an inner impulse to seek out paths in the world whereby he might be able to come to an experience concerning the immortality of the soul. Later on, in the Middle Ages, when we desired to learn something concerning the spiritual world, it was customary that we would sink down into our own inner natures. In more modern times, we could say that a still more inward process is followed. In those olden times of which we are speaking, however, it was a matter of clear and exact knowledge that the Earth is not the mere lump of rock which the geology books would lead us to imagine, but rather that the Earth is a living being—a living being, moreover, endowed with soul and spirit. As a tiny insect that runs over a human being as it passes over his nose and forehead, or through his hair; as the insect acquires its knowledge in this way by making a journey over the human being, so in those times it was by setting forth upon journeys over the Earth and by learning to know the Earth with its different configurations in different places that we gained insight into the spiritual world. And this he was able to do, whether access to the Mysteries were permitted to him or not. It is in truth no merely superficial account that relates how Pythagoras[21] and others wandered far and wide in order to attain their knowledge. Humans went about the Earth in order to receive what was revealed in its manifold configurations, in all that they could observe from the different forms and shapes of the Earth in different places; and not of the Earth in its physical aspect alone, but also of the Earth as soul and spirit.

Today we may travel to Africa, to Australia, and yet, with the exception of external details, at which we gape and stare, our experiences in these places may be very little different from our experiences at home. For our sensitiveness to the deep differences that subsist between different places of the Earth has died.

In the period with which we are now dealing, it had not died out. Thus the impulse to wander over the Earth, and thereby receive something that should help gain a solution of the problem of immortality, betokened something filled with meaning for Gilgamesh.

So he set forth upon his wanderings. And the result for him was of very great significance. He came to a region that is nearly the same as we now call Burgenland, a district much talked of in recent times and concerning which there has been a good deal of contention as to whether it should belong to Hungary or not. The whole social conditions of the country have of course greatly changed since those far-off times. Gilgamesh came thither and found there an ancient Mystery—the High Priest of the Mystery is called Xisuthros in the Epic—an ancient Mystery that was a genuine successor of the old Atlantean Mysteries—only, of course, in a changed form, as must necessarily be the case after so long a time had elapsed.

And it was so that in this ancient Mystery centre they knew how to judge and appraise the faculty of knowledge that Gilgamesh possessed. He was met with understanding. A test was imposed upon him, one that in those days was often imposed on pupils of the Mysteries. He had to go through certain exercises, wide awake, for seven days and seven nights. It was too much for him, so he submitted himself to a substitute test. Certain substances were prepared for him, of which he then partook, and by means of them received a certain enlightenment; although, as is always the case when certain exceptional conditions are not assured, the enlightenment might be doubtful in some respects. Nevertheless a degree of enlightenment was there, a certain insight into the great connections in the universe, into the spiritual structure of the universe. And so, when Gilgamesh had ended his wandering and was returning home again, he did in fact possess a high spiritual insight.

He travelled along the Danube, following the river on its northern bank, until he came again to his home. Because he did not receive the initiation into the post-Atlantean Mystery in the other way that I described, but instead in a somewhat uncertain way, he succumbed to the first temptation that assailed him and fell into a terrible fit of anger over an event that came to his notice—something, in effect, which he heard had taken place in the city. He heard of the event before he reached the city, and burst out into a storm of anger; and in consequence, the enlightenment he had received was almost entirely darkened, so that he arrived home without it.

Nevertheless—and this is the peculiar characteristic of this personality—he still had the possibility, through the connection with the spirit of his dead friend, of looking into the spiritual world, or at least of receiving information from it.

It is, however, one thing by means of an initiation to acquire direct vision into the spiritual world, and another thing to receive information from a personality who is dead. Still, we may say with truth that something of an insight into the nature of immortality did remain with Gilgamesh. I am setting aside just now the experiences that are undergone by us after death; these do not yet play very strongly into the consciousness of the next incarnation, nor did they in those days—into life, into the inner constitution they work very strongly, but not into consciousness.

You now have before you these two personalities whom I have described and who together bring to expression the mental and spiritual constitution of humans in the third post-Atlantean period of civilization at about the middle point of its development. These two personalities still lived in such a way that the whole manner of their life was in itself strong evidence of the duality in human nature. The one—Gilgamesh—was conscious of this duality; he was one of the first to experience the descent of the 'I'-consciousness, the descent of the ego into human physical and etheric nature. The other, inasmuch as he had experienced few incarnations on Earth, had a clairvoyant knowledge, by means of which he was able to know that there is no such thing as matter, but that everything is spiritual and the so-called material is only another form of the spiritual.

Now you can imagine that, if our being were so constituted, we certainly could not think and feel what we think and feel today. His whole thinking and feeling was indeed totally different from ours. And what such personalities could receive in the way of instruction was of course quite unlike what is taught today at school or in the universities. Everything of a spiritual or cultural nature that we received in those days came to us from the Mysteries, whence it was spread abroad as widely as possible among humans by all manner of channels. It was the wise, the priests in the Mysteries, who were the true teachers of humanity.

Now it was characteristic of these two personalities that in the incarnation that we have described they were unable, just because of their special psychic constitution, to approach the Mysteries of their own land. The one who is named Eabani in the Epic stood near the cosmos; the one who is called Gilgamesh experienced a kind of initiation into a post-Atlantean Mystery, which however only partially bore fruit in him. The result of all this was that both felt in their own being, as it were, something that made them kin to the primeval times of earthly humanity. Both were able to put the question to themselves: How have we become what we are? What share have we had in the evolution of the Earth? We have become what we are through the evolution of the Earth; what part have we played in its evolution?

The question of immortality that was the occasion of such suffering and conflict to Gilgamesh, was connected in those days with a necessary vision into the evolution of the Earth in primeval times. We could not think or feel (using the words in the sense of those times) the immortality of the soul unless we had at the same time some vision of how human souls who were already there in very early phases of the Earth's evolution, during the Ancient Sun and Ancient Moon embodiments, saw approaching them what later became what we call earthly. We felt we belonged to the Earth. We felt that to know ourselves, we must behold and recognize our connection with the Earth.

Now the tacit knowledge that was cultivated in all Mysteries of Asia, was first and foremost cosmic knowledge; its wisdom and its teachings unfolded the origin of the evolution of the Earth in connection with the cosmos. So that in these Mysteries there appeared before us in a living way, in such a way that it could become living ideas in them, a far-spread vision, showing them how the Earth evolved, and how in the heave and surge of the substances and forces of the Earth, all through the Sun, Moon, and Earth periods of evolution, we have been evolving together with all these substances. All this was set before us extremely vividly.

One of the Mysteries where such things were taught was continued on into much later times. It was the Mystery centre of Ephesus, the Mystery centre of Artemis of Ephesia. This Mystery had in the very middle of its sanctuary the image of the Goddess Artemis. When we look today at pictures of the goddess Artemis, we have perhaps only the grotesque impression of a female form with many breasts.

This is because we have no idea how such things were experienced in olden times; and it was the inner experience evoked by these things that was all-important. The pupils of the Mysteries had to go through a certain preparation before they were conducted to the true centre of the Mysteries. In the Ephesian Mysteries, the centre was this image of the Goddess Artemis. When the neophytes were led up to the centre, they became one with such an image. As they stood before the image, they lost the consciousness that they were there in front of it, enclosed in their skin. They acquired the consciousness that they themselves were what the image is. They identified themselves with the image. This identification of themselves in consciousness with the divine image at Ephesus had the following effect. The neophytes no longer merely looked out upon the kingdoms of the Earth that were round about them—the stones, trees, rivers, clouds, and so forth—but when they felt themselves one with the image, when they entered into the image of Artemis, they received an inner vision of their connection with the kingdoms of the ethers. They felt themselves one with the world of the stars, one with the processes in the world of the stars. They did not feel themselves as earthly substance within a human skin; rather they felt their cosmic existence. They felt themselves within the etheric.

And as they did so, there rose before them earlier conditions of earthly experience and of our experience on Earth. They began to see what these earlier conditions had been. Today we look upon the Earth as a great piece of rock or stone, covered with water over a large part of its surface and surrounded by a sphere of air containing oxygen and nitrogen and other substances—containing, in fact, what the human being requires for breathing. And so on, and so on. And when thinkers begin to explain and speculate on what passes today for scientific knowledge, then we get a fine result indeed! For only by means of spiritual vision can we penetrate to the conditions that prevailed in the earliest primeval times. Such a spiritual vision, however, concerning primeval conditions of the Earth and of humanity, was attained by the pupils of Ephesus when they identified themselves with the divine image; they beheld and understood how formerly what surrounds the Earth today as atmosphere was not as it now is;

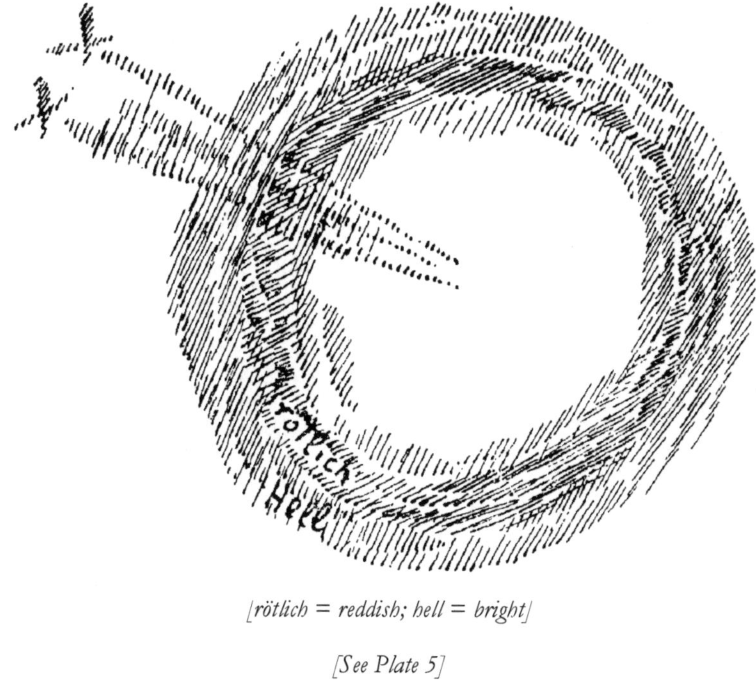

[rötlich = reddish; hell = bright]

[See Plate 5]

surrounding the Earth, in the place where the atmosphere is today, was an extraordinarily fine albumen, a volatile-fluid,[22] albuminous substance [Plate 5]. And they saw how everything that lived on the Earth required for its own genesis the forces of this volatile-fluid, albuminous substance, that was spread over the Earth, and how everything also lived in it. They saw too how what was in a certain sense already finely diluted within this substance, but everywhere exhibiting the tendency to crystallize, what was there as silicic acid was in reality a kind of sensory-organ for the Earth, and could take up into itself from all sides the Imaginations and influences from the surrounding cosmos. And thus in the silicic acid contained in the earthly albuminous atmosphere were everywhere Imaginations, real and externally present.

These Imaginations had the form of gigantic, vegetable organisms. Out of what incorporated itself into the earthly as Imagination the plant kingdoms later developed, through the assimilation of atmospheric substance. This was originally a fleeting form within the circumference of the Earth. Only later did it sink down into the earth and become the plants. And besides the silicic acid, there was also imbedded in this atmosphere of albumen another substance, something chalk-like in an extremely diluted condition. Again, out of this chalky substance, under the influence of the congelation of the albumen there arose the animal kingdom. And humans felt themselves within all this. They felt one with the whole Earth in primordial times. They lived in what formed itself as plant in the Earth through Imagination, and they also lived in what was developing on Earth as animal, in the way I have described. Humans felt themselves to be spread out over the whole Earth; they felt themselves to be at one with the Earth. So that the human beings were all—as I have described it for the Platonic[23] teaching in my book *Christianity as Mystical Fact*,[24] in reference to the human capacity for ideas—were all each within the other.

Now destiny brought it about that the two personalities, of whom I spoke in Stuttgart and of whom I am speaking of to you again here, were reincarnated as adherents of the Mystery of Ephesus, and there received with deep devotion into their souls the things that I have here pictured to you in brief outline. Thereby their souls were, in a manner, inwardly consolidated. Through the Mystery they now received as earthly wisdom what had formerly been accessible to them only in experience for the most part unconscious experience. Thus the human experience of these personalities was divided between two separate incarnations. And thereby they bore within them a strong consciousness of humanity's connection with the higher, with the spiritual world, and at the same time a strong, an intense capacity for feeling and experiencing all that belongs to the Earth.

For if you have two things that perpetually flow together, so that you cannot keep them apart, then they merge and lose themselves in each other. If, on the other hand, they show themselves clearly distinct, then you can judge the one by the other. And so these two personalities were able on the one hand to judge the spiritual of the higher world that came to them as a result of their experiences of life, and that lived in them as an echo from their earlier incarnations. And now, as the origin of the kingdoms of nature was communicated to them in the Mysteries of Ephesus under the influence of the Goddess Artemis, they were able to judge how the things external to humanity on the Earth came into being, how gradually everything external to humanity on the Earth was formed out of a primeval substance, a substance that also included the human being. And the life of these two personalities—it fell partly in the latter end of the time when Heraclitus[25] was still living in Ephesus, and partly in the time that followed—became particularly rich inwardly and was powerfully lit up from within with the life of great cosmic secrets. There was in them, moreover, a strong consciousness of how humans in their life of soul may be connected, not merely with what lies spread out around us on the Earth, but with that which also extends upward—when we ourselves reach upward with our being. Such were the inner psychic configurations of these two personalities who had worked together in the earlier Egypto-Chaldean epoch and then lived together at the time of Heraclitus and after, in connection with the Mystery of Ephesus. And now this working together was able to continue still further. The configuration of soul that had been developed in both, passed through death, through the spiritual world, and began to prepare itself for an earthly life that must needs again bring problems which will now of course present themselves in quite a different way. And when we observe in what manner these two personalities had to find their part later in the history of earthly evolution, we may see how through the experiences of the soul in earlier times—these experiences having their karmic continuation in the next life on Earth—things are prepared which afterwards appear in totally different form in the later life, when the personalities are once more incorporated into the evolution of humanity on Earth.

I have brought forward this example, because these two personalities make their appearance later in a period that was of extraordinary importance in the history of humanity. I indicated this in my lectures at Stuttgart 13 years ago; in fact, I dealt with all these matters from a certain point of view. These personalities who had first gone through what I may call a widely-extended cosmic life during the Egypto-Chaldean epoch, and had then deepened this cosmic experience within them, thereby in a sense establishing their souls, now lived again in a later incarnation as Aristotle[26] and Alexander the Great.[27] When we understand the underlying depths in the souls of Aristotle and Alexander the Great, then we can begin to understand, as I explained in Stuttgart, all that was working so problematically in the time when Greek culture was falling into decay and Roman rule beginning to have dominion.

Lecture 4

DORNACH, 27 DECEMBER 1923

It was my task yesterday to show from the example of individual personalities how the historical evolution of the world runs its course. If we seek to come further in the direction of anthroposophy, we cannot represent things otherwise than by showing the consequences of events as they reflect themselves in humans. For not until our own epoch do we feel ourselves, for reasons which we will discuss in the course of these lectures, shut off as an individual being from the rest of the world. In all previous epochs we felt—and, be it expressly noted, in all subsequent epochs we will again feel ourselves—to be members of the whole cosmos, as belonging to the entire world, even as a finger (as I have often said) can have no independent existence for itself, but can only exist on the human being as a whole. For the moment a finger is separated from us, it is no longer a finger; it begins to decay; it is something quite different, subject to very different laws than it is when attached to a human organism. And as a finger is only a finger in unison with the organism, so in the same way we are only a being having some form or other, whether in the earthly life or in the life between death and a new birth, in connection with the entire cosmos. This consciousness was present in earlier epochs, and will again be present at a later time; only it is darkened today because, as we shall hear, it was necessary that it should be eclipsed in order that we might develop to the full the experience of freedom. The farther back we go, however, into ancient times, the more do we find individuals possessing this consciousness of belonging to the whole cosmos.

I have given you a picture of two personalities, the one called Gilgamesh in the famous Epic, and the other Eabani. I have shown you how these personalities lived in the ancient Egypto-Chaldean epoch[28] in accordance with what was possible at that time, and how they afterwards experienced a deepening through the Mysteries of Ephesus. And I told you at the end of my lecture yesterday that the same human beings played their part later in the historical evolution of the world as Aristotle and Alexander.

In order now to understand fully the course of earthly evolution at the time when all these things were taking place, we must look more closely into what such souls were able to receive into themselves in these three successive epochs.

I have told you how the personality who is concealed behind the name of Gilgamesh undertook a journey to the West, and went through a kind of Western, post-Atlantean initiation.

Let us first form an idea of the nature of such an initiation, so that we may better understand what came later. We will naturally turn to a place where echoes of the old Atlantean initiation remained on for a long time. This was the case with the Hibernian Mysteries, of which I have recently spoken to the friends who are here in Dornach.[29] I must now repeat some of what I said then so that we can come to a clear and full understanding of the subject that we are treating.

The Mysteries of Hibernia, the Irish Mysteries, were in existence for a long time. They were still there at the time of the foundation of Christianity. And they are the Mysteries that in some respects preserved most faithfully the ancient wisdom of the Atlantean peoples. Let me give you a picture of the experiences of a person who was initiated into the Irish Mysteries in the post-Atlantean epoch. Before they were able to receive initiation, they had to be strictly prepared. The preparation that had to be undergone before entering the Mysteries was always in those times extraordinarily strict and rigorous. The important thing in the Hibernian Mysteries was that pupils should learn to become aware in powerful, inward experience of what is *illusory* in their environment—all the things, that is to say, which they attributed to their sensory perception. Then they were made aware of all the difficulties and obstacles which meet us when we search after the *truth*, the real truth. And they were shown how, fundamentally, everything which surrounds us in the world of the senses is an illusion, that what the senses provide is illusion, and that the truth conceals itself behind the illusion, so that in fact true being is not accessible to us through sensory perception.

Now, very likely you will say that you yourselves have held this conviction for a long time; you know this quite well. But all the knowledge we can have in present-day consciousness of the illusory nature of the sensory world is as nothing compared with the inner shattering, the inner tragedy that individuals of that time suffered in their preparation for the Hibernian initiation. For when we say theoretically that everything is maya,[30] everything is illusion, we take it quite lightly! But the training of the Hibernian pupils was carried through to such a point that they had to say to themselves: there is for humans no possibility of penetrating the illusion and coming to real, true Being.

The pupils were led by this means to content themselves, as it were in desperation, with the illusion. They adopted an attitude of despair. The illusory character, they felt, is so overpowering and so penetrating that we can never get beyond it. And in the life of these pupils we always find the feeling: Very well then, we must remain in the illusion. That means, however, that we must lose the very ground from under our feet, for there is no standing firmly on illusion! In truth, my dear friends, we can scarcely form any idea today of the strictness and severity of the preparation in the ancient Mysteries. Individuals shrink in terror before what inner development actually demands.

Such was the experience that came to the pupils in regard to Being and its illusory character. And now a similar experience regarding the search for truth awaited them. They learned to know the hindrances we have in our emotions that keep us from coming to the truth, all the dark and overwhelming feelings that trouble the clear light of knowledge. And so once more that culminated in a great moment when they said to themselves: If truth is inaccessible, well, then, we live—we must live—in error, in untruth. To arrive at a time in their lives when they despair of Being and truth means, in short, that they are stripped of their own humanity.

All this was given in order that, through experiencing the opposite of what we were finally to reach as our goal, we might approach that goal with a proper and deep human feeling. For unless one has learned what it means to live with error and illusion, then one cannot value Being and truth. And the pupils of Hibernia had to learn to value Being and truth.

And then, when they had gone through all this, when they had, as it were, experienced to the bitter end the entire opposite of what they were eventually to reach, the pupils were led (and here I must describe what happened in a pictorial language that can represent what really took place in the Hibernian Mysteries), they were then led into a kind of sanctuary where there were two statues like pillars of infinitely strong suggestive force, and of gigantic size. One of these pillar-like statues was inwardly hollow; the surface that surrounded the hollow space, the whole substance, that is, of which the statue consisted, was elastic throughout. Wherever one pressed, one could make an indentation into the statue; but the moment one ceased to press, the form restored itself.

The whole pillar-shaped statue was made in such a way that the head was more particularly developed. When someone approached the statue, they had the feeling: Forces are streaming forth from the head into the colossal body. Of course, they did not see the space within; they only became aware of it when they pressed. And the pupil was exhorted to press. The neophyte had the feeling that the forces of the head rayed out over the whole of the rest of the body, that in the statue the head does everything.

I willingly admit, my dear friends, that if a modern individual in our present-day, prosaic life were led before the statue, they would scarcely be able to experience anything but very abstract ideas about it. That is certainly so. But it is a different matter when we first experience with our whole inner being, with soul and spirit—yes, and with blood and nerves—the might of illusion and the might of error, and then, after that, we experience the suggestive force of such a gigantic figure.

This statue had male characteristics.

Beside it stood another that had female characteristics. It was not hollow. It was composed of a substance that was not elastic, but rather plastic. When the neophyte pressed this statue—and again they were exhorted to do so—they destroyed the form. They dug a hole in the body.

After the pupil had found how in the one statute, owing to its elasticity, the form was always re-established, and how in the other they defaced the statue by pressing it, and after something else had also taken place, of which I shall speak presently, he left the place, and was only led back there again when all the deformations he had caused in the plastic, non-elastic female figure had been restored, and the statue was intact. Thanks to all the preparations which the neophyte had undergone—and I can give them here only in brief—in connection with the statue having female characteristics, they were able to receive a deep, inner experience in the whole of their being—body, soul, and spirit.

This inner experience had of course already been prepared in the neophyte earlier, but it was established and confirmed in full measure through the suggestive influence of the statue. They received into them a feeling of inward numbness, of hard and frozen numbness. This worked in them such that they saw their souls filled with Imaginations. And these Imaginations were pictures of the Earth's winter, pictures that represented the winter of the Earth. Thus the pupil was led to perceive reality, in the spirit, from within.

With the other, the male statue, they had a different experience. They felt as though all the life in them, which was generally spread out over the whole body, went into their blood, as if their blood were permeated with forces and pressing against their skin. Whereas before, the one statue made them feel that they were becoming a frozen skeleton, they now had to feel before the other that all the life in them was being consumed in heat, and they were living in a tightly-stretched skin. This experience of their entire inwardness pressing against the surface enabled the pupils to receive a new insight. They were able to say to themselves: You now have a feeling of what you would be if, of all the things in the cosmos, the Sun alone worked upon you. In this way, they learned to recognize the working of the Sun in the cosmos, and how the Sun's effects are distributed throughout it. They learned to know our relationship to the Sun. And they learned that the reason why they are not really what they now felt themselves to be under the suggestive influence of the statue of the Sun was because other forces, working in from other corners of the cosmos, modified this working of the Sun. In this way, the neophytes learned how to find their bearings in the cosmos, to be, as it were, at home in the cosmos.

And when the neophytes felt the suggestive influence of the statue of the Moon, when they had in them the hard frost of numbness, and experienced a winter landscape within (in the case of the statue of the Sun, they experienced a summer landscape in the spirit), then they felt what they would be like if only the lunar influences were present.

What do we really know about the world in the present day? We know, let us say, the chicory flower is blue, that the rose is red, the sky blue, and so forth. But these facts make no violent or overwhelming impression upon us. They merely tell us of what is nearest at hand, of what is in our immediate environment. If we would know the secrets of the cosmos, then we must become in our whole being a sensory organ—and that to an intense degree.

Through the suggestive influence of the statue of the Sun, the whole of the neophytes' being was concentrated in the circulation of the blood. They learned to know themselves as solar beings, as they experienced within them this suggestive influence. And they learned to know themselves as lunar beings by experiencing the suggestive influence of the female statue. And then they were able to tell from these inner experiences they had received how Sun and Moon work upon us; even as we today can say, from experience of our eyes, how the rose affects us, or from the experience of our ears can tell the workings of the sound of C sharp, and so on.

Thus the pupils of these Mysteries experienced still, even in post-Atlantean times, how we are placed, as it were, in the cosmos. It was for them an immediate and direct experience.

Now what I have related to you today is but a brief sketch of the sublime experience that came to us in the Mysteries of Hibernia, and continued to arrive until the first centuries of the Christian era. It was cosmic, this experience of the Sun and the Moon.

In the Mysteries of Ephesus in Asia Minor, the neophytes had to undergo experiences of a very different character. Here they experienced in a particularly intense manner, with the whole of their being, what later found such perfect expression in the opening words of the Gospel of St. John: 'In the beginning was the Word. And the Word was with God. And a God was the word.' In Ephesus, the neophytes were led, not before two statues, but before one, the statue that is known as Artemis of Ephesia. Identifying themselves, as I said yesterday, with this statue, which represented the fullness of life, which abounded with life, the neophytes lived into the cosmic ether. With the whole of their inner feeling and experience, they raised themselves out of merely earthly life, raised themselves up into the experience of the cosmic ether. And now they were guided to new knowledge. First of all, the real nature of human speech was imparted to them. And then from human speech, from the human image, that is, of the cosmic Logos, from the humanly imagined Logos, the neophyte was shown how the cosmic Word works and weaves creatively throughout the universe.

Again, I can only describe these things in barest outline. The process was such that the attention of the neophytes was drawn especially to what happens when we speak, when we impress the mark of our word on the outgoing breath. We were led to experience what happens with what, through our own inner deed, we lead over into life—and moreover, how further processes are united with what takes place in the element of air.

Imagine that we have here the expired air [see drawing, right part, bright blue with a red line], on which are impressed certain words that the human being speaks. While this breath, formed into words, streams outward from the breast, the rhythmic vibration descends and passes over into the whole watery element that permeates the human organism [bright, water]. Thus at the level of our throat, our organs of speech, we have the rhythms of the air when we speak. But along with our speaking goes a surging and seething of our whole body of fluids. The fluid in us that is below the region of speech, comes into vibration, and vibrates in harmony. This is what it really means to say that our speech is accompanied by feelings. If the watery element in the human being did not vibrate in harmony in this way, our speech would proceed neutrally, indifferently; we would

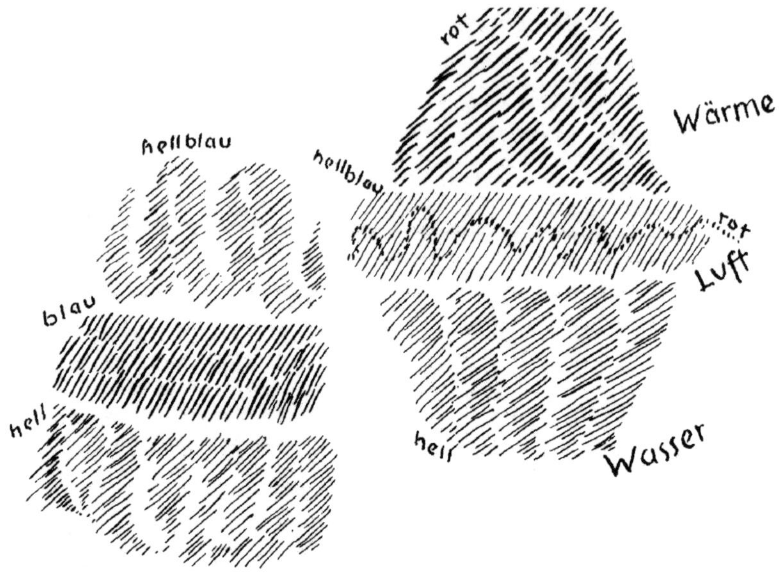

[rot = red; hellblau = bright blue; Wärme = warmth; Luft = air; Wasser = water; hell = bright; blau = blue]

[See Plate 6]

not be able to penetrate what we say with feeling. But upwards in the direction of the head rises the element of warmth [red], and accompanying the words that we impress upon the air are upward-streaming waves of warmth that permeate the head and make it possible there for our words to be accompanied by thought.

Thus, when we speak, we have to do with three things: air, warmth, and water. This process, which alone presents a complete picture of what lives and weaves in human speech, was taken as the starting point for the pupil of Ephesus. It was then made clear to him that what takes place in us is a cosmic process made human, and that in a certain far-off time, the Earth itself worked in that way, only it was not then the airy element, but rather the watery element, the fluid element [left part of the drawing, blue]—which I described yesterday as a volatile, fluid albumin—that had this wave-like moving and surging. Like the air in us, in the microcosm, when we speak on the outgoing breath, so there once existed the volatile, fluid element, the albumin which surrounded the Earth like an atmosphere. And as today the air passes over into the element of warmth, so the albumin rose upwards into a kind of airy element [left, bright blue], and downwards into a kind of earthly element. And as our feelings arise in our body through the fluid element, so in the Earth the earthly formations, the forces of the Earth sprang into existence, all the forces that work and seethe within the Earth. And above, in the airy element, the cosmic thoughts were born, the soaring cosmic thoughts that inhabited earthly substance creatively.

Majestic and powerful was the impression that humans received at Ephesus when we were shown how the microcosmic echo of what had once been macrocosmic lives in our speech. And when the neophytes of Ephesus spoke, they felt an insight into the working of the cosmic Word come to them through the experience of speech. We could perceive how the cosmic Word set in motion the volatile fluid element, giving it movement full of meaning and import. We saw also how it went upwards to the creative, cosmic thought, and downwards to the earthly forces coming into being.

Thus the neophytes lived their way into the cosmos by learning to understand rightly what was in their own being. 'Within thee is the human Logos. The human Logos works from within thee during thy time on Earth. Thou art the human Logos.' (For indeed, through what streams downwards in the fluid element, we are ourselves formed and moulded out of speech, while through what streams upwards, we have our human thoughts during our time on Earth.) 'And even as in thee the essence of humanity is the microcosmic Logos, so once in the far-off beginning of things was the Logos, and It was with God and Itself was a God.'

In Ephesus, this was profoundly understood, for they understood it in and through the human being.

In considering such a personality as is concealed behind the name of Gilgamesh, you must remember how he led his life in the whole milieu, in the whole environment that radiated out from the Mysteries. For all culture, all civilization, emanated in earlier times from the Mysteries. Thus, when I name Gilgamesh to you, you must think of him—as long as he was living in Uruk—not indeed as himself initiated into the Mysteries of Uruk, but as living in a civilization that was permeated with the feeling of an experience we could enjoy from our relationship with the cosmos.

And the experience then came to this personality during his journey to the West, which made him directly acquainted, not with the Hibernian Mysteries themselves—he did not travel so far afield—but with what was cultivated in a colony of the Hibernian Mysteries, situated, as I told you, where the Burgenland[31] now is. What he experienced there lived in his soul and then developed further in the life between death and new birth. And in the next earthly life he underwent a deepening of the soul at Ephesus in connection with this same experience.

The psychic deepening took place for both the individuals of whom we have been speaking. Verily, it was as though a torrent surged up from the depths of the civilization of that time and broke like a great wave over both souls. They experienced in vivid and intense reality what survived in Greece after the Homeric period only as a beautiful semblance, as the glory of something that had gone.

In Ephesus, the place where Heraclitus also lived, and where so much of the old reality was felt into later Greek times, into the sixth or fifth centuries CE, precisely in Ephesus could one still sense the whole reality in which humanity had once lived when we still stood in an immediate relationship to the divine. Then Asia was still the lowest of the heavens through which we still had a relationship to the higher heavens that bordered it, because in Asia the elemental beings were experienced, and above them the Angeloi, Archangeloi and so forth; above them, the Exusiai and so forth. And thus we can say: While already in Greece only the echoes formed of what had once been a reality; what had once been reality was transformed into the images of the heroic legends, in which you can still see clearly that they point to archetypal realities. While in Greece the dramatic elements gained archetypal realities in Aeschylus,[32] in Ephesus it was still the case that, immersed in the deep darkness of the Mysteries, one felt echoes of old realities through which humanity lived in direct contact with the divine beings. And that is what is essential about Greece, namely that the Greeks immersed in the more intimate myths and more intimate beauty and art, thus in an image, what was once experienced in cosmic context by humans.

Now we must turn our thoughts to a time when, on the one hand, the Greek civilization had reached its zenith, when it had probably pushed back, in the Persian wars, the last thrust as it were of the old Asiatic reality, a time when on the other hand Greece itself was already beginning to decline. And we must picture to ourselves what the people of such a time would experience if they still bore in their soul the unmistakable echoes of what had once been the divine, spiritual reality on Earth in the body, soul, and spirit of humanity.

We will have to see how Alexander the Great and Aristotle lived in a world that was not altogether adapted to them, in a world indeed that held great tragedy for them. The fact is, Alexander and Aristotle stood in an altogether different relationship to the spiritual world from those around them, for although they cannot be said to have concerned themselves very much with the Samothracian Mysteries, they had nevertheless a strong affinity in their souls to interactions with the Cabiri[33] in those Mysteries. And right on into the Middle Ages there were those who understood what this meant. We of the present day build up altogether false ideas of the Middle Ages: we do not realize that there were individuals of all classes in life, on into the thirteenth and fourteenth centuries, who possessed a clear spiritual vision, at any rate in that realm which in the ancient East was designated as 'Asia'. The *Song of Alexander* that was composed by a certain priest[34] in the early Middle Ages is a very significant document; in comparison with the account history gives today of the doings of Alexander and Aristotle, the poem by Lamprecht the Priest is a sublime and grand conception, still akin to the old understanding of all that had come to pass through Alexander the Great.

Take for instance a passage in the poem where a wonderful description is given in the following style. When springtime comes, you go out into the woods. You come to the edge of the wood. Flowers are blooming there, and the Sun stands where it lets the shadow fall from the trees onto the flowers. There you may see how in spring, in the shadow of the trees, spiritual flower-children come forth from the calices of the flowers and dance in chorus at the edge of the wood.

We can perceive distinctly shining through this description by Lamprecht the Priest an old and real experience which was still accessible to individuals of that time. They did not go out into the woods, saying prosaically: Here is grass, and here are flowers, and here the trees begin. Rather, when they approached the wood while the Sun stood behind it, and the shadow fell across the flowers, then in the shadow of the trees there came towards them from the flowers a whole world of flower-beings—beings that were actually present to them before they entered into the wood. For when they entered the wood itself, they perceived quite other elemental spirits. This dance of the flower-spirits appeared to Lamprecht the Priest, and he delighted especially in picturing it. It is indeed significant, my dear friends, that when Lamprecht, even as late as the twelfth or the beginning of the twelfth century, had this wish to describe the campaigns of Alexander, he permeates them everywhere with descriptions of nature that still contain the manifestations of the elemental kingdoms. Underlying his *Song of Alexander*, there was this consciousness: 'To describe what took place once upon a time in Macedonia when Alexander began his journeys into Asia, when Alexander was taught by Aristotle, we cannot merely describe the prosaic earth as the environment of these events. No, to describe them worthily we have to include with the prosaic earth the kingdoms of the elemental beings.' How different from a modern book of history, which is, of course, entirely justified for present times. There you will read how Alexander, against the counsel of his teacher Aristotle whom he disobeyed, conceived himself to have the mission to reconcile the barbarians with civilization, creating, as it were, an average of culture; the civilized Greeks, the Hellenes, the Macedonians, and the barbarians.

That, no doubt, is right enough for modern times. And yet how puerile it is compared to the real truth! On the other hand, we have a wonderful impression when we look at the picture Lamprecht gives us of the campaigns of Alexander, attributing to them quite a different goal. We feel as though what I have just described—the entry of the elemental kingdoms of nature, of the spirit into the physical in nature—were intended merely as an introduction. For what is the aim of Alexander's campaigns in Lamprecht's *Song of Alexander*?

Alexander comes to the very gates of Paradise. Translated as it is into the Christian language of his time, this corresponds to a high degree, as I shall presently explain, to the real truth. For the campaigns of Alexander were not undertaken for the mere sake of conquest, still less against the advice of Aristotle to reconcile the barbarians with the Greeks. No, they were permeated by a real and lofty spiritual goal. Their impulse came out of the spirit. Let us read of it in Lamprecht's poem, who in his own way with great devotion, albeit fifteen centuries after the life of Alexander, tells the heroic story. He tells us how Alexander came up to the gates of Paradise, but could not enter in, for, as Lamprecht says, he alone can enter Paradise who has attained true humility, and Alexander, living in pre-Christian times, had not attained that. Only Christianity could bring to humanity true humility.

Nevertheless, if we conceive the thing not in a narrow, but rather in a broad-minded way, we shall see how Lamprecht, the Christian priest, still feels something of the tragedy of Alexander's campaigns.

It is not without purpose that I have spoken of this *Song of Alexander*. For now you will not be surprised if we take our start from the campaigns of Alexander in order to describe what went before and what went after in the history of Western humanity and its connection with the East. For the real underlying feeling in these matters was still widely present, as we have seen, at a comparatively late period in the Middle Ages. Not only so; it was present in so concrete a form that the *Song of Alexander* could arise, describing as it does with wonderful dramatic power the events that were enacted through the two souls I have characterized.

The significance of this moment in the history of Macedonia reaches on the one hand far back into the past, and on the other hand far on into the future. And it is essential to bear in mind how something of a cosmic tragedy hangs over all that has to do with Aristotle and Alexander. Even externally, the tragedy comes to light. It shows itself in this, my dear friends. Owing to peculiar circumstances—circumstances that were fateful for the history of the world—the writings of Aristotle have come into Western Europe, and there have been further studies preserved by the Church. In point of fact, it is only the writings that deal with logic or are clothed in logical form.

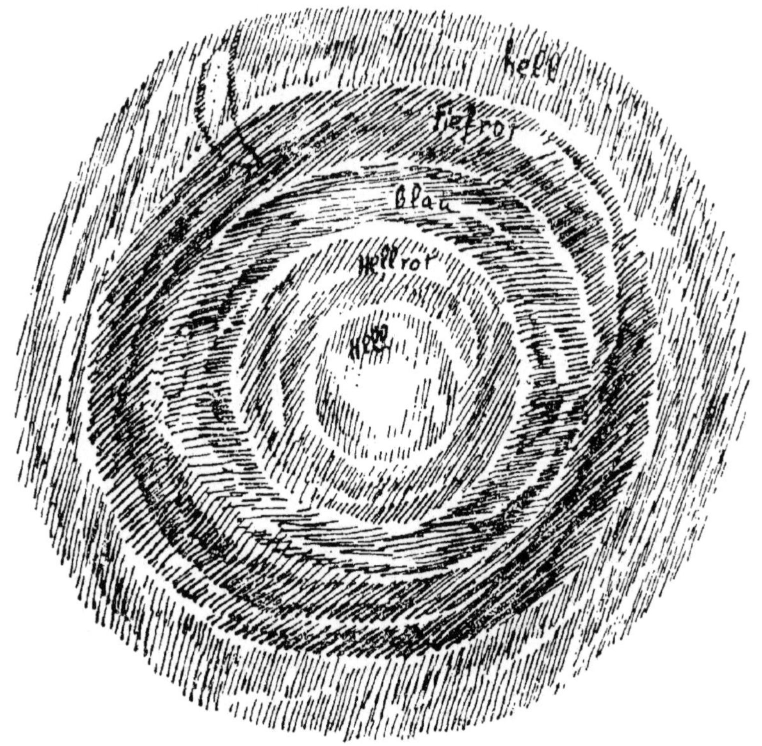

[hell = bright; tiefrot = deep red; blau = blue; hell rot = bright red]

[See Plate 7]

A serious study, however, of the little that is preserved of Aristotle's scientific writings will show what a powerful vision he still had of the connection of the whole cosmos with the human being. Let me draw your attention to a single passage.

We speak today of the elements of earth, of water, of air, of fire or warmth, and then of the ether. How does Aristotle represent all this? He shows the earth, the firm earth [see drawing; bright nucleus]; the fluid earth, water [bright red]; and the whole permeated and surrounded with fire [blue]. But for Aristotle, the 'earth' in this sense reaches up as far as the Moon. And from the cosmos, reaching from the stars to the Moon, and not, that is to say, into the earthly realm, but only as far as the Moon, coming towards us, as it were, from the zodiac, from the stars—is the remaining ether, filling cosmic space [bright, outer]. The ether reaches downwards as far as the Moon.

All this may still be read by scholars in the books that have been written about Aristotle. Aristotle himself, however, said to his pupil, Alexander, again and again: The ether that is way out there beyond the realm of earthly warmth—the light-ether, the chemical ether, and the life-ether—was once upon a time united with the Earth. It came in as far as to the Earth. And when the Moon withdrew in an ancient epoch of evolution, then the ether withdrew from the Earth. And Aristotle told his pupil, Alexander: all that is around us in space as the dead world is not permeated by the ether. When, however, springtime approaches, and plants, animals, and human beings come forth to new life on the Earth, then the elementary spirits bring down again the etheric form from out of the realm of the Moon, bring it down into these new-born beings. Thus the Moon is the shaper and moulder of beings.

Standing before that great female figure in the Hibernian Mysteries, the neophyte had a most vivid experience of how the ether does not really belong to the Earth, but is brought down by the elementary spirits, every year, to the extent that it is needed for the springing-up into life.

And this was so for Aristotle. He also had deep insights into the connection of the human being with the cosmos. His pupil, Theophrastus, did not allow the writings that treat of these things to come westwards. Some of them, however, went to the East, where there still was an understanding for such truths. Thence they were brought by Jews and Arabs through North Africa and Spain to the West of Europe, where they met, in a manner that I will yet describe, with the emanations of the Hibernian Mysteries, as these expressed themselves in the civilization and the cultures of the various peoples.

But now all that I have been describing to you was no more than the beginning of the teaching that Aristotle gave to Alexander. It was a teaching that belonged entirely to the inner experience. I might describe it in outline somewhat as follows. Alexander learned from Aristotle to understand how the earthy, watery, airy, and fiery elements that live outside the human being in the world around us live also within us ourselves, and how we are in this regard a true microcosm. We learned how the earthly element lives in the bones of the human being, and how in our circulation and in all the fluids and humours within us there lives the watery element. The airy element works in all that has to do with the breathing, and the fiery element lives in human thought. Alexander still had the conscious knowledge of living in the elements.

But with this experience of living in the elements of the world also went the experience of our intimate relationship with the Earth. Today we travel eastward, westward, northward, and southward, but we have no feeling for what streams into our being the while. We only see what our external senses perceive; we only see what the earthly substances in us perceive. We do not see what the elements in us perceive.

Aristotle, however, was able to teach Alexander: When you go eastwards, you pass more and more into an element that dries you up. You pass into the dry.

You must not imagine this meant that when one travels to Asia, one becomes completely dried up. We have here, of course, to do with fine and delicate workings that Alexander was perfectly able to feel in himself after he had received the guidance and instruction of Aristotle. When he was in Macedonia he could feel: I have a certain measure of dampness or moistness in me that diminishes as I go eastward. In this way, as he wandered over the Earth, he felt its configuration, as you may feel a human being by touch, let us say by drawing your hand caressingly over some part of the human body, feeling the difference between nose and eye and mouth. In this way, persons such as I have described you were able to perceive a difference between the experience they had when they came more and more into the dry, and the experience that was theirs on the other hand and going westward and coming more and more into the moist.

We still experience the other differentiations today, though crudely. In the direction of the North, we experience the cold; in the direction of the South the warm, the element of fire. But the interplay

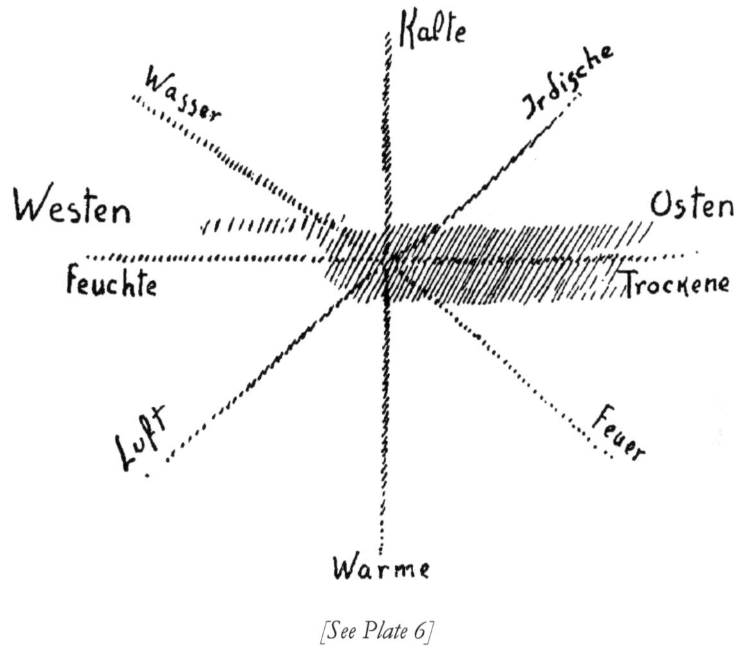

[See Plate 6]

of moist and cold, when one goes Northwest—that is no longer experienced.

Aristotle awakened in Alexander all that Gilgamesh had passed through when he undertook the journey to the West. And the result was that his pupil could perceive in direct inner experience what is felt in the direction of the Northwest, in the intermediate zone between moist and cold, namely water. A man like Alexander not merely could, but did actually speak in such a manner that he did not say: There goes the road to the Northwest, but instead: There goes the road to where the watery element holds dominion. In the intermediate zone between moist and warm lies the element where the air holds dominion.

Such was the teaching in the ancient Greek Chthonian Mysteries, and in the ancient Samothracian Mysteries; and thus did Aristotle teach his own immediate pupil.

And in the zone between cold and dry—that is to say, looking from Macedonia towards Siberia—humans had the experience of the region of the Earth where the earth itself, the earthy, holds dominion—the element of Earth, the hard and firm. In the intermediate zone between warm and dry, that is, towards India, was experienced the region of the Earth where the element of fire ruled.

And so it was that the pupil of Aristotle pointed Northwest and said: There I feel the watery spirits working upon the Earth; pointed Southwest and said: There I feel the airy spirits; pointed Southeast towards India, and saw the spirits of fire hover over the earth, saw them there in their element.

And in conclusion, my dear friends, you will be able to feel the deep and intimate relationship both to the natural and to the moral when I tell you how Alexander began to speak in this way: I must leave the cold and moist element and throw myself into the fire—I must undertake a journey to India! That was a manner of speaking that was as closely bound up with the natural as it was with the moral. I'll have more to say about this tomorrow.

I wanted to give you a picture today of what was living in those times. For in all that took place between Alexander and Aristotle, we may see at the same time a reflection of the great and mighty change that was taking place in the world's history. In those days it was still possible to speak in an intimate way to pupils of the great Mysteries of the past. But then humanity began to acquire in increasing measure logic, abstract knowledge, categories, and to push back the other.

Therefore we have to see in these events the working of a tremendous and deep change in the historical evolution of humanity, and at the same time an all-important moment in the whole progress of European civilization and its connection with the East.

Lecture 5

DORNACH, 28 DECEMBER 1923

Among the Mysteries of ancient times, Ephesus holds a unique position. You will remember that in considering the part played by Alexander in the evolution of the West, I had to mention also this Mystery of Ephesus.

We can only grasp the significance of the events of earlier and more recent times when we understand and appreciate the great change that took place in the character of the Mysteries (which were in reality the source whence all the older civilizations sprang) and passing from the East to the West, and, in the first place, to Greece. This change was of the following nature.

When we look back into the older Mysteries of the East, we have everywhere the impression: The priests of the Mysteries were able, out of their own vision, to reveal great and important truths to their pupils. The farther back we go in time, the more were these wise priests in a position to call forth in the Mysteries the immediate presence of the gods themselves, the spiritual beings who guide the worlds of the planets, who guide the events and phenomena of Earth. The gods were actually present there.

The connection of the human being with the macrocosm was revealed in many different Mysteries in an equally sublime manner to what I pictured for you yesterday, in connection with the Mysteries of Hibernia, and also with the teachings that Aristotle had still to give to Alexander the Great. An outstanding characteristic of all ancient, oriental Mysteries was that moral impulses were not sharply distinguished from natural impulses. When Aristotle points Alexander to the Northwest, where the spirits of the element of water held dominion, it was not only physical impulses that came from that quarter—as we today feel how the wind blows from the Northwest and so forth—but with the physical came also moral impulses. The physical and the moral were one. This was possible, because through the knowledge that was given in these Mysteries—the spirit of nature was actually perceived in the Mysteries—humans felt themselves to be one with the whole of nature. Here we have something in the relationship between humans and nature that was still living and present in the time that intervened between the life of Gilgamesh and the life of the individuality Gilgamesh became, who was also in close contact with the Mysteries, specifically with the Mystery of Ephesus. There was still alive in the people of that time a vision and perception of the connection between humans and the spirit of nature. This connection they perceived in the following way. Through all that humans learned concerning the working of the elementary spirits in nature, and the working of the intelligent Beings in the planetary processes, people were led to this conclusion: All around me I see displayed on every side the world of plants—the green shoots, the buds and blossoms, and then the fruit. I see the annual plants in the meadows and in the countryside that grow up in springtime and fade away again in autumn. I see, too, the trees that go on growing for hundreds of years, forming a bark on the outside, hardening to wood, and reaching downwards far and wide into the earth with their roots. But all that I see out there—the annual herbs and flowers, the trees that take firm hold of the earth—once upon a time, I, as a human being, have borne it all within me.

You know how today, when there is carbon dioxide in the air that has arisen through the breathing of human beings, we can feel that we ourselves have breathed out the carbon dioxide, we have breathed it into space. We have today therefore still a slight connection with the cosmos. Through the airy part of our nature, through the air that gives rise to the breathing and other airy processes that go on in the human organism, we have a living connection with the great universe, with the macrocosm. Human beings today can look upon their exhaled breath, upon the carbon dioxide that was in them and is now outside them. But just as we are able today to look upon the carbon dioxide we have breathed out—we do not generally do so, but we could—so the initiates of olden times looked upon the whole world of plants. Those who had been initiated in the oriental Mysteries, or had received the wisdom that streamed forth from the oriental Mysteries, were able to say: I look back in the evolution of the world to an ancient Sun epoch. At that time I still bore within me the plants. Then afterwards, I let them stream forth from me into the far circles of earthly existence. But as long as I bore the plants within me, while I was still that Adam Kadmon[35] who embraced the whole Earth and the plants with it, so long was this whole vegetable world watery and airy in substance.

Then human beings separated this plant world off from themselves. Imagine that you were to become as big as the whole Earth, and then to separate off, to secrete, as it were, inwardly something plant-like in nature, and this vegetable substance were to go through metamorphoses in the watery element—coming to life, fading away, growing up, being changed, taking on different shapes and forms—and by this Imagination you will call up again in your soul feelings and experiences that once lived in it. Those who received their education and training in the East at about the time of Gilgamesh were able to say to themselves that these things had once been so.

And when they looked abroad upon the meadows and beheld all the growth of green and flowers, then they said: We have separated the plants from ourselves, we have put them forth from us in an earlier stage of our evolution; and the Earth has received them. It is the Earth that has lent them roots, and has given them their woody nature; what in the world of plants tends toward trees comes from the Earth. But the whole vegetative kingdom as such has been cast off, as it were, by humans, and received by the Earth. In this way we felt an intimate and near relationship with everything of the nature of plants.

Humans did not feel a relationship of this kind with the higher animals. For we knew that we could only work our way rightly and come to our true place on the Earth by overcoming the animal form, by leaving the animals behind us in our evolution. We took the plants with us as far as the Earth, then gave them over to her so that she might receive them into her bosom. For the plants, we were on Earth the mediator of the gods, the mediator between the gods and the Earth.

Those who had this great experience acquired a feeling that may be put quite simply in a few words. Humans came hither to the Earth from the universe [yellow]. The question of number does not come into consideration; for, as was said yesterday, we were all within the other. What afterwards became the kingdom of plants separates off from the human being, the Earth receives it, and gives it roots [dark green stripes]. Humans felt as though they had surrounded the Earth with the garment of plant growth, and as though the Earth were thankful for this enfolding [red husk], and took from us the watery and airy plant element that we were able, as it were, to breathe into her.

In entering into this experience, humans felt themselves intimately associated with the god, with the chief god, Mercury. Through the feeling that they had themselves brought the plants onto the earth, humans entered into a special relationship with the god Mercury.

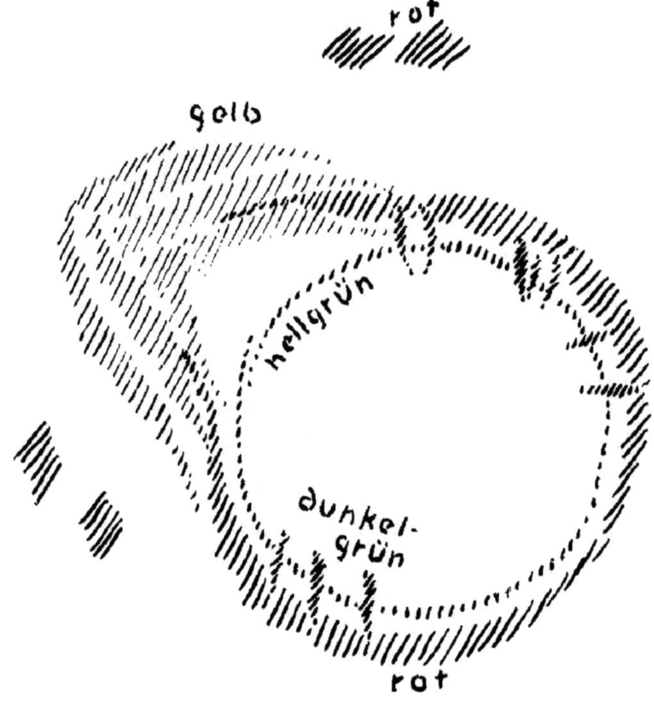

[rot = red; gelb = yellow; hellgrün = bright green; dunkel-grün = dark green]

[See Plate 8]

Towards the animals, on the other hand, humans had a different feeling. They knew that they could not bring them along to Earth; they had to cast them off; they had to make themselves free from them. Otherwise, they would not be able to evolve their human form in the right way. They thrust the animals from them; they were pushed out of the way [red stripes outward] and then had to go through an evolution on their own account on the lower level than the level of humanity. Thus the humans of olden times—of the time of Gilgamesh and later—felt themselves placed between the animal kingdom and the plant kingdom. In relation to the plant kingdom they were the bearers, who bore the seed to the Earth and fructified the Earth with it, doing this as representatives of the gods. In relation to the animal kingdom, they felt as though they had pushed it away from them, in order that they might become human without the encumbrance of the animals, who have consequently been stunted and retarded in their development.

The worship of animals in Egypt has to do with this perception. The deep fellow-feeling, too, with animals that we find in Asia is connected with it. It was a sublime conception of nature that humans had, feeling their relationship on the one hand with the plant world, and on the other hand with the world of animals. In relation to the animals, we had a feeling of emancipation. In relation to the plant kingdom, we felt a close and intimate kinship. The plant world was to us a bit of ourselves, and we felt a sincere love for the Earth, inasmuch as the Earth had received into herself that part of humanity that gave rise to the plants, and let these take root in her, had even given of her own substance to clothe the trees in bark. There was always a moral element present when we took cognisance of the physical world around us. When they beheld the plants in the meadow, it was not only the natural growth that they perceived. In this growth they perceived and felt a moral relationship to humanity. With the animal, they felt again another moral relationship: they had fought their way up beyond them.

Thus we find in the Mysteries over in the East a sublime conception of nature and of spirit in nature. Later there were Mysteries in Greece, too, but these offered a much less real perception of nature and of spirit in nature. The Greek Mysteries are grand and sublime, but they are essentially different from the oriental Mysteries. It is characteristic of the oriental Mysteries that they did not tend to make us feel ourselves a part of the Earth, but rather, through them, we felt ourselves a part of the cosmos, a part of the universe. In Greece, on the other hand, the character of the Mysteries had changed, and the time was come when we began to feel ourselves united with the Earth. In the East, the spiritual world itself was either seen or felt in the Mysteries. It is absolutely true to say that in the ancient oriental Mysteries the gods themselves appeared among the priests, who did sacrifice there and made prayers. The temples of Mysteries were at the same time the earthly guesthouses of the gods, where the gods bestowed upon humans, through the priests, what they had to give them from the treasures of heaven. In the Greek Mysteries, on the other hand, there appeared the images of the gods, the pictures, as it were, the phantoms—true and genuine, but phantoms nonetheless; no longer the divine beings, no longer the realities, but phantoms. And so the Greek had a wholly different experience from those who belonged to the ancient oriental culture. The Greeks had the feeling: There are indeed gods, but for humans it is only possible to have pictures of these gods, just as we have in our memory pictures of past experiences, no longer the experiences themselves.

That was the fundamental feeling that arose in the Greek Mysteries. The Greeks felt that they had, as it were, memories of the cosmos. Not the appearance of the cosmos itself, but pictures; pictures of the gods, and not of the gods themselves. Pictures, too, of the events and processes on Saturn, Sun, and Moon,[36] no longer a living connection with what actually took place on Saturn, Sun, and Moon—the kind of living connection the human being has with his own childhood. Members of the oriental civilization had this real connection with Sun, Moon, and Saturn; they had it from their Mysteries. But the Mysteries of the Greeks had a pictorial or iconic character. The shadowy spirits of divine, spiritual reality appeared in them. And something else accompanied this as well that was very significant. For there was yet another difference between the oriental Mysteries and the Greek.

In the oriental Mysteries, if one wanted to know something of the sublime and tremendous experience that was possible in these Mysteries, one had always to wait until the right *time*. Some experience or other could perhaps only be found by making the appropriate sacrifice, the appropriate supersensible 'experiments', as it were, in autumn, another only in spring, another again at midsummer, and another in the depths of winter. Again it might be that sacrifices were made to certain gods at a time determined by a particular phase of the Moon. At that special time, the gods would appear in the Mysteries, and the people would come there to be present at their manifestations. When the time had gone by, one would have to wait, perhaps 30 years, until the opportunity would come again when those divinities should once more reveal themselves in the Mysteries. All that related to Saturn, for example, could only enter the region of the Mysteries every 30 years; all that was concerned with the Moon, about every 18 years. And so on. The priests of the oriental Mysteries were dependent on time, and also on place, and on all manner of circumstances for receiving the sublime and tremendous knowledge and vision that came to them. Quite different manifestations were received deep in a mountain cave and high on the mountaintop. Or again, the revelations were different, according to whether one was far inland in Asia or on the coast. Thus a certain dependence on place and time was characteristic of the Mysteries of the East.

In Greece, the great and awful realities had disappeared. But images persisted. And the images were dependent not on the time of year, on the course of the century, or on place. Rather, they could receive the images when they had performed this or that exercise, or had made this or that personal sacrifice. If someone had reached a certain stage of sacrifice and of personal ripeness, then for the very reason that he had accomplished all this, they were able to perceive the shadows of the great, cosmic events and of the great, cosmic Beings.

That is the important change in the nature of the Mysteries that meets us when we pass from the ancient East to Greece. The ancient oriental Mysteries were subject to the conditions of space in the locality, while in the Greek Mysteries, human beings themselves came into consideration, and what they brought to the gods. The gods came, so to speak, in their shadow-picture, as a spectre, when humans, through the preparations they had undergone, had been made worthy to receive the god in phantom form. In this way, the Mysteries of Greece prepared the road for modern humanity.

Now, the Mystery of Ephesus stood midway between the ancient oriental Mysteries and the Greek Mysteries. It held a unique position. For in Ephesus, those who attained to initiation were still able to experience something of the tremendous, majestic truths of the ancient East. Their souls were still stirred with the deep, inward experience of the connection of the human being with the macrocosm and with the divine, spiritual Beings of the macrocosm. In Ephesus, humans could still have sight of the supra-earthly, and in no small measure. Self-identification with Artemis, with the goddess of the Mystery of Ephesus, still brought to us a vivid sense of our relationship to the kingdoms of nature. The plant world, so it was taught, is yours; the Earth has only received it from you. You have overcome the animal world. You have had to leave it behind. You must look back on the animals with the greatest possible compassion: they have had to remain behind, in order that you might become human. To feel oneself at one with the macrocosm: this was an experience that was still granted to the initiate of Ephesus. He could still receive the experience straight from the realities themselves.

At the same time, the Mysteries of Ephesus were the first to be turned Westward. As such, they had attained that independence from the seasons, or from the course of years and centuries; that independence from location on Earth. In Ephesus, the important things were the exercises that the humans went through, making themselves ripe, through sacrifice and devotion, to approach the gods. So that on the one hand, in the content of its Mystery truths, the Mystery of Ephesus harked back to the Ancient East, while on the other hand it was already directed to the development of humanity itself, and was thus adapted to the nature and character of the Greeks. It was the very last of the Eastern Mysteries of the Greeks, where the great and ancient truths could still be brought near to humans; for in the East generally the Mysteries had already become decadent.

It was in the Mysteries of the West that the ancient truths remained longest. The Mysteries of Hibernia still existed, centuries after the birth of Christianity. These Mysteries of Hibernia are nevertheless doubly secret and occult, for you must know that even in the so-called Akashic Record,[37] it is by no means easy to search into the hidden mysteries of the statues of which I told you yesterday—the statues of the Sun and Moon, the male and the female. To approach the pictures of the oriental Mysteries and to call them forth out of the astral light is, comparatively speaking, easy for one who is trained in these things. But let anyone approach, or want to approach, the Mysteries of Hibernia in the astral light, and he will at first be dazed and stupefied. He will be beaten back. These Irish, these Hibernian Mysteries will not willingly let themselves be seen in the Akashic pictures, albeit they continued longest in their original purity.

Now you must remember, my dear friends, that the individuality who was in Alexander the Great had come into close contact with the Hibernian Mysteries during the time of Gilgamesh, when he made his journey Westward to the neighbourhood of the modern Burgenland. These Mysteries had lived in him, lived in him after a very ancient manner, for it was in the time when the West resounded still with powerful echoes of the Atlantean age. And not all this experience was carried over into the condition of human existence that runs its course between death and a new birth. Then later the two friends, Eabani and Gilgamesh, found themselves together again in life in Ephesus, and there they entered into a deeply conscious experience of what they had experienced formerly during the time of Gilgamesh more or less unconsciously or subconsciously, in connection with the divine worlds.

Their life during this time of Ephesus was comparatively peaceful. They were able to digest and ponder what they had received into their souls in more stormy days.

Let me remind you of what it was that passed over into Greece before these two appeared again in the decadence of the Greek epoch and the rise of the Macedonian. The Greece of olden time, the Greece that had spread abroad and embraced Ephesus also within its bounds, and had even penetrated right into Asia Minor, had still in her shadowy pictures the after-echo of the ancient time of the gods. The connection between humans and the spiritual world was still experienced, though in shadows. Greece was however gradually working herself free from the shadows; we may observe how step by step the Greek civilization was wresting its way out of what we may call divine civilization and taking on more and more the character of a purely earthly one.

My dear friends, it is only too true that the very most important things in the history of human evolution are simply passed over in the materialistic, external history of today! Of extraordinary importance for the understanding of the whole Greek character and culture is this fact: that in the Greek civilization we find no more than a shadowy picture, a phantom of the old divine presence wherein we had contact with the supersensible worlds, for we were already gradually emerging out of this divinity and learning to make use of our individual and personal spiritual faculties. Step by step we can see this taking place. In the dramas of Aeschylus[38] we may see placed before us in an artistic picture the feeling that yet remained to humans of the old time of the gods. Scarcely however has Sophocles[39] come forward when humanity begins to tear itself away from this conscious sense of union with divine existence. And then something else appears that is coupled with a name which, from one point of view, we cannot overestimate—but of course there are many points of view to be considered.

In the older Greek times there was no need to make written history. Why was this? Because we had the living shadow of everything of divine importance that had happened in the past. History could be read in what came to view in the Mysteries. There we had the shadowy pictures, the living, shadowy pictures. What was there then to write down as history?

But now came the time when the shadowy pictures became submerged in the lower world, when human consciousness could no longer perceive them. Then came the impulse to make records. Herodotus,[40] the first prose historian, appeared. And from this time onward, many could be named who followed him, the same impulse working in them all—to tear mankind away from the divine, and to set him down in the purely earthly. Nevertheless, as long as Greek culture and civilization lasted, there is a splendour and a light shed abroad over this earth-directed tendency, a light of which we shall hear tomorrow that it did not pass over to Rome nor to the Middle Ages. In Greece, a light was there. Of the shadowy pictures, even the fading shadowy pictures of the evening twilight of Greek civilization, we still felt that we were divine in our origin.

In the midst of all this, like a heaven of refuge where humanity found clear enlightenment concerning what was present, as it were in fragments, in Greek culture—in the midst stood Ephesus. Heraclitus received instruction from Ephesus, as did many another great philosopher; Plato, too, and Pythagoras. Ephesus was the place where the old oriental wisdom was preserved up to a certain point. And the two souls who dwelt later in Aristotle and Alexander the Great were in Ephesus a little after the time of Heraclitus, and were able to receive there the heritage from the old knowledge of the oriental Mysteries that the Mystery of Ephesus still retained. Notably, the soul of Alexander entered into an intimate union with the very Being of the Mysteries as far as it was living in the Mystery of Ephesus.

And now we come to one of those historical events which people may think are mere chance, but which have their foundations deep down in the inner connections of the evolution of humanity. In order to gain an insight into the significance of this event, let us call to mind the following. We must remember that in the two souls who afterwards became Aristotle and Alexander the Great, there was living in the first place all that they had received in a far-off time in the past, and had subsequently elaborated and pondered. And then there was also living in their souls the treasure of untold value that had come to them in Ephesus. We might say that the whole of Asia—in the form that it had assumed in Greece, and in Ephesus in particular—was living in these two, and more especially in the soul of Alexander the Great, that is to say, of him who afterwards became Alexander the Great.

Picture to yourselves the part played by this personality. I described him for you as he was in the time of Gilgamesh; and now you must imagine how the knowledge that belonged to the ancient East and to Ephesus, a knowledge which we may also call a 'beholding', a 'perceiving'—this knowledge was called up again in the intercourse between Alexander the Great and Aristotle, in a new form. Picture this to yourselves, and then think what would have happened if Alexander, in his incarnation as Alexander, had come again into contact with the Mystery of Ephesus, bearing within him in his soul the tremendous document of the Mystery of Ephesus, for this majestic document of knowledge lived with extraordinary intensity in the souls of these two. If we can form a idea of this, we can rightly estimate the fact that on the day on which Alexander was born, Herostratus threw the flaming torch into the Sanctuary of Ephesus; on the very day on which Alexander was born, the Temple of Diana of Ephesus was treacherously burnt to the ground. It was gone, never to return. Its monumental document, with all that belonged to it, was no longer there. It existed only as a historical mission in the soul of Alexander and in his teacher Aristotle.

And now you must bring all this that was alive in the soul of Alexander into connection with what I said yesterday, when I showed you how the mission of Alexander the Great was inspired by an impulse coming from the configuration of the Earth. You will readily understand how what in the East had been real revelation of the divine was, as it were, extinguished with Ephesus. The other Mysteries were at bottom only Mysteries of decadence, where traditions were preserved, though it is true these traditions did still awaken clairvoyant powers in specially gifted natures. The splendour and the glory, the tremendous majesty of the olden times, were gone. With Ephesus, the light that had come over from the East was finally extinguished.

You will now be in a position to appreciate the resolve that Alexander made in his soul: to restore to the East what she had lost; to restore it at least in the form in which it was preserved in Greece, in the phantom or shadow-picture. Hence his idea of making an expedition into Asia, going as far as it was possible to go, in order to bring to the East once more—albeit in the shadow form in which it still existed in the Greek culture—what she had lost.

And now we see what Alexander the Great is really doing, indeed in a most wonderful way, when he makes this expedition. He is not bent on the conquest of existing cultures; he is not trying to bring

Hellenism to the East in any external sense. Wherever he goes, Alexander the Great not only adopts the customs of the land, but is also able to enter right into the minds and hearts of the human beings who are living there, and to think their thoughts. When he comes to Egypt, to Memphis, he is hailed as a saviour and deliverer from the spiritual fetters that have hitherto bound the people. He permeates the kingdom of Persia with a culture and civilization which the Persians themselves could never have produced. He penetrates as far as India.

He conceives the plan of effecting a balance, a harmony between Hellenic and oriental civilizations. On every hand he founds academies. The academies founded in Alexandria, in Northern Egypt, are the best known and have had the greatest significance for later times. Of the first importance, however, is the fact that all over Asia larger and smaller academies were founded, in which the works of Aristotle were preserved and studied for a long time to come. What Alexander began in this way continued to work for centuries in Asia Minor, repeating itself again and again, as it were, in feebler echoes. With one mighty stroke Alexander planted the Aristotelian knowledge of nature in Asia, even as far as India. His early death prevented his reaching Arabia, though that had been one of his chief aims. He went however as far east as India, and also into Egypt. Everywhere he implanted the spiritual knowledge of nature that he had received from Aristotle, establishing it in such a way that it could become fruitful for humanity. For everywhere he let the people feel it was something that was their own—not a foreign element, a piece of Hellenism, that was being imposed upon them. Only a nature such as Alexander's, able to fire others with his own enthusiasm, could ever have accomplished what he did. For everywhere others came forward to carry on the work he had begun. In the years that followed, many more scholars went over from Greece. Apart from Edessa,[41] it was one academy in particular, that of Gondishapur,[42] which received constant reinforcements from Greece for many centuries to come.

A marvellous feat was thus performed! [Plate 8] The light that had come over from the East, extinguished in Ephesus by the flaming torch of Herostratus, this light, or rather its phantom shadow, now

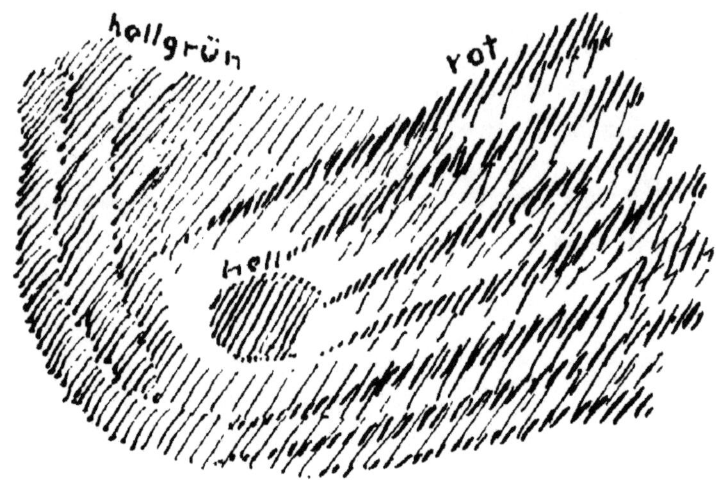

[hellgrün = light green; rot = red]

[See Plate 8, detail]

shone back again from Greece, and continued so to shine until the dramatic moment when beneath the tyranny of Rome the schools of the Greek philosophers were ultimately closed. In the sixth century CE the last of the Greek philosophers fled away to the academy of Gondishapur.

In all this we see two elements interworking; one that had gone so to speak, in advance, and one that had remained behind. The mission of Alexander was founded, more or less unconsciously, upon this fact: the waves of civilization had advanced in Greece in a luciferic manner, whilst in Asia they had remained behind in an ahrimanic manner.[43] In Ephesus was the balance. And Alexander, on the day of whose birth the physical Ephesus had fallen, resolved to found a spiritual Ephesus that would send its solar rays far out to East and West. It was in very truth this purpose that lay at the root of all he undertook: to found a spiritual Ephesus, reaching out across Asia Minor Eastward to India, covering also Egyptian Africa and the East of Europe.

It is not really possible to understand the spiritual evolution of Western humanity unless we can see it against this background. For soon after the attempt had been made to spread abroad in the world the ancient and venerated Ephesus, so that what had once been present in Ephesus might now be preserved in Alexandria—be it only in pale instead of in large, shining letters—soon after this second blooming of the flower of Ephesus, an altogether new power began to assert itself, the power of Rome. Rome, and all the word implies, is a new world, a world that has nothing to do with the shadowy pictures of Greece, and suffers us to keep no more than memories of these olden times. We can study no graver or more important incision in history than this. After the burning of Ephesus, through the instrumentality of Alexander, the plan is laid for the founding of a spiritual Ephesus; and this spiritual Ephesus is then pushed back by the new power that is asserting itself in the West, first as Rome, later under the name of Christianity, and so on. And we only understand the evolution of humanity aright when we say: We, with our way of comprehending things through the intellect, with our way of accomplishing things by means of our will, we with our feelings and moods can look back as far as ancient Rome. Thus far we can look back with full understanding. But we cannot look back to Greece; neither can we look back to the East. There we must look in Imaginations. Spiritual vision is needed there. Yes, we can look Southward, as we go back along the stream of evolution; we can look Southward with the ordinary prosaic understanding, but not Eastward. When we look Eastward, we have to look in Imaginations. We have to see standing in the background the mighty Mystery Temples of primeval, post-Atlantean Asia, where the wise men, the priests, made plain to each one of their pupils his connection with the divine in the cosmos, and where a civilization was to be found that could be received from the Mysteries in the time of Gilgamesh, as I have described it to you. We have to see these wonderful temples scattered over Asia, and in the foreground Ephesus, preserving still within its Mystery much that had faded away in the other temples of the East, whilst at the same time it had already itself made the transition and become Greek in character. For in Ephesus, a person no longer needed to wait for the constellations of the stars or for the right time of year, nor to wait until he himself had attained a certain age, before he could receive the revelations of the gods. In Ephesus, if he were ripe for it, he might offer up sacrifices and perform certain exercises that enabled him so to approach the gods that they drew graciously near to him.

It was in this world that stands before you in this picture that the two personalities of whom we have spoken were trained and prepared, in the time of Heraclitus. And now, in 356 BCE on the birthday of Alexander the Great, we behold the flames of fire that burst forth from the Temple of Ephesus.

Alexander the Great is born, and finds his teacher Aristotle. And it is as though from out of the ascending flames of Ephesus a mighty voice went forth for those who were able to hear it: Found a spiritual Ephesus far and wide over the Earth, and let the old physical Ephesus stand in human memory as its centre, as its midmost point.

Thus we have before us this picture of ancient Asia with her Mystery centres, and in the foreground Ephesus and her pupils in the Mysteries. We see Ephesus in flames, and a little later we see the expeditions of Alexander that carried over into the East what Greece had to give for the progress of humanity, so that there came into Asia in pictorial form what she had lost in its reality.

Looking across to the East and letting our imaginations be fired by the tremendous events that we see taking place, we are able to view in a true light that ancient chapter in human history—for it needs to be grasped with the imagination. And then we see gradually rise up in the foreground the Roman world, the world of the Middle Ages, the world that continues down to our own time.

All other divisions of history into periods—ancient, medieval and modern, or however else they may be designated—give rise to false conceptions. But if you will study deeply and intently the picture that I have here set before you, it will give you a true insight into the hidden workings that run through European history down to the present day.

Lecture 6

DORNACH, 29 DECEMBER 1923

Of peculiar importance for the understanding of the history of the West in its relation to the East is the period that lies between three or four hundred years before, and three or four hundred years after, the Mystery of Golgotha. The real significance of the events we have been considering, events that culminated in the rise of Aristotelianism and in the expeditions of Alexander to Asia, is contained in the fact that they form, as it were, the last act in that civilization of the East which was still immersed in the impulses derived from the Mysteries.

A final end was put to the genuine and pure Mystery-impulse of the East by the criminal burning of Ephesus. After that we find only traditions of the Mysteries, traditions and shadowy pictures—the remains, so to speak, that were left over for Europe and especially for Greece, of the old, divinely-inspired civilization. And four hundred years after the Mystery of Golgotha another great event took place, which serves to show what was still left of the ruins—for so we might call them—of the Mysteries.

Let us look at the figure of Julian the Apostate.[44] Julian the Apostate, Emperor of Rome, was initiated in the fourth century, as far as initiation was then possible, by one of the last of the hierophants of the Eleusinian Mysteries. This means that he entered into an experience of the old, divine secrets of the East, in so far as such an experience could still be gained in the Eleusinian Mysteries.

At the beginning of the period we are considering, stands the burning of Ephesus; and the day of the burning of Ephesus is also the day on which Alexander the Great was born. At the end of the period, in 363, we have the day of the death—the terrible and significant death—of Julian the Apostate far away in Asia. Midway between these two days stands the Mystery of Golgotha.

And now let us examine a little this period of time as it appears in the setting of the whole history of human evolution. If we want to look back beyond this period into the earlier evolution of humanity, we have first to bring about a change in our power of vision and perception, a change that is very similar to one of which we hear in another connection. Only we do not often bring these things together in thought.

You will remember how in my book *Theosophy*[45] I had to describe the different worlds that come under consideration for humans. I described them as the physical world; a transition world bordering on it, namely, the world of the soul; and then the world into which only the highest part of our nature can find entrance, the land of the spirit. Leaving out of account the special qualities of this land of the spirit, through which we today pass between death and a new birth, and looking only at its more general qualities and characteristics, we find that we have to give a new orientation to our whole thought and feeling before we can comprehend the land of the spirits. And the remarkable thing is that we have to change and re-orientate our inner life of thought and feeling in just the same way when we want to comprehend what lies beyond the period I have defined. We shall do wrong to imagine that we can understand what came before the burning of Ephesus with the conceptions and ideas that suffice for the world of today. We need to form other concepts and other ideas to enable us to look across the years to human beings who still knew that as surely as humans are united through breathing with the air outside them, so surely are they in constant union through their souls with the gods.

Starting then from this world, the world that is a kind of earthly Devachan,[46] the earthly land of the spirit—for the physical world fails us when we want to picture it—we came into the interim period, lasting from about 356 BCE to about 363 CE. And now what follows? Over in Europe we find the world from which present-day humanity is on the point of emerging into something new, even as the humanity of olden times came forth from the oriental world, passed through the Greek world, and then into the realm of Rome [see Plate 9].

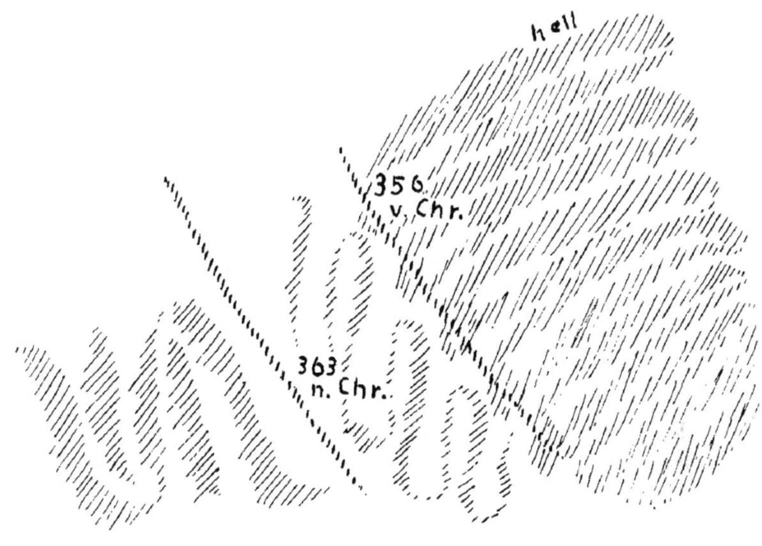

[hell = bright; 356 v. Chr. = 356 BCE; 363 n. Chr. = 363 CE]

[See Plate 9, detail]

Setting aside for the moment what went on in the inner places of the Mysteries, we have to see in the civilization that has grown up through the centuries of the Middle Ages and developed on into our own time a civilization that has been formed on the basis of what humans themselves can produce with the help of their own conceptions and ideas. We may see a beginning in this direction in Greece, from the time of Herodotus onward. Herodotus describes the facts of history in an external way; he makes no allusion, or at most very slight allusion, to the spiritual. And others after him go further in the same direction. Nevertheless, in Greece we always feel a last breath, as it were, from those shadowy pictures that were there to remind us of the spiritual life. With Rome, on the other hand, begins the period to which we today may still feel ourselves related, the period that has an altogether new way of thought and feeling, different even from what we have observed in Greece. Only here and there in the Roman world do we find a personality such as Julian the Apostate who feels something like an irresistible longing after the old world, and evinces a certain honesty in getting himself initiated into the Eleusinian Mysteries.

What Julian, however, is able to receive in these Mysteries has no longer the force of knowledge. And what is more, he belongs to a world where individuals are no longer able to grasp in their soul the traditions from the Mysteries of the East.

Present-day humanity would never have come into being if Asia had not been followed first by Greece and then by Rome. Present-day humanity is built upon personality, upon the personality of the individual. Eastern humanity was not formed in this way. Individuals of the East felt themselves part of a continuous. divine process. The gods had their purposes in Earth evolution. The gods willed this or that, and this or that came to pass on the Earth below. The gods worked on the human will, inspiring them. Those powerful and great personalities in the East of whom I spoke to you—all that they did was inspired from the gods. Gods willed; humans carried it into effect. And the Mysteries were ordered and arranged in olden times to this end—to bring divine will and human action into line with each other.

In Ephesus we first find a difference. There the pupils in the Mysteries, as I have told you, had to be watchful for their own condition of ripeness and no longer to observe seasons and times of year. There the first sign of personality makes its appearance. There in earlier incarnations, Aristotle and Alexander the Great had received the impulse towards personality.

But now comes a new period. It is in the early dawn of this new period when Julian the Apostate experiences, as it were, the last longing to partake, even in that late age, in the Mysteries of the East. Now the human soul begins to grow different again from what it was in Greece.

Picture to yourselves once more individuals who have received some training in the Ephesian Mysteries. Our constitution of soul was not derived from these Mysteries: they owe their constitution of soul to the simple fact that we were living in that age. When people today recollect, when, as we say, they bethink themselves, what can they call to mind? They can call to mind something that they themselves experienced in person during their present life, perhaps something that they experienced 20 or 30 years ago. This inward recollection in thought does not of course go further back than their own personal lives. With individuals who belonged, for instance, to the Ephesian civilization it was otherwise. If they had received, even in a small degree, the training that could be had in Ephesus, then it was so with them that when they bethought themselves in recollection, there emerged in their souls, instead of the memories that are limited to personal life, events of pre-earthly existence, events that preceded Earth evolution. They beheld the Moon evolution, the Sun evolution, beholding them in the several kingdoms of Nature. They were able, too, to look within themselves, and see the union of humans with the cosmic all; they saw how humans depend on and are linked with the cosmos. And all this that lived in his soul was true memory of self; it was the cosmic memory of humanity.

We may therefore say that we are here dealing with a period when in Ephesus we were able to experience the secrets of the universe. The human soul had memory of the far-past ages of the cosmos.

This remembering was preceded in evolution by something else: it was preceded by an actual living within those earlier times. What remained was a looking back. In the time, however, that the Epic of Gilgamesh relates, we cannot speak of a *memory* of past ages in the cosmos; we must speak of a *present experience* of what was past.

After the time of cosmic memory came what I have called the interim time between Alexander and Julian the Apostate. For the moment we will pass by this period. Then follows the age that gave birth to the Western civilization of the Middle Ages and of modern times. Here there is no longer a memory of the cosmic past, still less an experience in the present of the past; nothing is left but tradition.

1. Experience of prehistory in the present.
2. Memory of prehistory by the human soul.
3. Tradition. [Plate 10.]

Now individuals can write down what has happened. History begins. History makes its first appearance in the Roman period. Think, my dear friends, what a tremendous change we have here! Think how the pupils in the Ephesian Mysteries *lived with* time. They needed no history books. To write down what happened would have been to them laughable. One only needed to ponder and meditate deeply enough, and what had happened would rise up before one from out of the depths of consciousness. Here was no demonstration of psychoanalysis such as a modern doctor might make: the human soul took the greatest delight in fetching up in this way out of a living memory that which had been in the past.

In the time that followed, however, humanity forgot, and the necessity arose of writing down what happened. But all the while that we had to let our ancient power of cosmic memory crumble away, and begin in a clumsy manner to write down the great events of the world—all this time personal memory, personal recollection was evolving in our inner being. For every age has its own mission; every age has its own task.

Here you have the other side of what I set before you in the very first lectures of this course, when I described the rise of what we designated 'memory in time'. This memory in time, or temporal memory, had, so to say, its cradle in Greece, grew up through the Roman culture into the Middle Ages and on into modern times. In the time of Julian the Apostate the seed was already sown for the civilization based on personality, as is testified by the fact that Julian the Apostate found it, after all, of no avail to let himself be initiated into the Eleusinian Mysteries.

We have now come to the period when the individuals of the West, beginning from the third or fourth century after Christ and continuing down to our own time, lived their life on Earth entirely outside the spiritual world, lived in concepts and ideas, in mere abstractions. In Rome the very gods themselves became abstractions. We have reached a time when humanity no longer has any knowledge of a living connection with the spiritual world. The Earth is no longer Asia, the lowest of the heavens; the Earth is a world for itself, and the heavens are far away, dim and darkened to humanity's view. Now is the time when humanity evolves personality, under the influence of the Roman culture that is spread abroad over the lands of the West.

As we had to speak of a world of soul bordering on the spiritual world, on the land of the spirits that is above—so, bordering on this spiritual, oriental world is the civilization of the West; we may call it a kind of psychic world in time. This is the world that reaches right down to our own day. And now, in our time, although most humans are not at all alive to the fact, another stupendous change is again taking place.

Some of you who often listen to my lectures will know that I do not readily call any period a period of transition, for in truth every period is such—every period marks a transition from what comes earlier to what comes later. The point is that we should recognize for each period the nature of the transition.

What I have said will already have suggested that in this case it is as though, having passed from the land of spirit into the world of soul, one were to come thence into the physical world. In modern civilization as it has evolved up until now, we have been able to catch again and again *echoes* of the spiritual. Materialism itself has not been without its echoes of the spirit. True and genuine materialism in all domains has only been with us since the middle of the nineteenth century, and is still understood by very few in its full significance. It is there, however, with gigantic force, and today we are going through a transition to a third world, that is in reality as different from the preceding Roman world as this latter was different from the oriental.

Now there is one period of time that has had to be left out in tracing this evolution: the period between Alexander and Julian. In the middle of this period fell the Mystery of Golgotha. Those to whom the Mystery of Golgotha was brought did not receive it as individuals who understood the Mysteries, otherwise they would have had quite different ideas of the Christ Who lived in the man Jesus of Nazareth. A few there were, a few contemporaries of the Mystery of Golgotha, who had been initiated in the Mysteries, and these were still able to have such ideas of Him. But by far the greater part of Western humanity had no ideas with which to comprehend spiritually the Mystery of Golgotha. Hence the first way by which the Mystery of Golgotha found a place on Earth was the way of external tradition. Only in the very earliest centuries were there those who were able to comprehend spiritually, from their connection with the Mysteries, what took place at the Mystery of Golgotha.

Nor is this all. There is something else, of which I have told you in recent lectures,[47] and we must return to it here. Over in Hibernia, in Ireland, were still the echoes of the ancient Atlantean wisdom. In the Mysteries of Hibernia, of which I have given you a brief description, were two statues that worked suggestively on us, making it possible for us to behold the world exactly as the people of ancient Atlantis had seen it. Strictly guarded were these Mysteries of Hibernia, hidden in an atmosphere of intense earnestness. There they stood in the centuries before the Mystery of Golgotha, and there they remained at the time of the Mystery of Golgotha. Over in Asia, the Mystery of Golgotha took place; in Jerusalem the events came to pass that were later made known to people in the Gospels by the way of tradition. But in the moment when the tragedy of the Mystery of Golgotha was being enacted in Palestine, in that very moment it was known and beheld clairvoyantly in the Mysteries of Hibernia. No report was brought by word of mouth, no communication whatever was possible; but in the Mysteries of Hibernia the event was fulfilled in a symbol, in a picture, at the same time that it was fulfilled in actual fact in Jerusalem. Individuals came to know of it, not through tradition, but by a spiritual path. Whilst in Palestine that most majestic and sublime event was being enacted in concrete physical reality, over in Hibernia, in the Mysteries, the way had been so prepared through the performance of certain rites that at the very time when the Mystery of Golgotha was fulfilled, a living picture of it was present in the astral light.

The events in human evolution are closely linked together; there is, as it were, a kind of valley or chasm moving at this time over the world, into which humanity's old nearness to the gods gradually disappears.

In the East, the ancient vision of the gods fell into decay after the burning of Ephesus. In Hibernia it remained until some centuries after Christ, but even there also the time came when it had to disappear. Tradition developed in its stead. The Mystery of Golgotha was transmitted by the way of oral tradition, and we find growing up in the West a civilization that rests wholly on oral tradition. Later it comes to rely rather on external observation of nature, on an investigation of nature with the senses; but this after all is only what corresponds in the realm of nature to tradition, written or oral, in the realm of history.

Here then we have the civilization of personality. And in that civilization, the Mystery of Golgotha, with all that pertains to the spirit, is no longer perceived by humans [see Plate 9]. It is merely handed down as history.

We must place this picture vividly before us, the picture of a civilization from which the spiritual is excluded. It begins from the time that followed Julian the Apostate, and not until towards the end of the nineteenth century, beginning from the end of the 'seventies, did there come, as it were, a new call to humanity from the spiritual heights. Then began the age that I have often described as the Age of Michael. Today I want to characterize it as the age when humanity, if it wishes to remain in the old materialism—and a great part of humanity does wish so to remain—will inevitably fall into a terrible abyss. Such individuals have absolutely no alternative but to go under and become sub-human; they simply cannot maintain themselves on the human level. If we would maintain the human level, we must open our senses to the spiritual revelations that have again been made accessible since the end of the nineteenth century. That is now an absolute necessity.

Certain spiritual forces were at work in Herostratus, of which he was only the expression. He was, so to speak, the last dagger stretched out by certain spiritual powers from Asia. When he flung the burning torch into the Temple of Ephesus, demonic beings were behind him, holding him as one holds a sword—or as it might be, a torch; he was but the sword or torch in their hands. For these demonic beings had determined to let nothing of the spirit go over into the coming European civilization. The spiritual was to be absolutely debarred from entry there.

Aristotle and Alexander the Great placed themselves in direct opposition to the working of these beings. For what was it they accomplished in history? Through the expeditions of Alexander,

Aristotle's knowledge of nature was carried over into Asia; a fundamental knowledge of nature was spread abroad. Not in Egypt alone, but all over Asia Alexander founded academies, and in these academies made a home for the ancient wisdom, where the study of it could still continue. Here too, the Greek sages were ever and again able to find a refuge. Alexander brought it about that a true understanding of nature was carried into Asia.

This deeper knowledge of nature could not find entrance into Europe in the same way. Europe could not in all honesty receive it. She wanted only external knowledge, external culture, external civilization. Therefore, Aristotle's pupil Theophrastus[48] took out of Aristotelianism what the West could accept and transmitted that. It was the more logical writings that the West received. But that meant a great deal. For Aristotle's works have a character all their own; they read differently from the works of other authors, and his more abstract and logical writings are no exception. Just make the experiment of reading first Plato and then Aristotle with inner concentration, and in a meditative spirit, and you will find that each gives you quite a different experience.

When we moderns read Plato with true spiritual feeling and in an attitude of meditation, after a time we begin to feel as though our head were a littler higher than our physical head actually is—as though it had, so to speak, grown out beyond our physical organism. That is absolutely the experience of anyone who reads Plato, provided he is not read in an altogether dry manner.

With Aristotle it is different. With Aristotle you never have the feeling that you are coming out of your body. When you read Aristotle after having prepared yourself by meditation, you will find that he works right down into our physical nature. Our physical nature makes a step forward through the reading of Aristotle. His logic has an effect. It is not a logic that one merely observes and considers; rather, it is a logic that works in our inner being. Aristotle himself is a stage higher than all the pedants who came after him, and who developed logic from him. In a certain sense we may say with truth that Aristotle's works are only rightly comprehended when they are taken as books for meditation. Think what

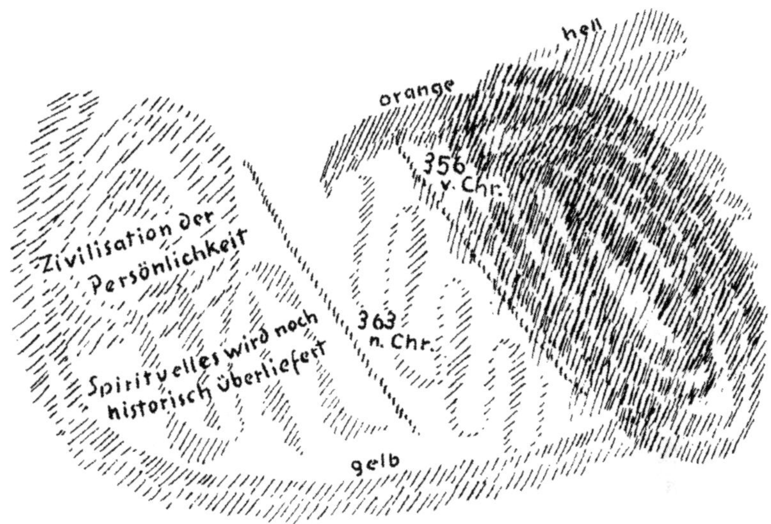

[hell = bright; Zivilisation der Persönlichkeit = civilization of personality; 356 v. Chr = 356 BCE*; 363 n. Chr. = 363* CE *Spirituelles wird noch historisch überliefert = spiritual matters still transmitted historically; gelb = yellow]*

[See Plate 9, detail]

would have happened if the natural scientific writings of Aristotle had gone over to the West as they were and come into Middle and Southern Europe. Humanity would, no doubt, have received a great deal from them, but in a way that did them harm. For the science that Aristotle was able to pass on to Alexander needed for its comprehension souls that were still touched with the spirit of the Ephesian age, the time that preceded the burning of Ephesus. Such souls could only be found over in Asia or in Egypt; and it was into these parts that this knowledge of nature and insight into the essence of nature were brought, by means of the expeditions of Alexander [further drawing on the board, Plate 9; orange toward the right]. Only later in a diluted form did they come over into Europe by many and diverse ways—especially, for example, by way of Spain—but always in a very diluted or, as we might say, sifted form [yellow from left to right].

The works of Aristotle that came over directly into Europe were his writings on logic and philosophy. These lived on, and found fresh life again in medieval Scholasticism.

Therefore we have these two streams. On the one hand, we always have there a stream of wisdom that spreads far and wide, unobtrusively, among simple folk—the secret source of much of medieval thought and insight. Long ago, through the expeditions of Alexander, it had made its way into Asia, and now it came back again into Europe by diverse channels, through Arabia, for instance, and later on following the path of the returning Crusaders. We find it in every corner of Europe, inconspicuous, flowing silently in hidden places. To these places came men like Jacob Boehme[49], Paracelsus[50] and a number more, to receive that which had come to us by many a roundabout path and was preserved in these scattered primitive circles of European life. We have had amongst us in Europe far more folk-wisdom than is generally supposed. The stream continues even now. It has poured its flood of wisdom into reservoirs like Valentin Weigel[51] or Paracelsus or Jacob Boehme—and many more, whose names are less known. And sometimes it met there—as for example, in Basil Valentine[52]—new influences that came over later into Europe. In the cloisters of the Middle Ages lived a true alchemistic wisdom, not an alchemy that demonstrates transformations in matter merely, but an alchemy that demonstrates the inner nature of the changes in the human being himself within the universe. The recognized scholars meanwhile were occupying themselves with the other Aristotle, with a misstated, sifted, 'logicized' Aristotle. This Aristotelian philosophy, however, which the Schoolman and subsequently the scientists studied, brought nonetheless a blessing to the West. For only in the nineteenth century, when individuals could no longer understand Aristotle and simply studied him as if he were a book to be read like any other, and not a book whereon to exercise oneself in meditation—only in the nineteenth century has it come about that humanity no longer received anything from Aristotle because he no longer lives and works in them. Until the nineteenth century, Aristotle was a book for the exercise of meditation, but since the nineteenth century the whole tendency has been to change what was once exercise, work, active power into abstract knowledge—to change practice and capacities into abstract knowledge.

Let us look now at the line of development, that leads from Greece through Rome to the West. It will illustrate for us from another angle the great change we are considering. In Greece there was still the confident assurance that insight and understanding proceed from the whole human being. The teacher is the *gymnast.*[53] From out of the whole human being in movement—for the gods themselves work in human bodily movements—something is born that then comes forth and shows itself as human understanding. The gymnast is the teacher.

In Rome the *rhetorician* steps into the place of the gymnast. Already something has been taken away from the human being as a whole; nevertheless, we still have at least a connection with a deed that is performed by humans in a part of their organism. What movement there is in our whole being when we speak! We speak with our heart and with our lungs; we speak right down to our diaphragm and further below it! We cannot say that speaking lives as intensely in the whole human being as do the movements of the gymnast, but it lives in a great part of us. (As for thoughts, they of course are but an extract of what lives in speech.) The rhetorician steps into the place of the gymnast. The gymnast has to do with the whole human being. The rhetorician excludes the limbs, and has only to do with a part of the human being and with what is sent up from this part into the head, and there becomes insight and understanding.

The third stage appears only in modern times, and that is the stage of the *professor* who trains nothing but the head of his pupils, who cares for nothing but thoughts. Professors of Eloquence were still appointed in some universities even as late as the nineteenth century, but these universities had no use for them, because it was no longer the custom to set any store by the art of speaking; thinking was all that mattered. The rhetorician died out. The doctors and professors, who looked after the least part of the human being, namely his head, these became the leaders in education.

As long as the genuine Aristotle was still there, it was training, discipline, exercise that we gained from our study of him. The two streams remained side by side. And those of us who are not very young and who shared in the development of thought during the later decades of the nineteenth century, know well, if we have gone about among the country folk in the way that Paracelsus did, that a last remnant of the medieval popular knowledge, from which Jacob Boehme and Paracelsus drew, was still to be found in Europe even as late as the 'seventies and 'eighties of the last century. Moreover, it is also true that within certain orders and in the life of a certain narrow circle a kind of inner discipline in Aristotle was cultivated right up to the last decades of the nineteenth century. So that it has been possible in recent years still to meet here and there the last ramifications, as it were, of the Aristotelian wisdom that Alexander carried over into Asia and that returned to Europe through Asia Minor, Africa, and Spain. It was the same wisdom that had come to new life in such men as Basil Valentine and those who came after him, and from which Jacob Boehme, Paracelsus, and countless others had drawn. It was brought back to Europe also by yet another path, namely through the Crusaders. This Aristotelian wisdom lived on, scattered far and wide among the common people. In the later decades of the nineteenth century, one is thankful to say, the last echoes of the ancient nature knowledge carried over into Asia by the expeditions of Alexander were still to be heard, even if sadly diminished and scarcely recognizable. In the old alchemy, in the old knowledge of the connections between the forces and substances of nature that persisted so remarkably among simple country folk, we may discover again its last lingering echoes. Today they have died away; today they are gone, they are no longer to be heard.

Similarly, in these years we could still find isolated individuals who gave evidence of Aristotelian spiritual training, though today they, too, are gone. And thus what was carried eastward as well as westward was preserved [Plate 9; red from right to left], for what was carried eastward came back again to the West [Plate 9; blue from the middle leftwards]. And it was possible in the 'seventies and 'eighties of the nineteenth century for one who could do so with new, direct spiritual perception, to make contact with what was still living in these last and youngest children of the great events we have been describing.

There is, in truth, a wonderful interworking in all these things. For we can see how the expeditions of Alexander and the teachings

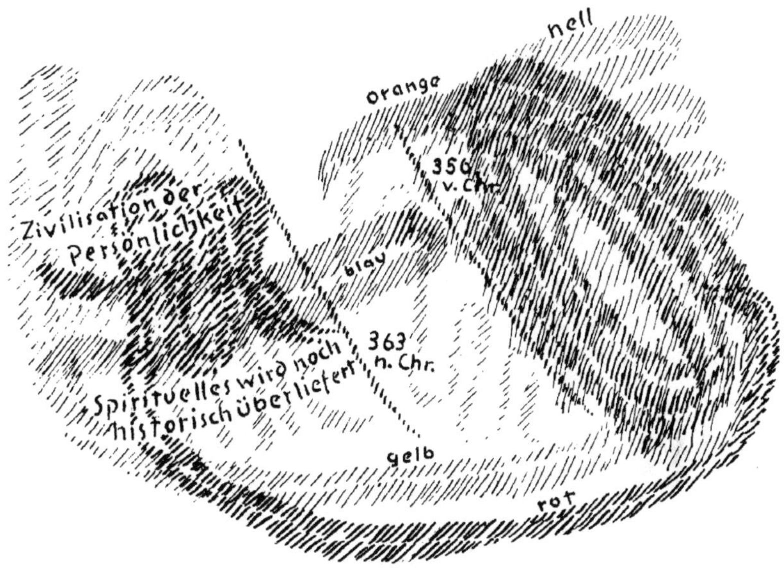

[See Plate 9, detail]

of Aristotle had this end in view, to keep unbroken the threads that unite us with the ancient spirituality, to weave them, as it were, into the material civilization that was to come, that so they might endure until such time as new spiritual revelations should be given.

From this point of view, we may gain a true understanding of the events of history, for it is often so that seemingly fruitless undertakings are fraught with deep significance for the historical evolution of humanity. It is easy enough to say that the expeditions of Alexander to Asia and to Egypt have been swept away and submerged. It is not so. It is easy to say that Aristotle ceased to be in the nineteenth century. But he did not. Both streams have lasted up to the very moment when it is possible to begin a renewed life of the spirit.

I have told you on many occasions how the new life of the spirit was able to begin at the end of the 1870s, and how from the turn of the century onwards, it has been able to grow more and more. It is our task to receive in all its fullness the stream of spiritual life that is poured down to us from the heights.

And so today we find ourselves in a period that marks a genuine transition in the spiritual unfolding of humanity. And if we are not conscious of these wonderful connections and of how deeply the present is linked with the past, then we are in very truth asleep to important events that are taking place in the spiritual life of our time. And numbers of people are fast asleep today in regard to the most important events of all. But anthroposophy is there for that very purpose, to awaken us from sleep.

You who have come here for this Christmas Conference—I believe that all of you have felt an impulse that calls you to awaken. We are nearing the day—as this Meeting goes on, we shall have to pass the actual hour of the anniversary—we are coming to the day when the terrible flames burst forth that destroyed the Goetheanum. Let the world think what it will of the destruction by fire of the Goetheanum: in the evolution of the anthroposophical movement, the event of the fire has a tremendous significance.

We shall not however be able to judge of its full significance until we look beyond it to something more. We behold again the physical flames of fire flaring up on that night, we see the marvellous way in which the fusing metal of the organ pipes and other metallic parts sent up a glow that caused that wonderful play of colour in the flames. And then we carry our memory over the year that has intervened. But in this memory must live the fact that the physical is *maya*, that we have to seek the truth of the burning flames in the spiritual fire that it is ours now to kindle in our hearts and souls. In the midst of the physically burning Goetheanum shall arise for us a spiritually living Goetheanum.

I do not believe, my dear friends, that this can come to pass in the full, world-historic sense unless we can on the one hand look upon the flames mounting up in terrible tongues of fire from the Goetheanum that we have grown to love so dearly, and behold at the same time in the background that other treacherous burning of Ephesus, when Herostratus, guided by demonic powers, flung the flaming brand into the Temple. When we bring these two events together, setting one in the background and one in the foreground of our thought, we shall then have a picture that will perhaps have power to write deeply enough in our hearts what we have lost and what we must strive our utmost to build again.

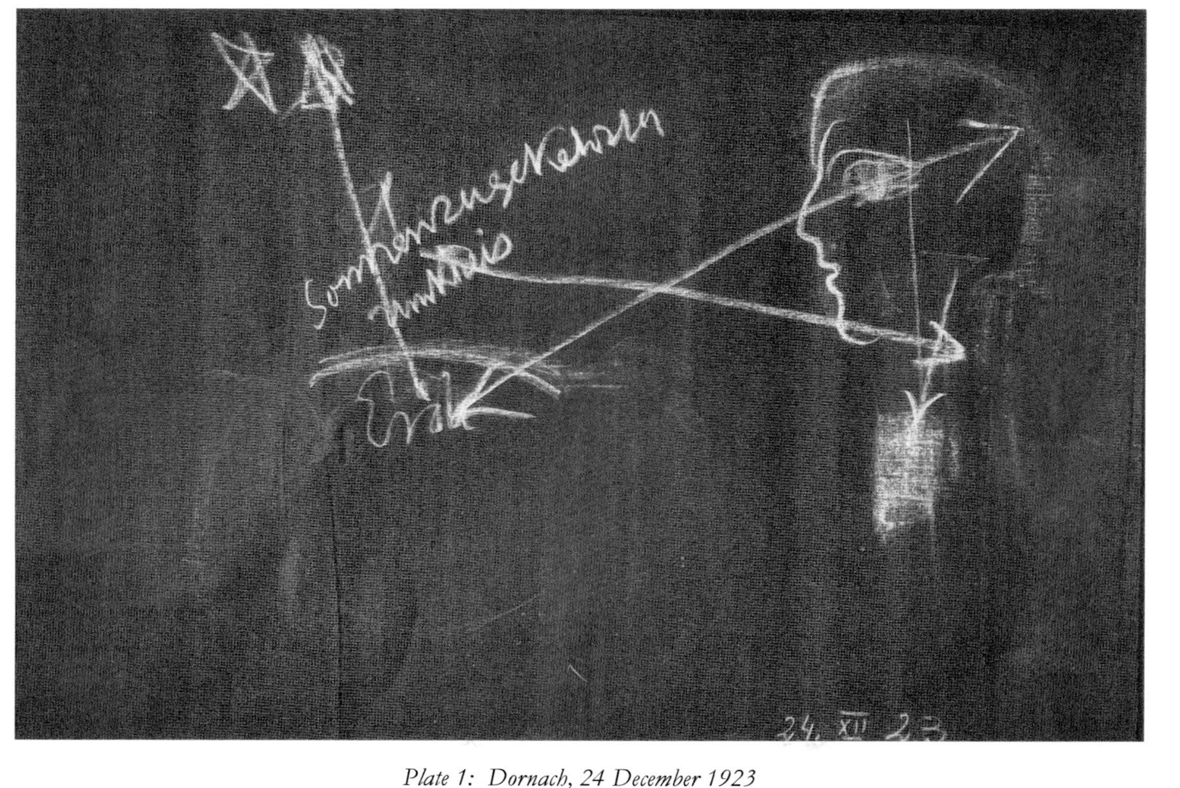

Plate 1: Dornach, 24 December 1923

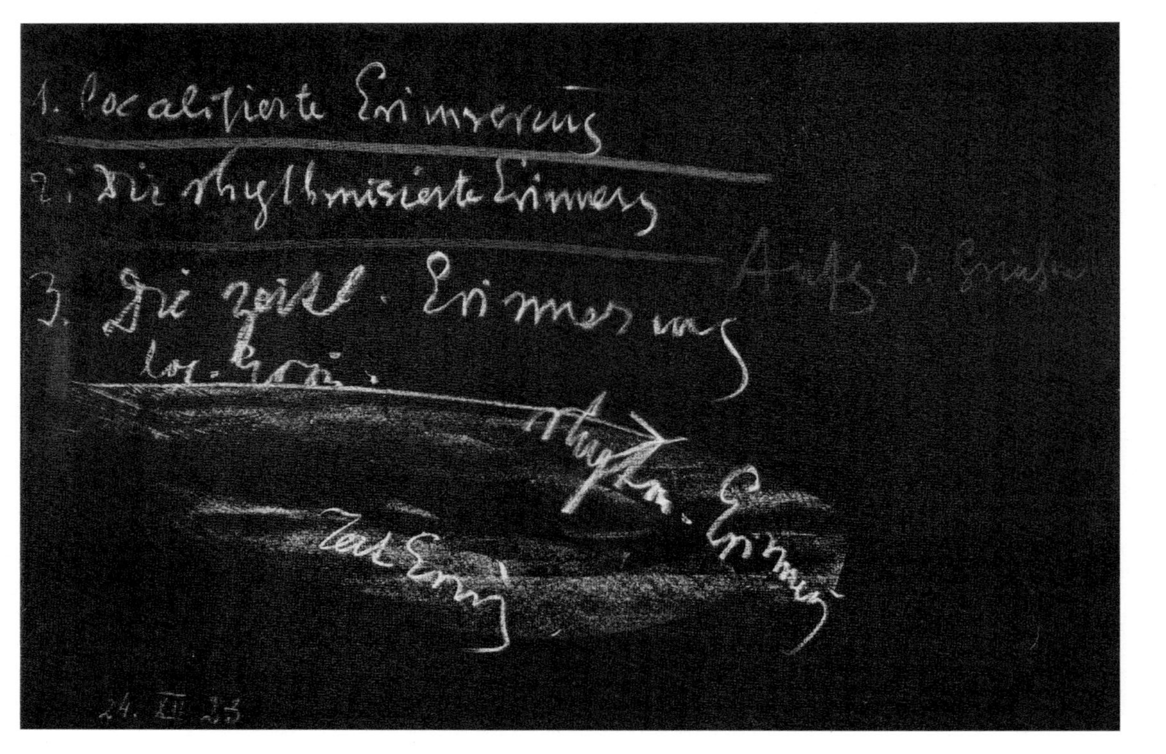

Plate 2: Dornach, 24 December 1923

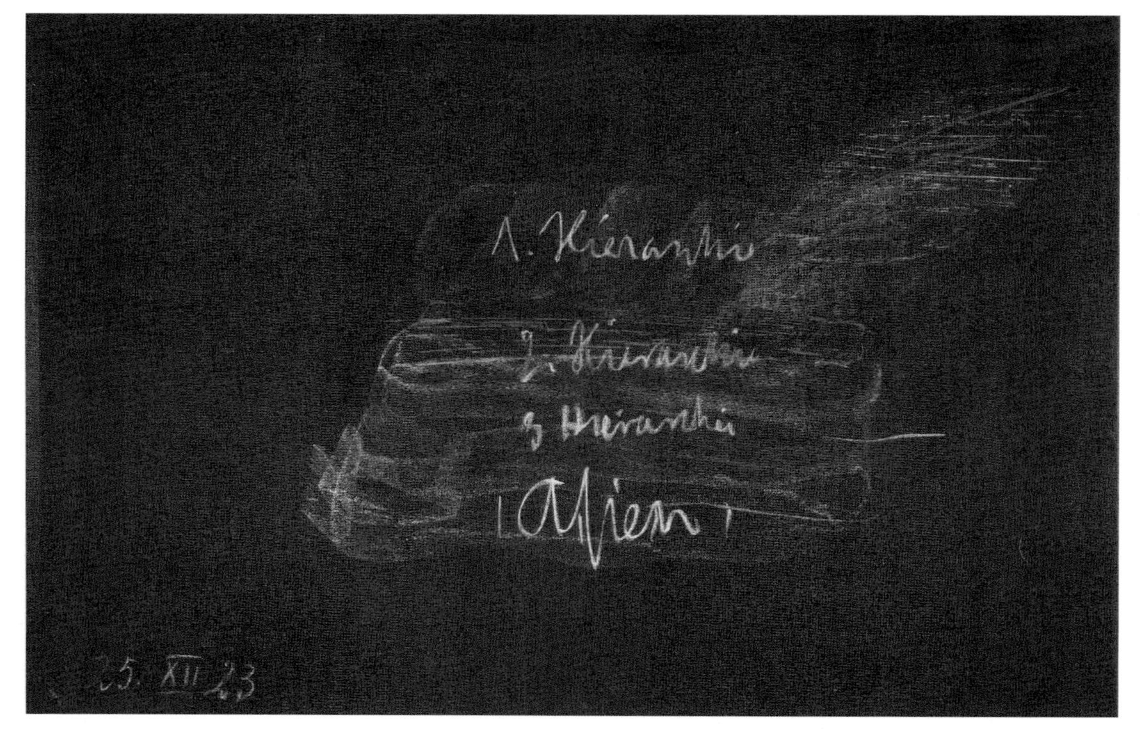

Plate 3: Dornach, 25 December 1923

Plate 4: Dornach, 25 December 1923

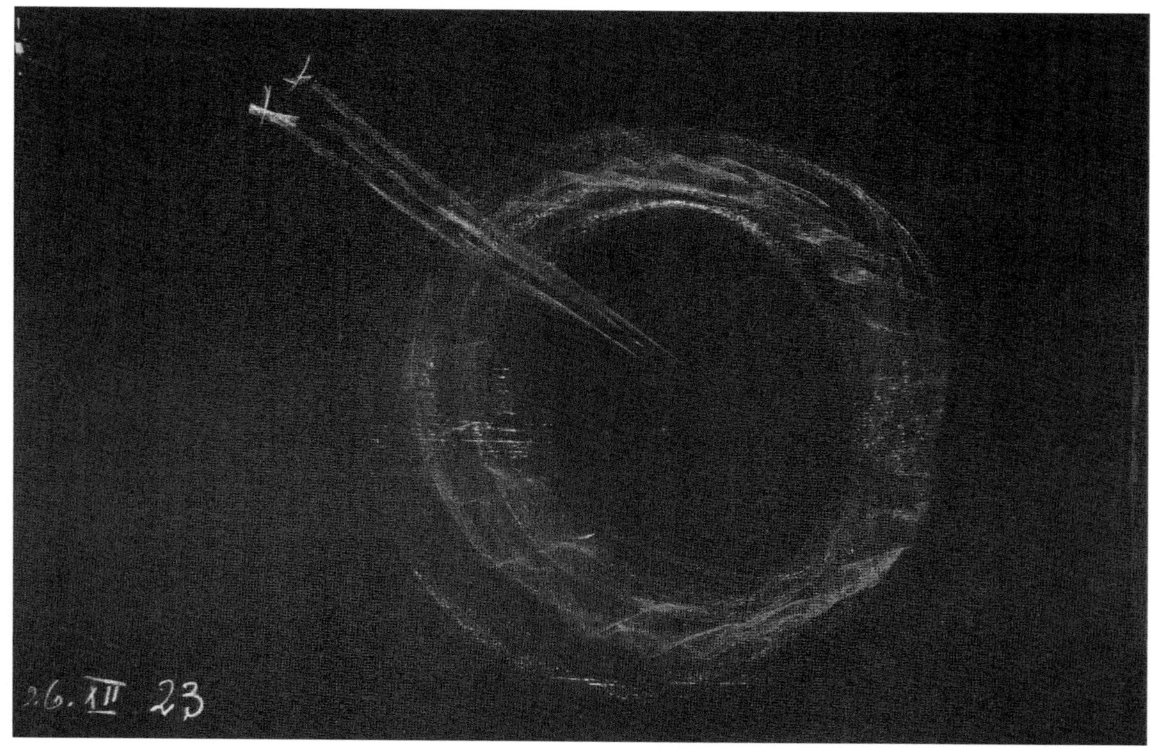

Plate 5: Dornach, 25 and 26 December 1923

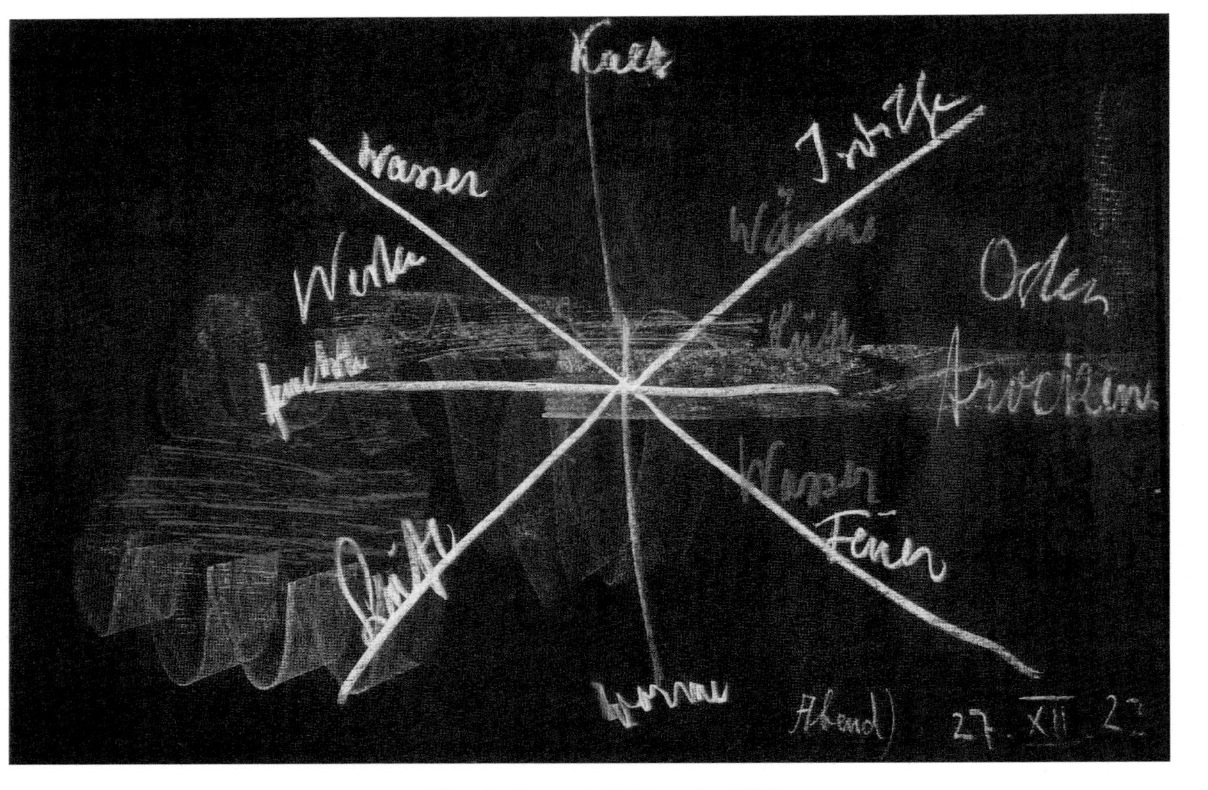

Plate 6: Dornach, 27 December 1923

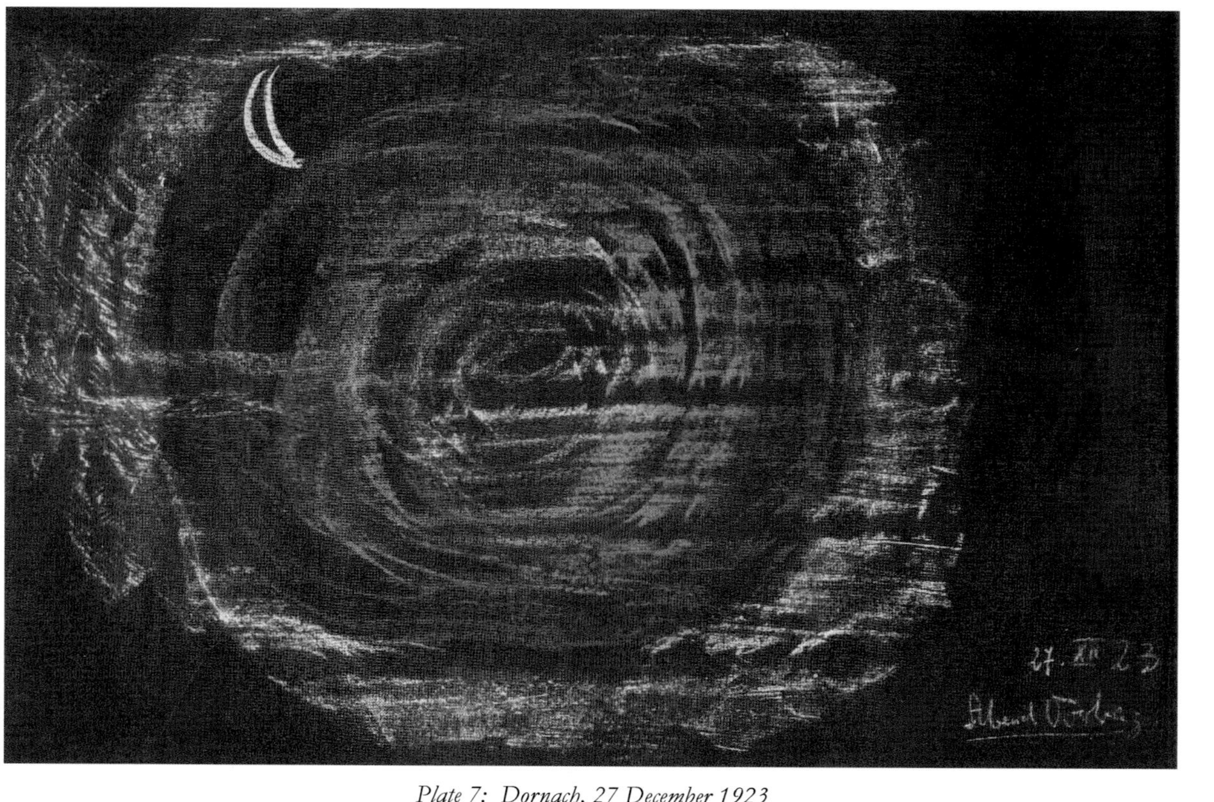

Plate 7: Dornach, 27 December 1923

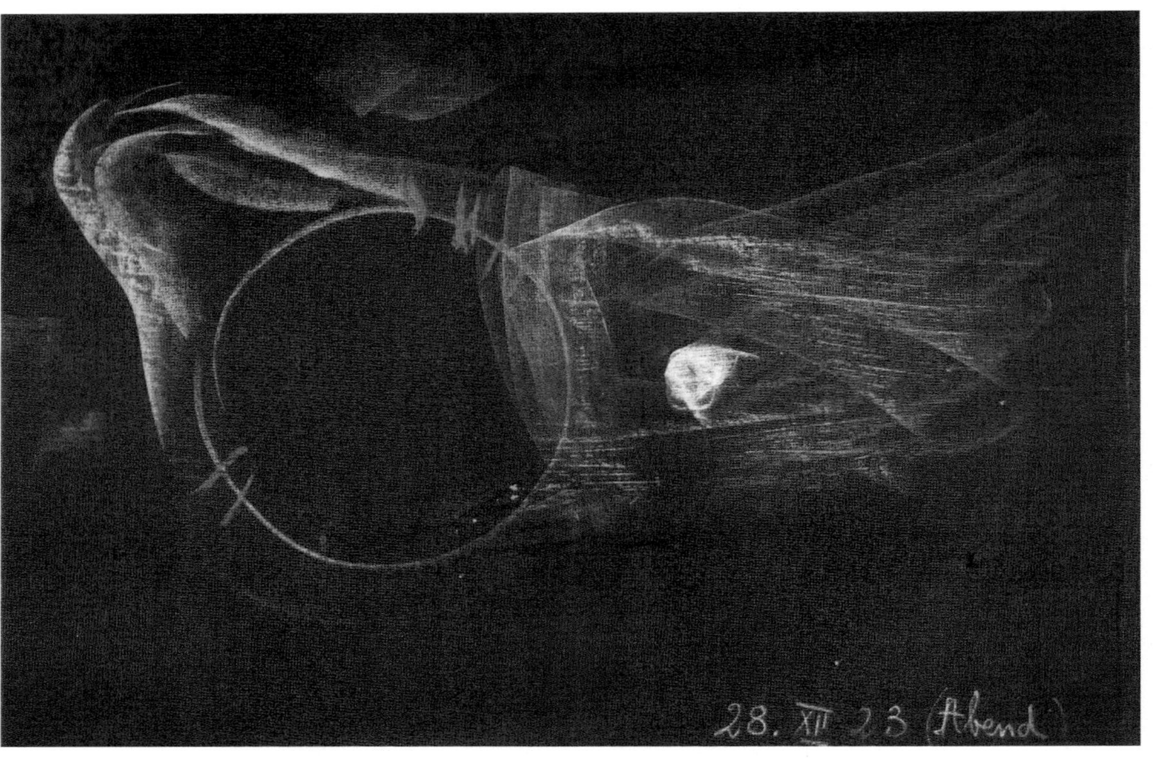

Plate 8: Dornach, 28 December 1923

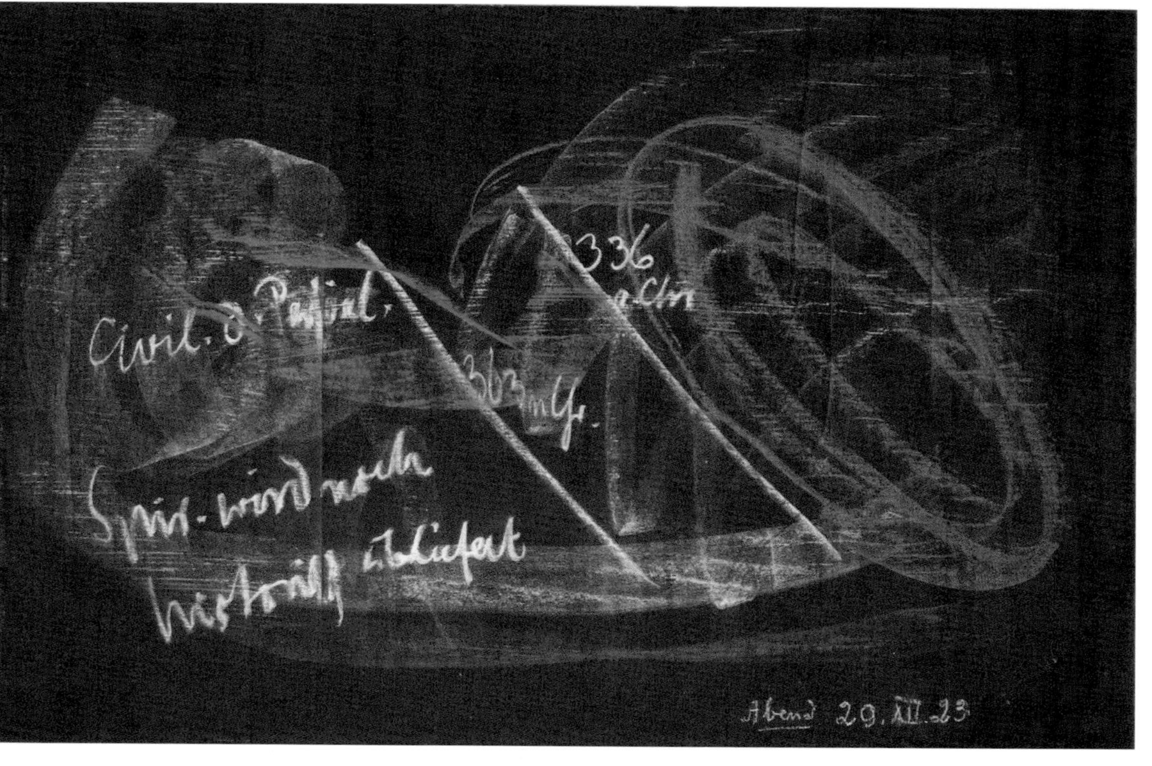

Plate 9: Dornach, 29 December 1923

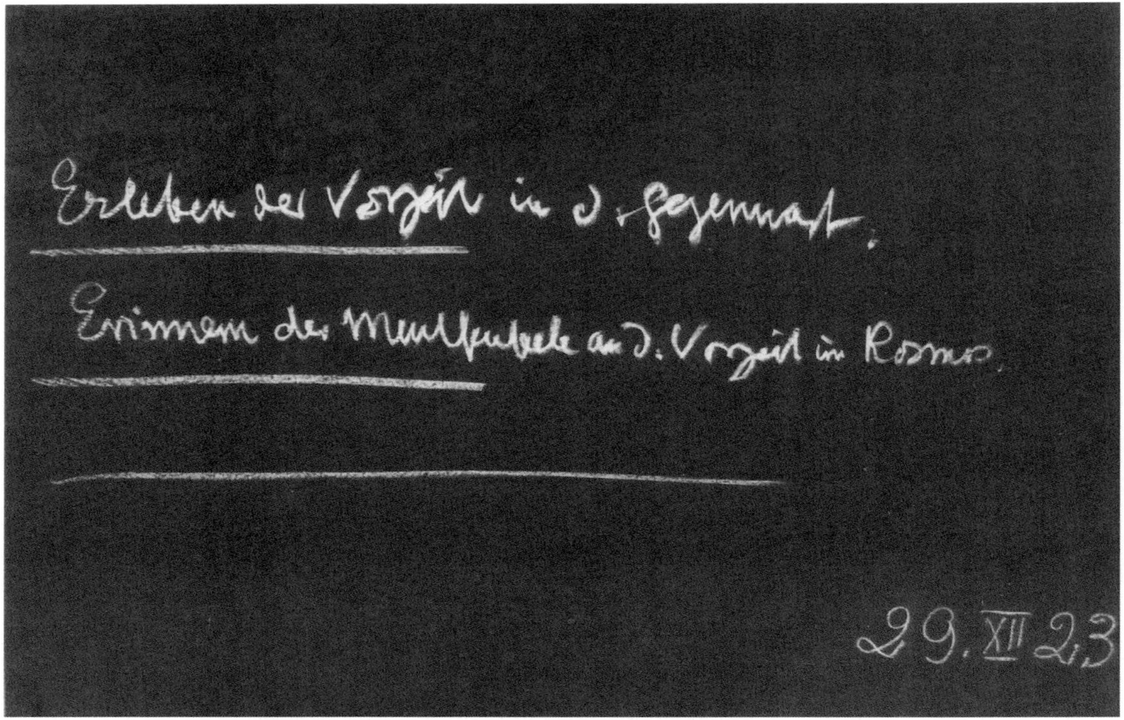

Plate 10: Dornach, 29 December 1923

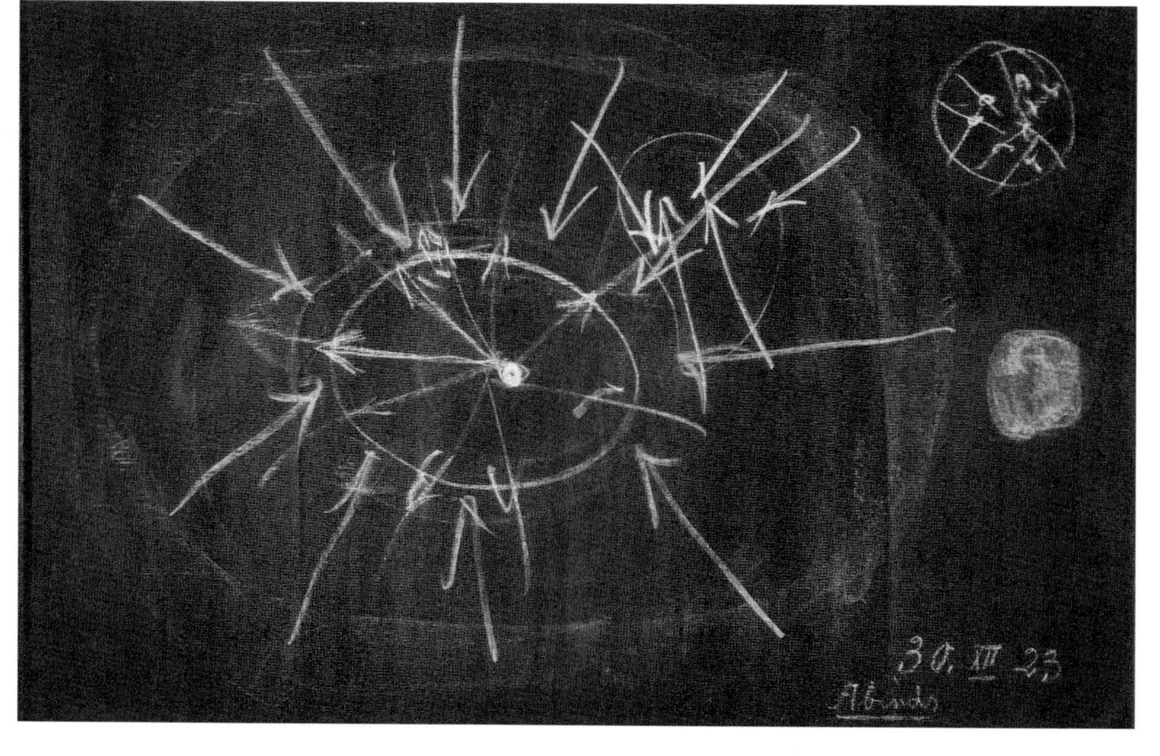

Plate 11: Dornach, 30 December 1923

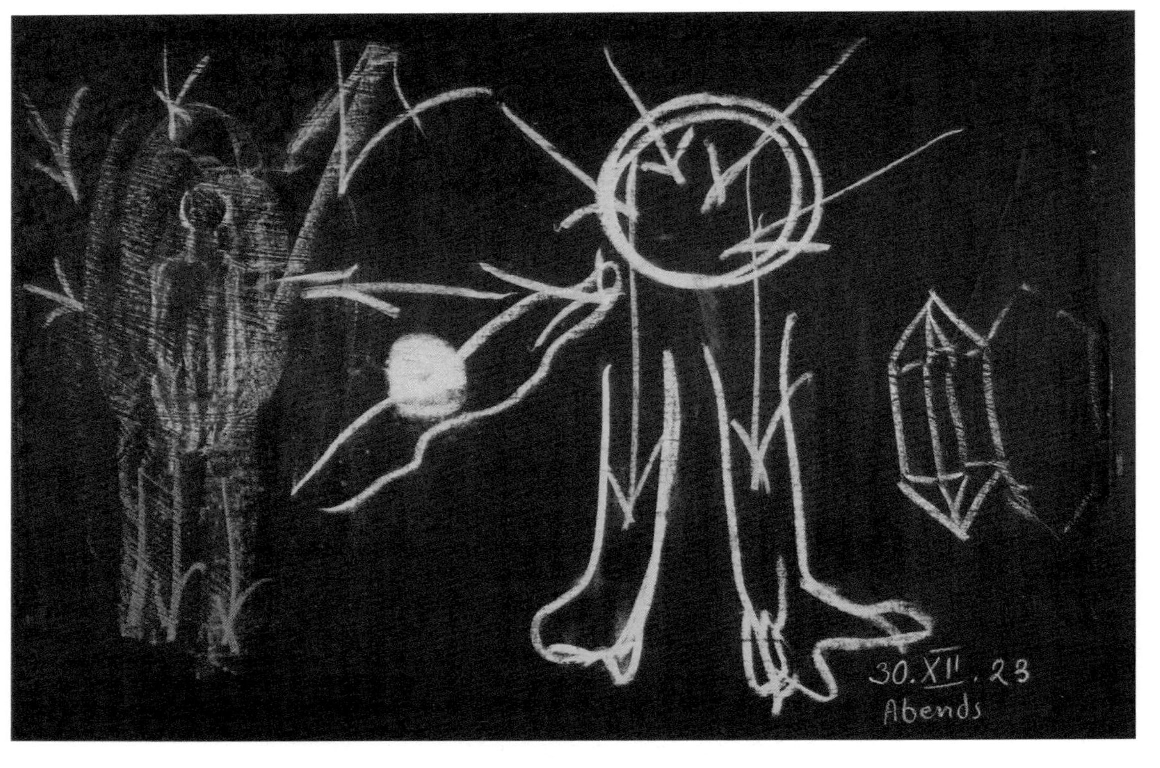

Plate 12: Dornach, 30 December 1923

Lecture 7

DORNACH, 30 DECEMBER 1923

THE last great incision into the historical evolution of humanity is the one that took place—we have often spoken of it—in the first third of the fifteenth century, and that marks the transition from the evolution more particularly of the intellectual soul[54] to that of the consciousness soul.[55] For we live in an age when the evolution of the consciousness soul is taking place, and it is an age that is entirely bereft of true insight into the connections of the human being with the deeper impulses and forces of nature, or rather of the spirit that is in nature. Today, when we speak of humans and their constitutions as physical, we speak, for instance, of the chemical substances, enumerating them under the heading of what the chemist calls the elements. But it is of about as much value to know that something we eat contains carbon and nitrogen as it is for a watch repairer to know that the watch he has in his hand consists of glass and, shall we say, silver and some other substances. All this kind of knowledge that traces back the real substance of human nature to these material abstractions—hydrogen, oxygen and the like—affords no true knowledge of the human being. The mechanism of the watch has to be understood by seeing in it a connected system of forces; and similarly, if we would understand human nature, we must recognize how the various impulses that are to be found working in all the kingdoms of nature work in the human being, for there they work differently than in the other kingdoms of nature. In modern times, however, there is no longer any true vision of the connection between humans and the universe. Until the fourteenth or fifteenth centuries this vision and knowledge persisted; though degenerate, it was still present in greater or less degree, and instinctively gifted natures were able still to make use of it. But later on, save for a few individuals like Paracelsus, Jacob Boehme and others, true insight into humanity's connection with the universe, little by little, died completely away.

What does the newer natural science, that has gradually grown up since the fifteenth century, know of the relation, let us say, of the world of plants or animals to the human being? Scientists examine plants in their chemical constitution and try by some means or other to study these same chemical constituents of the plant as they appear in human nature. Finally, perhaps, we try to form an idea—generally, we fail!—of the influence of the substances on the healthy and on the diseased human being. All this investigation however results in a darkening of knowledge. The important thing today, if we are desirous of going forward in our knowledge of humanity on the foundation of historical insight, is that we should learn to know again what is the real relation between human beings and nature that we find around us.

Until the time of the last great revolution in human consciousness that took place in the fifteenth century, there was still a clear feeling of the great difference that exists in the metals, as between those that are found in the human being and those that are found in nature. When we set out to consider the various substances in physical human nature, certain metals show themselves in greater or lesser degree. For example, iron is present in the human organism, in combination with various other substances; magnesium is also present, and we could name many others. Before the fifteenth century, people were keenly alive to the difference between such metals as these we have mentioned, that are found when we examine the human organism, and such metals as are present in external nature but are not at any rate quickly apparent in the human organism. People of those earlier times said: Humans are a microcosm; whatever is present in the world outside them, in the macrocosm, is present in some form or other in them. And this was for them no mere general principle in the abstract: had they gone but a little way in initiatory knowledge, it followed inevitably from what they knew of human nature and of the nature of the universe. They knew that we can only come to a true understanding of human nature when we bring together in one the whole of nature, with all her impulses, with all the substances that she contains. Then we have a picture, an Imagination of human nature. And a disturbing element enters the picture when we meet with something outside in nature that cannot be found in humans.

So thought a researcher into nature of the ninth, tenth or eleventh century. In those times, however, something else was known, namely, that what humans receive by way of physical nourishment is only a part, perhaps not even the most important part, of all that serves to maintain our physical organism, or rather our whole human organism throughout.

Now, to go beyond physical nourishment and include also breathing presents no difficulty to the individual of the present day; for breathing too is a form of metabolism. But it would not occur to us to go any further. The researcher into nature before the fifteenth century went further. It was clear that when we use our eyes to perceive things, we do not merely see with the eye, but during the process of perception we receive through the eye in infinitely minute quantities something of the substance of the cosmos. And not through the eye alone, but through the ear and through other portions of the organism. And the medieval student of nature was fully aware of the very great importance of those substances which occur in a slight measure only in the human organism, such as, for example, lead, and which we receive in infinitely minute quantities that may be found where we little suspect their presence.

Lead is a metal that cannot immediately be shown as occurring in us. But lead is, as a matter of fact, distributed throughout the entire physical cosmos in a state of very fine dilution, and humans assimilate lead from the cosmos by means of processes that are many times more delicate than the process of breathing. Humans are perpetually excreting substances, throwing them off in the direction of the periphery. You not only cut your nails, you continually throw off substances from your skin. But while substances are thus given off, other substances are taken up and received into the organism.

This was the kind of thought in which a researcher into nature who belonged to medieval times lived until the ninth, tenth, eleventh or twelfth centuries. We had no balances, we had none of the coarser measuring instruments with which to determine how the substances and forces worked; for us it was a matter of entering deeply into the inner qualities of nature, of understanding her inner impulses and her connection with humans. And up to the fifteenth century, humans were able in this way to know many things that they will one day begin to know again. For, if truth be told, nothing is known today of the real nature of the human being.

You know how when we investigate the human constitution, we sum it up in the following way, in order to have some kind of classification and plan: The human being is composed of physical body, etheric body, astral body, and ego, or ego-organization. Well and good. In the first instance, these terms are mere words, but it is good to begin with them. Each person can form from them some small idea of the truth. But if we want to make use of this classification in practical life, especially if we want to use it in medicine—admittedly a highly important 'practice' in life, and one that depends at every step on our knowledge of the human being—then we cannot possibly be satisfied with the words. We must enter into what is behind the words and gives them their content. We ask first: What about the physical body? How can we gain a true idea of it? (You will see presently why I am developing this line of thought.) Take any object on the Earth, outside the human being; let us say, for instance, a stone. A stone falls to the ground. We say, the stone is heavy, it is attracted by the Earth, it has weight. We discover other forces working in the stone. If it is formed into a crystal, then formative forces work in it. These are also related to the earthly forces. In short, when we look around in the world, we find all about us substances that are subject to the earthly nature.

Keep that clearly in mind: we have, to begin with, substances that are subject to earthly nature.

Someone whose thoughts on these things are not clear will perhaps come and show you a piece of coal, a piece of black coal. What is it in reality? In the neighbourhood of the Earth, it is coal; but the moment you were to take it but a short distance—comparatively speaking—away from the Earth, it would cease to be coal. What makes it coal is nothing but the forces of the Earth. Thus you can say: Here is the Earth, and the forces of the Earth are within it; but

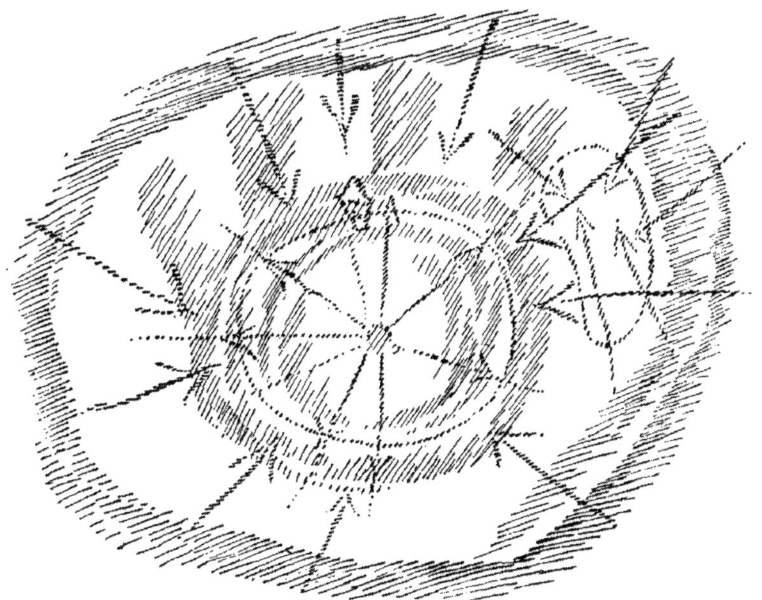

[See Plate 11, detail]

the forces of the Earth are also in every single object that I find here on the Earth. And the physical human body, although of course it is marvellously combined and held together, is nevertheless essentially such an object, standing in subjection to these physical forces of the Earth, the forces that come from the centre of the Earth. The physical body of the human being can therefore be described as that which is subject to the forces coming from the centre of the Earth [arrows pointing outwards].

Now there are other forces on the Earth in addition. These other forces come from the far periphery [arrows pointing inwards]. Imagine for a moment that you are going out and out, away from the Earth into unmeasured distances. From these unmeasured distances forces work upon the Earth, inverse to the forces of the Earth, working inwards from every direction. Yes, it is a fact, such forces do exist, coming from all directions of the cosmos and working in everywhere towards the centre of the Earth. It is possible to gain quite a clear and concrete representation of them in the following way.

You will remember that the most important substance that forms the basis everywhere of the organism, whether it be of plant, animal or human, is albumen. And albumen also forms the basis for the germ of a new plant, animal, or human organism. From a fructified germ cell proceeds what evolves into an organism, and the substance of the germ is albumen. In these days, instead of pursuing true science, people construct all kinds of imaginations, and they represent to themselves this albumen as composed of substances in intricate chemical combination. It is composed, so they say, of carbon, oxygen, hydrogen, nitrogen, sulphur, and a trace also of phosphorus, all in complicated combinations. And so the atomist comes to see in albumen the example *par excellence* of chemical combination. The atoms and molecules have to be thought of as arranged in a most complicated manner. And this complicated albumen-molecule, or whatever you choose to call it, arises in the maternal animal or maternal plant; it develops

[See Plate 11, detail]

further and the new animal comes to birth from it, arising, that is, purely through inheritance.

From the spiritual point of view, all this is sheer nonsense. The truth is that the albumen of the maternal animal is not a complicated chemical combination at all; it is all broken up, destroyed and reduced to chaos. The albumen that is otherwise contained in the body is still to some extent organized, but albumen that forms the basis for propagation is distinguished by this very characteristic, that it is in a condition of complete disorganization. The substances that are contained in it are reduced to chaos and have no sort of structure. They are tossed and jumbled together to form a mere accumulation without order or proportion. And on this very account the albumen is no longer subject to the Earth. So long as the albumen can by some means or other be held together in inward cohesion, so long is it subject to the forces that work from the centre of the Earth. The moment the albumen is inwardly split up and destroyed, it comes under the influence of the whole sphere of the cosmos. Forces work in upon it from every quarter. And then we have the tiny particle of albumen that forms the basis for reproduction. This tiny particle is an image of the entire cosmos, because albumen substance has been split up, destroyed and reduced to chaos—converted, that is, into cosmic dust and thereby fitted to become exposed to the working of the entire cosmos.

Of all this, people have today simply no knowledge at all. They imagine the old hen has the complicated albumen. This is included in the egg, and thence arises the new hen. It is the albumen continued; it has gone on evolving. Then the germinal substance is developed once again, and so it goes on from hen to hen. In actual fact, it is not so. Every time the transition takes place from one generation to the next, the albumen is exposed to the whole cosmos.

On the one hand, therefore, we have the earthly substances, subject to the earthly or central forces. But we can also imagine these earthly substances exposed in certain circumstances to the forces that work in from all quarters, from the farthest limits of the universe. The latter forces are the ones that work into the human etheric body. The etheric body is subject to the forces of the cosmos. These are real conceptions of the physical body and the etheric body.

Suppose you stand there and ask, what is my physical body? The answer is, it is that body which is subject to the forces proceeding from the centre of the Earth. What is my etheric body? It is that in you which is subject to the forces streaming in on all sides from the periphery. You can even show it in a drawing [Plate 12]. Imagine that this is the human being. Our physical body is the one that is subject to the forces that go towards the centre of the Earth [red]. Our etheric body [green] is the one that is subject to the forces streaming in from all sides, from the ends of the universe. Here we have a system of forces in humans. There are forces that pull downward—they are really present in all organs that are upright—and there are forces that pour in from without, tending inward [arrows]. You can actually perceive in the human form where the one kind and the other are more

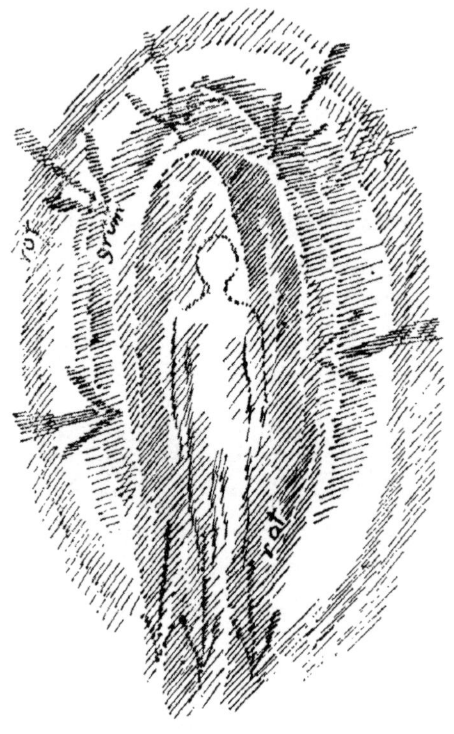

[rot = red; grün = green]

[See Plate 12, detail]

evident. Study the legs and it is obvious, their form is due to the fact that they are more adapted to the earthly forces [Plate 12]. The head is more adapted to the forces of the periphery. In like manner you may also study the arms. This is especially interesting. Hold your arms close to your body, and they are subject to the forces that go towards the centre of the Earth. Move them in a living way, and you yourself will be subjecting them to the forces streaming in from all sides of the periphery.

Such indeed is the difference between arms and legs. The legs are invariably subject to the central forces of the Earth, while the arms

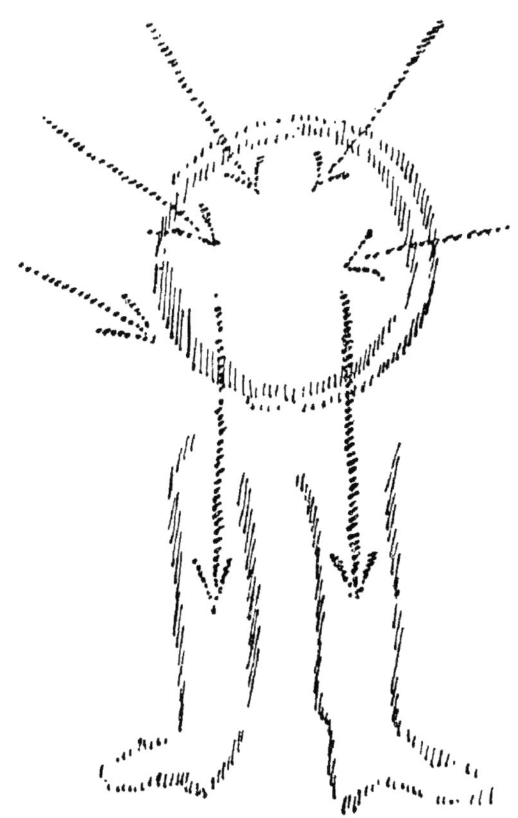

[See Plate 12, detail]

are so only in a certain posture, that is to say, conditionally. We are able to lift them out of the domain of the earthly, central forces and place them in the midst of what we call the etheric forces, the forces pouring in from the periphery. And so you can see for all the single organs how they are placed in the whole cosmos. Here then you have your physical body and your etheric body.

How is it with the astral body? In space, there is no other kind of force besides these two. The astral body receives its forces from beyond space. While the etheric body receives them from everywhere, from the periphery, the astral body receives them from beyond all space.

We can actually find certain places in nature where the physical forces of the Earth enter into the midst of the etheric forces that stream in from all sides. You may imagine albumen to begin with as a substance present in the physical Earth. So long as sulphur, carbon, oxygen, nitrogen, and hydrogen are in any way chemically recognizable in it, the albumen is in fact subject to the earthly forces. But the moment it enters the sphere of the reproductive process, it is lifted out of the physical forces. The forces of the circumference of the universe begin to work upon it in its disorganized condition. New albumen comes into being as an image of the whole universe.

[See Plate 12, detail]

But you see, sometimes the following situation emerges. The disorganization, the breaking down of the albumen cannot go far enough. You may have albuminous substance of this kind in connection with some animal, for instance. For reproduction to take place, it should be possible for it to be divided, broken down entirely, so that it may submit itself to the forces of the whole cosmos. But the animal is somehow prevented from delivering, for purposes of reproduction, such albuminous substance as would be able straightaway to submit itself to the whole macrocosm. To be capable of reproduction, albuminous substance must submit itself to the whole macrocosm. But the animal in this case is in some way unable to form albuminous substance capable of reproduction without further assistance. This is how it is with the gall-fly. What then does the gall-fly do? It lays its egg in some part of a plant. Again and again you may find these galls, in oaks, and in other trees where the gall-fly lays her eggs. In the leaf, for instance, you can see these strange formations. Within each one is the egg of a gall-fly. Why does it happen so? Why is the egg of a gall-fly laid in an oak leaf, with the result that the oak-apple is formed, holding within it the egg, which is *now* able to develop? The reason for this is as follows. The leaf of the plant contains within it an etheric body, which is adapted to the whole cosmic ether. It comes to the assistance of the egg of the gall-fly. Left alone, the gall-fly's egg is helpless. Hence the gall-fly lays it in a portion of a plant which contains already an etheric body included in the whole system of the cosmic ether. The gall-fly therefore approaches the oak in order to get help in the breaking down of its albumen, so that the cosmic periphery may be able to work *via* the oak leaf, *via* the oak. Alone, the egg of the gall-fly would be doomed to destruction, for it cannot be broken down. It holds together too strongly.

Here we can gain an insight into the strange workings of nature. But this same working is present in other places in nature, too. Suppose for instance that the animal is not merely incapable of providing germinal substance that can expose itself to the cosmic ether for the sake of reproduction; suppose it is not even able to transform any substances within it into inner means of nourishment—that is, to use them for its own inner nourishment. The example of the bee lies near to hand. The bee cannot eat anything and everything. It can only eat what the plant has already prepared for it. And now observe something very strange and remarkable. The bee goes to the plant, seeks out the honey juice, absorbs it, assimilates it within itself, and then builds up what we admire so, the wonderful cell structure of the beehive. Here we observe two most strange and wonderful processes: the bee sitting on the flower outside and sucking in the juice, and then, having gone into the beehive, building up from within itself in co-operation with the other bees the cells of wax that will be filled with honey.

What is it that really takes place? You must look carefully at the shape of the cells. They are like this, and here comes another joined on to it, and so on, and so on [Plate 12]. They are small cells, and similar in form to something else we find in nature, only there the hollow space is filled up; they are shaped like quartz crystals, like the crystals of silicic acid. If you go into the mountains and examine the quartz crystals, you will find you can draw them, too, in that form. The drawing will, it is true, show some irregularity of shape, but in

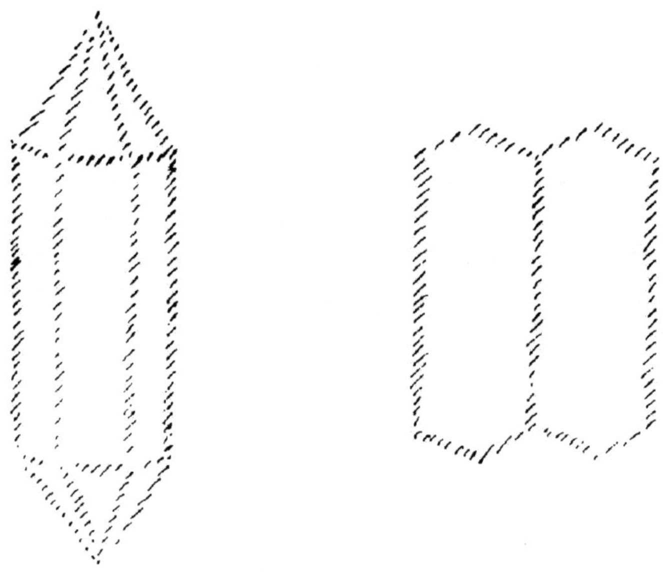

[See Plate 12, detail]

the main the form will be similar to the form of the bee-cells that are arranged side by side. Only, the cells of the bee are made of wax and the quartz is made of silicic acid.

When we follow up the matter, we find that long ago at a certain point of time in the evolution of the Earth the quartz-crystal was first formed in the mountains. It was formed under the prevailing etheric and astral influences, with the aid of silicic acid. There you have forces that come from the circumference, working, as ethereal-astral forces, and building the quartz crystals in the siliceous substance. Everywhere in the mountains you will find these crystals with their wonderful hexagonal forms. What you find in the solid crystals, you find again as *hollow* forms—as hollow spaces—in the cells of wax, in the beehive.

For what happens? The bee takes from the flower what once upon a time brought the quartz crystal into being. The bee fetches it up out of the flower and makes with the substance of her own body imitations of the quartz crystal. A process thus takes place between bee and flower that is similar to what took place long ago in the macrocosm.

I tell you these things so that you may understand how necessary it is not merely to take cognizance of the presence of carbon, nitrogen, hydrogen, and oxygen, all of which analysis is piteously abstract, but to observe and note the marvellous formative processes, the intimate inner conditions that prevail in nature and her processes. Once, long ago, science was instinctively built up on such observation. But that all passed away in the course of the historical evolution of humanity; it came to an end about the fifteenth century. We must win it back. We must find our way again into the intimate connections of nature and of her relationship with the human being. Only when we are able once more to recognize such connections can we hope to find again a true insight into the healthy as well as into the diseased human being. Otherwise all pharmacology remains merely a matter of testing and experimenting, without any perception of the inner connections that are at work.

The period from the fifteenth century until now may be described as an unfruitful period in the evolution of the human spirit. It has borne humans down beneath its weight. We have looked out upon plant and animal, upon human being and upon mineral, and all the while without any real knowledge of them whatsoever; we have been brought right out of connection with the world and the universe. Now at length it has landed us in chaos as far as our relationship to the great world is concerned; we live without knowing that we are in any sort of connection with the world around us. In the days when people pondered and meditated upon such things, it was known that every time reproduction took place, the whole macrocosm speaks. In the germ or seed that is capable of reproduction there comes to birth a minute image of the whole macrocosm. All around is the great world; and in the tiniest germ is an offspring of the influences that stream in from the great world from every direction.

In the human being we may see working together, first of all the forces that are the physical-central forces of the Earth. These forces work in all the organs of the human being. But everywhere in us there work also, in an opposite direction, the forces that stream in from all sides, the etheric forces. Look at the liver, for example, or the lungs: you will only understand them when you know that in them are working together the forces that come from the centre of the Earth and the forces that come in from every direction from the circumference of the universe. Then we have also certain organs that are permeated by the astral body, or again by the ego-organization, whilst others are less permeated by these higher members. In the condition of sleep, of course, humans as a whole do not have their astral body and ego-organization in them at all. Now imagine that some organ, let us say one of the lungs, has through some circumstance become too strongly affected by the forces that stream in everywhere from the entire cosmos. The lung will in consequence become diseased, for a certain harmony and balance is necessary between what works in the lung from the centre of the Earth and what streams in upon it from all parts of the circumference. If you can succeed in finding mineral substances which will provide a counterpoise in the lung to the too strongly working etheric forces, then you will have a remedy wherewith to eliminate their over-activity. The reverse may also happen. The etheric forces may become too weak, and the physical forces that work from the centre of the Earth grow correspondingly too strong. This time you will search the whole kingdom of the plants to discover something that will strengthen the etheric forces in the organ where they are weak; and then you will have your remedy for this condition.

It is quite impossible to find even the slightest remedy by an observation of the physical body alone, for the human physical body has in itself no ground for telling anything about its own constitution. The so-called normal process that goes on in the physical body is a process of nature. But the process that goes on in illness is likewise a process of nature. If you have what is called a normal, healthy liver, you have a liver in which processes of nature take place. And if you have a liver in which there is an abscess, you also have a liver in which processes of nature take place. The difference can never be found by investigating the physical body. All you can do from investigation of the physical body is to establish the fact that the appearance is different in the one case from the other. You can learn nothing of the cause. If you have an abscess on the liver, you will only be able to discover the cause of it when you know that in such a case, for example, the astral body enters much more powerfully into the liver than it should. What you have to do is to drive out of the liver the astral body, which has taken possession there too strongly. From all this it is clear that there is really no possibility of speaking about the healthy and the diseased human being in a way that accords with the facts, unless we go beyond the physical body and include also in our consideration the higher members of the human being. We shall indeed only regain a pharmacology when we go beyond the physical body, for the nature of illness is simply not demonstrable from the physical body alone.

At the present time my purpose is merely to set forth these things in their historical aspect and connections. It must, however, be pointed out that with the gradual dimming and darkening of what has been brought over from olden times, all real knowledge of human nature has died right away. And now today we are faced with the necessity of acquiring once again a knowledge of the human being. Such knowledge will be attainable when we are once again in a position to understand the relationship of the human being to the surrounding kingdoms of nature.

Suppose, then, we take our start from the human ego-organization. If, through initiatory science, we have attained to imaginative cognition and are able to perceive the human ego-organization, then we may ask ourselves: With what portion of the human organism (in its present state) does this ego-organization stand in especially near relation? It stands in a special relation with all that is mineral in the human being. Hence when you receive into yourself some essentially mineral substance—for example, when you take some salt on your tongue—it is the ego-organization in you that immediately pounces upon this mineral substance. And as the substance is carried further into the body, all the while—even when the salt substance is in the stomach—the ego-organization remains with it. The salt goes still further, it undergoes various changes, it passes through the intestines—never once does the ego-organization leave hold of her salt! They behave like two closely related things, two things that belong to one another: the ego-organization, and the salt that enters the human being.

It is quite another matter when you eat, for example, a fried egg, or any substance of a similar—albuminous—consistency. The ego-organization is very little concerned when you have a piece of fried egg on your tongue. Afterwards, as it slips down into the stomach, the astral body concerns itself with it, but again only to a very small extent. Then it goes further. And now, first the etheric and then the physical body begin to act intensively upon it. They break down within you the albumen that you receive into your organism with the egg. The egg itself is now made entirely of mineral within you. It is broken down and destroyed. All life is driven out of it. It is destroyed within you. At the walls of the intestines the albumen substance that you have taken into you from outside ceases to be albumen in any sense, becomes entirely mineral in character. And now it passes over into the ego-organization; from this point the mineralized albumen is taken up by the ego-organization.

Thus, the ego-organization concerns itself only with what is mineral. And all mineral substances are changed through its action; in the human organism they become different from what they were outside it. No mineral substance can remain the same within the human organism as it is outside. The ego-organization has to look after this in a very thorough manner. Nor is it only such substances as cooking salt and the like that are seized upon by the ego-organization and inwardly changed to something quite different. The human being is surrounded by a certain condition of warmth, but that external condition of warmth must never be allowed to penetrate the human being. You can never have your finger full of what is all around you as external warmth. This warmth can but act as a stimulus, you yourself must create and produce the warmth that you have within you. The moment you are merely, so to say, an object and do not yourself create your own warmth or cold, but let the warmth from outside extend its influence into you exactly as it does into any external object—in that moment you become ill. The external warmth—not even a substance, but the warmth itself makes you ill. Suppose you have here a towel or a sponge, and over there is a fire. The warmth of the fire, which can spread out all around quite easily, will permeate the towel or the sponge. The towel or sponge only carries a little further the radiating warmth of the fire. When, however, the warmth of the fire reaches the skin of the human being and acts upon the senses, stimulating them, then it must no longer simply spread in this way; then the reaction must come, the inner warmth must be created from within. If we catch cold, our condition results from the fact that we have not merely let ourselves be stimulated to create our own inner warmth, but we have let the external cold enter to some extent beneath the skin. Thus we do not take our place in the world as fully active human beings who fill themselves with our own activity and our own impulses, but we play rather the part of an object that lets the activities and influences of the outer world pass through us. That is the essential nature of the ego-organization that it takes up into itself what is mineral and completely changes it from within, converting it into something altogether different.

Not until we have died does the mineral turn back again into the mineral of external nature. So long as we are alive on the Earth, and have the mineral enclosed in our skin, so long does the ego-organization continue to change it perpetually. Similarly, whatever we take up into ourselves that is of a vegetable nature is perpetually changed by the working of the astral body. It is in everything of a mineral nature that the ego-organization brings about a thorough metamorphosis; not merely in the solid mineral, but also in the liquid and gaseous mineral, and the mineral that is in the state of warmth or heat.

Of course, when we speak in quite an ordinary way, we may say: Here is some water. I drink it. Now I have the water inside me. The truth is, however, that the moment my organism receives the water, then by reason of the action of my ego-organization, the water inside me is no longer the same as the water outside. It only becomes the same again when I give it off in the form of perspiration, or in some other way convert it into water. Inside my skin water is not water; it is living fluid.

In this manner we shall have to alter our thoughts about a great many things. Today I have only been able to give you small indications. Think them over. Think how the albumen has to be broken down and disorganized in order that it may be exposed to the influences of the whole macrocosm. Think how the water I drink becomes in me living fluid and is no longer the inorganic water it was before, but rather becomes water permeated by the ego-organization. Think how, when you eat cabbage—outside you it was cabbage, inside you the astral body receives the cabbage into itself and transforms it into something new. And here we come to the consideration of very important processes in the human body. We learn to perceive how we have in our metabolic system processes that are only one evolutionary stage removed from the metabolisms that we have, for example, in our brain—the metabolisms that go to make up the nervous system, and so forth. I will speak further on this tomorrow and make clear, in connection with these processes, the radical difference between individuals of the twelfth and of the twentieth centuries. We shall thus come to see the necessity for new impulses to enter in, if there is to be progress in the understanding of health and disease, and if the knowledge of human nature is not to die out altogether and nothing more ever be known of the healthy or of the diseased human being.

Lecture 8

DORNACH, 31 DECEMBER 1923

We stand today under the sign of a painful memory, and I want to place what we have to take for the theme of our lecture today into the sign of that painful memory. The lecture I was able to give exactly a year ago in our old Goetheanum—those of you who were present will remember how it took its start from descriptions of nature, of relationships that can be observed in nature on Earth, and led from these up to the spiritual worlds and the revelations of the spiritual worlds in the writing of the stars. And you will remember how we were able then to bring the human heart, the human soul and spirit in their whole nature and being into close connection with what is found when one follows the path that leads away from the earthly into the distant stellar spaces, wherein the spiritual writes its cosmic script. And the words that I then wrote upon the blackboard, writing for the last time in the room that was so soon to be taken from us, bore within them this impulse and this purpose: to lift the human soul into spiritual heights.

So on that evening we were brought into direct and close touch with that to which our Goetheanum in its whole intention and character was devoted. And today you will allow me to speak to you again of these things, as it were in continuation of the lecture that was given here a year ago.[56]

In the days preceding the burning of Ephesus, when individuals spoke of the Mysteries, provided they were individuals who had some understanding and feeling for them, they spoke of them somewhat in the following manner. Human knowledge, human wisdom has a home and a dwelling place in the Mysteries. And when in those olden times the spiritual guides of the universe spoke of the Mysteries, when the Mysteries were spoken of in the supra-sensible worlds—I may be permitted this expression, although of course it is only a figure of speech to describe how thought and influence streamed down from the supra-sensible into the sensible worlds—when, therefore, the Mysteries were spoken of in the supra-sensible worlds, then it was somewhat in the following way: 'In the Mysteries humans erect places where we gods can find the individuals who do sacrifice and who understand us in the sacrifice.'

For in point of fact individuals of the old world, individuals of the old world who knew, were conscious that in the places of the Mysteries gods meet with human beings; they knew how all that carries and sustains the world depends on what takes place between gods and humans in the sacred Mysteries.

But there is a *word*—a word that has come down to us in history and that can speak powerfully to the human heart even in external historical tradition, but that speaks with peculiar force and earnestness when we see it shape itself out of strange and unparalleled events, when we see it written with eternal letters into the history of humanity, though the writing be only visible for a moment in the spirit. I declare to you that, wherever the eye of the spirit is turned to the deed of Herostratus, to the burning of Ephesus, then, in those flames of fire may be read the ancient words: The jealousy of the gods.

Among the many and diverse words that have come down to us from olden time, and that were in use in the life of olden times in the manner I have described—among all the words in this physical world, these words are, I verily believe, some of the most awful: The jealousy of the gods. In those times the term 'god' was applied to all beings of a supra-sensible nature—to every form of being that had no need to appear on Earth in a physical body. Many and varied kinds of gods were differentiated. The divine and spiritual beings who are most closely united with humanity, from whom we in our innermost nature originated and by whom we were launched into the stream of time, the same beings whom we recognize in the majesty of nature and in her smallest manifestations, and whom we discover too in that which lives in our own inmost selves—these divine-spiritual beings can never be jealous. Nevertheless, in that ancient time the 'jealousy of the gods' was something very real. If we study the period of human development that led up to the time of Ephesus, we find that the more advanced members of humanity received into themselves much of what the good gods held out to them in the Mysteries. For it is true to say that an intimate relationship exists between good human hearts and the good gods, and this intimate relationship was knit closer and closer in the Mysteries. And thus it came to pass that certain other divine beings, luciferic and ahrimanic divine beings, were made aware that humanity was being drawn nearer and nearer to the good gods. And there arose a jealousy on the part of the gods, a jealousy concerning humans. Over and over again in human history, we have to hear how an individual who strives after the spirit falls victim to a tragic destiny. In olden times such an event was spoken of as brought about by the jealousy of the gods.

The Greeks knew very well that this jealousy of the gods exists; they traced back to it much of what took place in human history. With the burning of Ephesus it was made manifest that further spiritual evolution was only possible if we became conscious that there are gods—that is, supra-sensible beings—who are jealous of the further advance of humanity.

It is this that gives the peculiar colouring to all history that follows the burning of Ephesus—or I may also say, the birth of Alexander. And it is essential for a right understanding of the Mystery of Golgotha. We have to see a world filled with the jealousy of certain kinds of gods. Ever since a time that follows soon after the Persian War, the psychic atmosphere of the world was filled with the effects of this jealousy of the gods. And what had to be done in the Macedonian time had to be done in the full consciousness that the jealousy of the gods pervades the spiritual atmosphere over the surface of the Earth. But it was done with courage and daring, and in spite of the misunderstandings of gods and humans.

Into this atmosphere, filled with the jealousy of the gods, sank then the deed of Him Who was capable of the greatest love that can exist in the world. We only see the Mystery of Golgotha in a true light when we add to everything else we have learned concerning it this picture: the dark bank of cloud that hung in olden time over Greece, Macedonia, Asia Minor, Northern Africa, and Southern Europe, the dark cloud that is the expression of the jealousy of the gods. And then into this cloud-filled atmosphere we behold streaming down the warm and gentle rays of the love that pours through the Mystery of Golgotha.

But when we come to our own time, then that which in earlier ages was—if I may put it so—an affair between gods and humans, must in this epoch of human freedom be played out below in the physical life of humanity. We can already describe how it is being played out. In olden times, when we thought of the Mysteries, it was in this sense that we spoke of them: In the Mysteries, we said, human knowledge, human wisdom has a home. And when the Mysteries were spoken of among the gods, it was said: When we descend into the Mysteries, we find the sacrifice done by human beings, and in the sacrificing human being we are understood.

The burning of Ephesus marks the beginning of the epoch that saw the gradual and complete disappearance of the Mysteries in their ancient form. I have told you how the Mysteries were continued here and there—in a sublime manner, for example, in the Mysteries of Hibernia, where the Mystery of Golgotha was celebrated in the ritual at the very time when it was taking place physically over in Palestine. They had knowledge of it not through physical, but through spiritual means of communication. Notwithstanding these survivals, the real being of the Mysteries retreated more and more within the physical world. The external centres which were the meeting places for gods and humans lost more and more of their significance. By the time of the thirteenth and fourteenth centuries, it had almost entirely gone. For whoever would find the way, for example, to the Holy Grail, must know how to tread *spiritual paths*. In the olden times, before the burning of Ephesus, we trod *physical paths*. In the Middle Ages, it was spiritual paths that we had to tread.

Spiritual paths above all were necessary from the thirteenth, fourteenth and especially the fifteenth century onwards, if we wanted to receive true Rosicrucian instruction. For the temples of the Rosicrucians were hidden from outer physical experience. Many a true Rosicrucian frequented these temples, it is true, but no outer physical eye could find them. Nonetheless there were disciples who came to these old Rosicrucians, for in scattered places the true Rosicrucians could indeed be found. They were like hermits of wisdom and of consecrated human action. And any person who was able to perceive the language of the gods in the gentle radiance of their eyes, would find them so. I am not speaking in mere pictures. I am relating a reality, and a reality which was of cardinal importance for that time. To find the Rosicrucian master the pupil must first attain the faculty to perceive the language of heaven in the gentle light of the physical eye. Then it was possible to find here and there in Central Europe, in the fourteenth and fifteenth centuries, these remarkable people, living in the most simple and unpretentious manner—people who were God-inspired, connected in their inner life with the spiritual temples which did indeed exist, albeit the access to them was no less difficult than the access to the Holy Grail, as described in the well-known legend.

Observing in the spirit what took place between such a Rosicrucian master and his pupil, we can hear many a conversation, wherein is shown once again—though in a form that belongs to a more modern age—how the wisdom of the gods lives and moves upon Earth. For the instructions of these masters were essentially objective and concrete. There in his loneliness some Rosicrucian master was found by the pupil who had spared no pains to seek him out. Gazing into the gentle eyes of the master out of which spoke the language of the gods, this pupil would receive in all humility an instruction somewhat as follows:

Look, my friend, at your own being! You carry about with you a body which your physical eyes can see. The centre of the Earth supplies this body with the forces which make it visible. This is your physical body.

But look around you at your environment on Earth. Behold the stones! They can exist on Earth by themselves, they are at home here. And if they have once assumed a certain form, they can preserve this form by virtue of the Earthly forces. Look at the crystal; it bears its form within it. The Earth enables it to keep the form which belongs to its own being. Your physical body cannot do that. When your soul leaves it, it is destroyed, dissolved in dust. The Earth has no power over your physical body. It has the power to form and also to maintain the transparent crystal mountains with their wonderful configuration; but the Earth has no power to maintain the form of your physical body, it must dissolve it into dust. Your physical body is not of the Earth, it is of high spirituality. To Seraphim, Cherubim, and Thrones belongs the form and figure of your physical body. Not to the Earth, but to the highest spiritual powers which are accessible to humans, does this physical body of yours belong. The Earth can destroy it, but never build it up.

And now, within this physical body dwells an etheric body. The day will come when your physical body will be received by the Earth for its destruction. Then your etheric body will dissolve in the wide expanse of the cosmos. The far spaces of the cosmos can indeed dissolve, but they again cannot build your etheric body. Only the divine, spiritual beings can build it up—the beings of the hierarchy of Dynamis, Exusiai, and Kyriotetes. To them you owe your etheric body.

With your physical body you unite the physical substances of the Earth. But what is within you transforms these substances into something utterly different from all that is physically present in the environment of the physical body. Your etheric body brings into movement all that is fluid within you, all that is water within you. The saps and fluids in their circulation stand under the influence of your physical body. Behold your blood! It is the Exusiai, Dynamis, and Kyriotetes who cause the blood to circulate as a fluid through your veins. It is only as a physical body that you are human; in the etheric body you are still animal, albeit an animal that is inspirited by the Second Hierarchy.

What I have here gathered up into a very few words was the substance of a prolonged instruction given by that master in the gentle light of whose eyes the pupils discerned the language of heaven. And then their attention was turned to the third member of the human being, which we call the astral body. And it was made clear to them that this astral body contains the impulse for the breathing—for all that is airy in the human organism, for all that pulsates as air within this body of ours. Now it is true that for a long time after we have passed through the gate of death, our earthly nature strives, as it were, to make disturbances in the airy element, so much so that the clairvoyant vision can observe in the atmospheric phenomena of the Earth for many years, the noising of the astral bodies of the dead. Nevertheless, the Earth with its encircling sphere also can only dissolve them in relation to the impulses of the astral body. For these again can only be created by Beings of the Third Hierarchy—the Archai, Archangeloi, and Angeloi.

And then the master said—and his words struck deep into the heart of the pupil: In your physical body, inasmuch as you receive within you the mineral kingdom and transform it, you belong to the Seraphim, Cherubim, and Thrones. In so far as you are an etheric body, you are like an animal. Here however you belong to the spirits whom we designated as those of the Second Hierarchy—the Kyriotetes, Exusiai, Dynamis. Inasmuch as you live and move in the fluid element, you belong not to the Earth, but to this Hierarchy. And as you live and move in the airy element, you belong not to the Earth, but to the Hierarchy of Archai, Archangeloi, and Angeloi.

When the pupils had received this instruction in sufficient measure, they no longer felt that they belonged to the Earth. They felt forces proceeding from their physical, etheric, and astral bodies which united them with the Hierarchies. For they felt how, through the mineral world, they were united with the First Hierarchy; through the water of the Earth, with the Second Hierarchy; and through the atmosphere, with the Third Hierarchy. And it was plain to them that they were an inhabitant of Earth purely and solely on account of the element of warmth that they bore within them. In this way, the Rosicrucian pupils came to the perception that the warmth, the physical warmth they had within them, is what made them human on Earth. And they learned increasingly to feel how closely related warmth of soul and warmth of spirit are to physical warmth.

People of later times gradually lost all knowledge of how their physical, etheric and astral contents are connected—through the solid, the fluid, and the aeriform—with the divine. The Rosicrucian pupils, however, knew this well; they knew that what made them earthly was not these elements at all, but the element of warmth. The moment the pupils of the Rosicrucian teacher perceived this secret of the connection of the element of warmth with their life on Earth as earthly beings, in that moment they knew how to link the human in them on to the spiritual.

Now the pupils who came to these often humble haunts where such Rosicrucian masters lived were prepared beforehand in a way that was frequently quite unsought by them, and that appeared no less than marvellous in their eyes. An intimation would come to them, to one in one way, to another in another; often to all outward appearance it came by a mere chance. The intimation would be given to them: You must seek out a place where you may be able to bring your own spiritual nature into contact with the spiritual of the cosmos. And after the pupils had received the instruction of which I told you, then, yes then, they were able to say to the master: We go from you with the greatest comfort that could ever be to us on Earth. For in that you have shown us how earthly humans have their own proper element in warmth, you have opened to us the possibility to connect our physical nature with soul and spirit. The hard bones, the flowing blood, the airy breath—into none of these do we bring our psychic nature, but only into the element of warmth.

It was with an infinite peace and rest that the pupils departed from their masters in those days. In their countenance was expressed the great comfort they had received, and from this look of peace developed gradually that mild and gentle gaze whence the language of heaven can speak. And so we find in those earlier times and on into the first third of the fifteenth century a profound psychic instruction being given in these humble and secluded haunts. It is indeed unknown as compared with the events of which external history relates. It went on nonetheless, and was an instruction that took deep hold of the entire human being, an instruction that made it possible for the human soul to link its own nature on to the sphere of the cosmic and spiritual.

This whole spiritual atmosphere has disappeared in the course of the later centuries. It is no longer present in our civilization. An external, God-estranged civilization has spread abroad over the countries that once upon a time saw such a civilization as I have just described to you. We stand here today bearing within us the memory of many a scene like that I have described, although the memory can only be created in the spirit in the astral light. And when we look back into the older times, that are so often pictured to us as times of darkness, and then turn our gaze upon our own times, a deep longing arises in our hearts. From out of the spiritual revelations that have been accessible to us since the last third of the nineteenth century, is born a longing to speak to us once more in a spiritual way. But to do so, it is not enough to speak with abstract words. To speak spiritually demands the use of manifold signs and symbols; our speech has to be wide and comprehensive. Such a language, my dear friends, such a form of speech as needed to be found for the spiritual beings who have to speak to modern humanity, was given to us in the forms of the Goetheanum that was destroyed by fire a year ago. In very truth, the forms were built and moulded to that end, that what was spoken from the platform in ideas should speak on further in them. And so in a certain sense we may say that in the Goetheanum we had something that could awaken in an altogether new form a memory of the old.

When the candidates for initiation entered the Temple of Ephesus, their attention was directed to the statue of which I have spoken to you in these lectures, and the statue called to them in the language of the heart with these words: Unite yourself with the cosmic ether, and you will behold the earthly from out of the etheric heights.

Many pupils at Ephesus did behold the earthly from out of the etheric heights. And certain gods were jealous. Centuries before the Mystery of Golgotha took place, brave people were already finding a way to meet this jealousy of the gods. They found a way to foster what had come down to them from ancient, holier years of humanity's history, and had worked powerfully in human evolution up to the time of the burning of Ephesus. True, it was dim now and feeble, but even in this enfeebled form it could still continue to work.

Had our Goetheanum been brought to completion, then as you entered from the west, your glance would have fallen on a statue that bade us know ourselves in our cosmic nature, know ourselves as beings set between the powers of Lucifer and Ahriman, God-maintained in the middle in inner balance. And when you looked upon the forms of the columns and of the architrave, these forms spoke a language that was a continuation of the language which was spoken in words from the platform, where the expression of the spiritual in ideas was sought. The sound of the words flowed on into the plastically moulded forms. And above in the dome were displayed the scenes which could bring before the eye of the soul the past evolution of humanity. Whoever looked upon this Goetheanum with feeling and understanding could find in it a memory of the Temple of Ephesus.

The memory, however, grew to be terribly painful. For in a manner not at all unlike that which befell Ephesus in earlier time, exactly at the moment in its evolution when the Goetheanum was ready to become the bearer of the renewal of spiritual life, in that very moment there was flung into it a burning brand.

My dear friends, our pain was deep and indescribable. But we made the resolve to go forward, unhindered by this tragedy that had befallen us, to continue our work for the spiritual world. For we were able to say to ourselves in the depths of our own hearts: When we look upon the flames that rose from Ephesus, we behold written into the flames these words: The jealousy of the gods. That was a time when humans were still unfree, and needed to follow the wills of the good and the evil gods.

In our day, humans are marked out for freedom. A year ago, on New Year's Eve, we beheld the destroying flames. The red glow rose to heaven. Tongues of flame, dark blue and reddish yellow, curled their way up through the sea of fire. They came from the metal instruments concealed in the Goetheanum; the gigantic sea of fire glowed with all manner of changing colours. And as one gazed into this sea of flame with its swift lines and tongues of colour, one had perforce to read these words, words that spoke pain for the soul: The jealousy of humanity.

Thus are the words that speak from epoch to epoch in human evolution bound together in deepest calamity and unhappiness. In the time when humans still looked up to the gods in unfreedom, but had it as their task to make themselves free, there were words that were significant of the deepest unhappiness and grief to them. They beheld inscribed into the flames: The jealousy of the gods. And by a thread of spiritual evolution our own calamity is linked with these words. We live in a time when we have to find in ourselves the power of freedom, and now we behold inscribed in the flames other words: The jealousy of humanity. In Ephesus, the statue of the gods; here in the Goetheanum the statue of humanity, the statue of the Representative of Humanity, Christ Jesus. In Him, identifying ourselves in all humility with Him, we thought to attain to knowledge, even as once in their way, a way that is no longer fully understood by humanity today, the pupils of Ephesus attained to knowledge of Diana of Ephesus.

The pain does not grow less when one beholds in the light of history what that New Year's Eve brought to us a year ago. When for the last time it was given to me to stand on the platform that was itself built in harmony with the whole Goetheanum, it was my intention and purpose to direct the gaze, the spiritual gaze of those present, away from earthly realms to the ascent into the starry worlds where the will and wisdom, where the light of the spiritual cosmos are brought to expression. I know well, godfathers and -mothers were there present at that time—spirits of those who in the Middle Ages taught their pupils in the manner I have described to you.

One hour after the last word had been spoken, I was summoned to the fire at the Goetheanum. At the fire of the Goetheanum we passed the whole of that New Year night.

One has but to speak these words, and thoughts unutterable surge up in all our hearts and souls. But whenever it has happened in the evolution of humanity that something sacred to that evolution has been torn away, then there have always been a few who have pledged themselves, after the dissolution of the physical, to continue the work in the spirit, to which the physical was dedicated. And gathered here as we are in the moment that marks the anniversary of the tragic loss of our Goetheanum, we do well to remember that we shall bring our souls into the right attitude for this gathering when we pledge ourselves one and all to bear onward in the spirit on the advancing wave of human progress what was expressed in physical form and in physical image in the Goetheanum, and which has been torn away from physical sight by a deed like the deed of Herostratus.

Our pain and grief cling to the old Goetheanum. But we shall only show ourselves worthy of having been permitted to build this Goetheanum, if we fulfil the task that yet remains to us, if we take today a solemn pledge, each one of us before the highest, the divine, that we bear within our soul, a pledge to hold faithfully in remembrance the spiritual impulses that have had their outward expression in the Goetheanum that is gone. The Goetheanum could be taken from us: the spirit of the Goetheanum, if in all sincerity we will to keep it, can never be taken from us. It will least of all be taken from us, if in this solemn hour, that is divided by but a short space of time from the actual moment a year ago, when the flames burst forth from our beloved Goetheanum—if in this solemn hour we not only feel a renewal of our pain, but out of the very pain pledge ourselves to remain loyal to the spirit to which we erected our Goetheanum, building it up through ten years of work. If this resolve wells up today in all sincerity from the depths of our hearts, if we are able to change the pain and grief into the impulse to action, then we shall also change the sorrowful event into blessing. The pain cannot thereby be made less, but it rests with us to find in the pain the urge to action, to action in the spirit.

Even so let us look back upon the terrible flames of fire that filled us with such unutterable sadness, but let us at the same time feel how today, as we dedicate ourselves with solemn vow to the highest divine forces that are within us, a spiritual flame lights up in our hearts. Yea, and the flame in our hearts shall shed new light and warmth on all that was purposed and willed in the Goetheanum, on all that we are now resolved to carry forward on the advancing wave of human evolution.

Let us then, my dear friends, recall at this time and write deeper in our hearts the words that I was able to speak to you over there in the Goetheanum almost in the very same moment of time a year ago. On that night I spoke somewhat in the following words: We are at the eve of a new year, we must go forward to meet an oncoming cosmic new year. If the Goetheanum were still standing, this demand and this call could in this moment be renewed. It is no longer standing. The same call can, however, be uttered again on this New Year's

Eve, can be uttered, as I believe, with redoubled power just because the Goetheanum is no longer there. Let us carry over the soul of the Goetheanum into the cosmic new year, let us try to erect in the new Goetheanum a worthy memorial to the old!

May our hearts be thus knit to the old Goetheanum, which we had perforce to give over to the elements. And may our hearts be closely knit to the spirit and the soul of this Goetheanum. And with this solemn pledge to the highest and the best that is in us, we will carry our life over not only into the New Year, but into the Cosmic New Year. We will go forward into it, strong for action, upheld and guided in soul and spirit.

My dear friends, you received me by rising in memory of the old Goetheanum. Let us now rise in token that we pledge ourselves to continue working in the spirit of the Goetheanum with the best and highest forces that we have within us. So be it. Amen.

And we will hold to this our solemn pledge, we will be true to it as long as we are able, we will hold to it with our will—for our will it is that unites these human souls of ours with the souls of the gods. We will remain faithful to the spirit in which at a certain moment of our life we first sought the anthroposophy of the Goetheanum.

And let us understand and know how to keep the promise we have made.

Lecture 9

DORNACH, 1 JANUARY 1924

As we are together for the last time during this Christmas Conference, which should be a source of strength and of vital importance for the anthroposophical movement, you will allow me to give this lecture as a supplement to the many vistas opened for us by the series of lectures just finished, while also giving tentative indications concerning the future of anthroposophical strivings.

When we look at the world today—and it has been the same for years now—destructive elements on a colossal scale are everywhere in evidence. Forces that are actively at work enable us to have forebodings of the abysses into which Western civilization will continue to steer. When we think of those individuals who are outwardly the spiritual leaders in various domains of life, we shall perceive that these individuals are in the throes of an ominous, universal sleep. They think, or at least most of them were still thinking only a short time ago, that until the nineteenth century, humanity was childish and primitive in respect of understanding and conceptions of the world. Then modern science appeared in its many branches and now—so it is thought—there exists something that must through all eternity be cultivated as the truth.

The people who think this are really giving way to extreme arrogance, only they are not aware of it. On the other hand there sometimes arises, even in people today, a premonition that things are not, after all, as I have described them.

Some little time ago it was still possible for me to give lectures in Germany organized by the Wolff Bureau. They attracted extraordinarily large audiences so that the existence of a desire for anthroposophy became obvious to many people. Among the many nonsensical utterances of opponents there was one voice which to be sure was not much cleverer than the others in respect of content, but which nevertheless indicated a remarkable premonition. It consisted in a newspaper report of one of the lectures I had given in Berlin. The notice was to this effect: When one listens to something of this kind, one becomes attentive to the fact that something is going on not only on the Earth—I am quoting the notice approximately—but in the whole cosmos something is happening which summons us to adopt a spirituality different from what existed previously. Now, the forces of the cosmos—not only earthly impulses—demand something from us. A kind of revolution is taking place in the cosmos, the result of which must be the striving for a new spirituality.

Such utterances were constantly to be heard and were very worthy of note. The fact of the matter is this: the impulse that must be working in what is now to go out from Dornach must—as I emphasized from every possible point of view during the Conference itself—be an impulse originating in the spiritual world, not on the Earth. Our striving here is to develop the strength to follow impulses from the spiritual world. That is why, in the evening lectures during this Christmas Conference, I spoke of manifold impulses at work in the course of historical evolution in order that hearts could be opened for the reception of the spiritual impulses which have yet to stream into the earthly world, which are not derived from that world itself. Everything for which the earthly world hitherto has rightly been the vehicle, proceeded from the spiritual world. And if we are to achieve anything fruitful for the earthly world, the impulses for it must be brought from the spiritual world.

This prompts the assertion that the impulses we ought rightly to take with us from the Conference for our further activity must be connected with great responsibility.

Let us think for a short time of the responsibility laid upon us by that Conference. Anyone with a sense of the reality of the spiritual world could encounter many personalities during recent decades, and observing them spiritually experience bitter feelings regarding the future destiny of humanity on Earth. One could encounter one's fellow human beings on the Earth in the way that is possible spiritually and observe these human beings during their sleep while they are in the spiritual world with ego and astral body, having left their physical and etheric bodies. During recent decades, explorations connected with the destinies of egos and astral bodies during the sleep of human beings have resulted in knowledge calling for great responsibility on the part of those who possess it. One often saw souls, who had left their physical and etheric bodies during sleep, approaching the Guardian of the Threshold.[57]

In the course of evolution the Guardian of the Threshold has been brought to human consciousness in very many different ways. Many a legend, many a saga—for it is in this form, not in the form of historical tradition that things of the greatest importance are preserved—many a legend tells of how, in earlier times, this or that personality met the Guardian of the Threshold and was instructed by him how to enter the spiritual world and return again into the physical world. Every legitimate entry into the spiritual world must include the possibility of being able at any and every minute to return into the physical world and to live there as a practical, thoughtful human being, not as a visionary or as an ecstatic mystic.

Fundamentally speaking, it was this that was demanded by the Guardian of the Threshold through all the ages of human endeavours to enter the spiritual world. But notably in the last third of the nineteenth century, hardly any human beings who succeeded in approaching the Guardian of the Threshold in waking consciousness were to be seen. In our present time, when it is historically incumbent upon the whole of humanity to encounter the Guardian of the Threshold in some form, one finds how souls during sleep approach the Guardian of the Threshold as egos and astral bodies, and the pictures that are revealed are full of significance. The stern Guardian of the Threshold has around him groups of human souls in the state of sleep, souls who in waking consciousness lack the strength to approach this Guardian of the Threshold. They approach him while they sleep.

When one watches the scene presented there, a thought connected with what I have called the seed of great and essential responsibility comes to one. The souls approaching the Guardian of the Threshold during the state of sleep plead with the consciousness then prevailing—in the waking state everything remains unconscious or subconscious—plead to be admitted into the spiritual world, to be allowed to cross the threshold. And in numberless cases one then hears the voice of the stern Guardian of the Threshold saying: For your own well-being you may not cross the threshold. You may not be allowed to enter the spiritual world. You must go back!—For if the Guardian of the Threshold were to permit such souls to enter the spiritual world, they would cross the threshold and enter that world with the concepts imparted to them by the schools, education, and civilization of today, with the concepts and ideas with which the human being is obliged to grow up from about the age of six to basically the end of his life on Earth.

The intrinsic character of these concepts and ideas is such that what a person has become through them in modern civilization and education means that we enter the spiritual world paralyzed in soul. Moreover, we would return to the physical world empty-headed in respect of thoughts and ideas. If the Guardian of the Threshold were not to reject many human souls of the modern age, but allow them to enter the spiritual world, they would feel on awakening: I am incapable of thinking, my thoughts do not connect with my brain, I am obliged to go through the world void of thoughts. For such is the effect of the abstract ideas which we apply to everything today. With these ideas we can enter the spiritual world, but not come forth from it again. And when we witness this scene which is experienced during sleep by more souls than is usually imagined, we feel: Oh! if only it were possible to protect these souls from having also to experience at death what they experience during sleep! For if the condition that is experienced in the presence of the Guardian of the Threshold were to be repeated for a sufficient length of time, if civilization were to remain long enough under the sway of what current education provides, then human souls would pass through the gates of death into the spiritual world, but would be unable to bring any mental vigour into the next earthly life. With the thoughts prevailing today it is possible for someone to enter the spiritual world, but they can only come out of it again paralyzed in soul.

You see, modern civilization adopts the form of spiritual life that has for so long been cultivated, but real life does not allow this. Civilization as it now is might continue to progress for a time. During waking life souls would have no inkling of the existence of the Guardian of the Threshold and during sleep would be rejected by him in order to avoid mental paralysis; and this would finally result in humans being born in the future with no understanding, no possibility of applying ideas in their future earthly life; and all thinking, all ideation would vanish from the Earth. A diseased, purely instinctive humanity would people the Earth. Evil feelings and unbridled emotions without the guiding power of ideas would take hold of the evolution of humanity. It is not only through observation of the souls confronting the Guardian of the Threshold—souls which can gain no entrance to the spiritual world—it is not only through observing this that a sorrowful picture is presented to the seer, but in a different connection there is another factor as well.

If on the journey of which I have spoken, when the souls of sleeping human beings confronting the Guardian of the Threshold can be observed, we are accompanied by a human being belonging not to Western but to Oriental civilization, a terrible reproach of the whole of Western civilization may be heard from him, to this effect: If things continue as they now are, when the human beings living today appear on Earth in new incarnations, the Earth will become barbaric. Human beings will live devoid of ideas, in instincts only. You Westerners have brought things to this pass because you have abandoned the ancient spirituality of the East.

A glimpse into the spiritual world such as I have described may well give rise to a sense of great responsibility. And here in Dornach there must be a place where for those human beings who have ears to hear, direct and significant experiences in the spiritual world can be described. Here there must be a place where sufficient strength is generated not merely to indicate in terms of the dialectical and empirical mentality of today that here or there little traces of spiritual reality exist. If Dornach is to fulfil its task, actual happenings in the spiritual world must be spoken of openly. Individuals must be able to hear of the impulses in the spiritual world which then pour into and control the natural world and nature itself. In Dornach, individuals must be able to hear of actual experiences, actual forces, actual beings of the spiritual world. Here there must be the School of Spiritual Science.[58] Henceforth we must not draw back when confronted by the shallowness of the scientific thoughts of today which, as I have described, lead in the state of sleep to the stern Guardian of the Threshold. In Dornach, the strength must be acquired to confront and experience the spiritual world in its reality.

There will be no dialectical tirades from me on the subject of the inadequacy of modern scientific theory. I was obliged, however, to call attention to the position in which human beings are placed when confronting the Guardian of the Threshold on account of these scientific theories and their offshoots in the orthodox schools of today. If what has been said at this Christmas Conference is sincerely applied in the life of soul, the Conference will be a forceful impulse which the soul can then apply in the activity that is needed in this age so that in their next incarnations, individuals may be able to confront the Guardian of the Threshold in the right way. This will ensure that civilization in its own right can enable us to face and hold our own when confronting the Guardian of the Threshold.

Just compare the civilization of today with that of earlier times during all of which human thoughts and concepts were directed primarily to the supra-sensible world, to the gods, to the world of productive, generative, creative forces. With concepts that were concerned primarily with the gods, we were able to contemplate the earthly world and also to understand it in the light of these concepts and ideas. If with these concepts—worthy of the gods as they were—an individual came before the Guardian of the Threshold, the Guardian would say to him: You may pass, for you bring over the threshold into the supra-sensible world thoughts that were already directed to the supra-sensible world during your earthly life in a physical body. Thus when you return into the physical world of the senses you will have enough strength to protect you from being paralyzed by the spectacle of the supra-sensible world.

Today we develop concepts and ideas which, in accordance with the genius of the age, we want to apply only to the material world.

These concepts and ideas are concerned with every possible aspect of weight, measure and the like, but they have nothing to do with the gods and are not worthy of the gods. Hence to souls who have completely succumbed to materialistic ideas that are unworthy of the gods, the voice of the Guardian of the Threshold thunders when they pass before him in the state of sleep: Do not cross the threshold! You have squandered your ideas on the world of the senses. Hence you must remain with them in the world of the senses. If you do not wish to be paralyzed in your life of soul, you may not enter the world of the gods as long as you hold such ideas.

These things must be said, not in order to be the subject of argument, but because every individual should let his mind and soul be permeated by them and thus develop the attitude of mind that should have been generated in him by this solemn Christmas Conference of the Anthroposophical Society. For more important than anything else we take with us is the recognition of the spiritual world which gives the certainty that in Dornach there will be created a living centre of spiritual knowledge.

Hence a really splendid note was struck this morning when Dr. Zeylmans[59] spoke in connection with the sphere of medicine, saying that it is no longer possible today for bridges to be built from orthodox science to what it is our aim to found in Dornach. If we were to speak of what it is hoped to develop in the sphere of medicine here by boasting that our products can stand the test of all modern clinical requirements, then we should never reach any definite goal. For then other people would simply say: That is just a new remedy; and we too have produced plenty of new remedies!

It is of essential importance that a branch of practical life such as medicine should be taken in the real sense into anthroposophical life. That is what I certainly understood to be Dr. Zeylmans' wish when he said this morning that an individual who becomes a doctor today really longs for something that gives impulses from a new corner of the world. In the domain of medicine this is just what will be done here in the future, together with many another branch of genuine anthroposophical activity. It will be worked out now, with Dr. Wegman[60] as my helper, as a system of medicine based upon anthroposophy. It is a dire need of humanity and will soon be available. It is also my intention to establish as soon as possible a close relationship between the Goetheanum and the Clinic in Arlesheim that is proving to be so beneficial. The work there will be oriented entirely towards anthroposophy. That is also Dr. Wegman's intention.

In speaking as he did, Dr. Zeylmans also indicated what attitude the *Vorstand*[61] in Dornach will adopt in all spheres of anthroposophical activity. In future we shall know exactly how matters stand. We shall not say: let us bring eurythmy to this or that town, for if people first see eurythmy without hearing anything about anthroposophy, eurythmy will please them. Then, later on perhaps, they will come to us, and because they have liked eurythmy and have heard that anthroposophy is behind it, anthroposophy too may please them! Or again, it may be said: In the practice of medicine people must be shown that ours are the right remedies and then they will buy them; later on they may discover that anthroposophy is behind them and then they will come to anthroposophy!

We must have the courage to realize that such procedure is dishonest and must be abandoned. Anthroposophy will then find its way in the world. Our striving for truth here in Dornach will in the future be without fanaticism, will be advocated honestly and candidly. Perhaps in this way we can make reparation for principles that have been gravely sinned against in recent years.

We must leave this Conference, which has led to the Founding of the General Anthroposophical Society, not with trifling, but with solemn thoughts. But I think that nobody need have experienced any pessimism as a result of what took place here at Christmas. We had, it is true, to pass the tragic ruins of the Goetheanum every day, but I think that all those who climbed the hill and passed the ruins during the Conference will have become aware of what our friends have understood in their hearts and that the following thought will have become a reality to them: Spiritual flames of fire will go forth from the new Goetheanum that will come into being in the future, for the blessing of mankind, will come into being through our activity and devotion. And the greater the courage with which to conduct the affairs of anthroposophy that we take with us from this Conference, the more effectively have we grasped the spiritual impulse of hope that has pervaded the Conference.

The scene that I have described to you—the scene that is so often to be seen of modern humanity with the results of this civilization and education facing the Guardian of the Threshold—this scene does not actually occur among perceptive anthroposophists. But it does sometimes happen that this warning is necessary: You must develop the resolute courage to become aware of and avow your obedience to this voice from the spiritual world, for you have begun to wake. Courage will keep you wakeful; lack of courage—that and that alone could cause you to sleep.

The voice of exhortation to unfold courage and wakefulness—that is the other variant for anthroposophists in the life of modern civilization. Non-anthroposophists hear the voice which says: Remain outside the spiritual world, for you have misused the ideas which are coined for purely earthly objects; you have amassed no ideas that are worthy of the gods. Hence you would be paralyzed on your return into the physical world of the senses. To the souls who are truly anthroposophical souls, however, it is said: You have now to be tested in respect only of your courage to avow adherence to the voice which because of the trend and inclination of your souls and hearts you can certainly hear and understand.

Yesterday, a year ago, we were watching the flames that were destroying the old Goetheanum, but just as we did not allow ourselves then to be interrupted in our continuation of the work, so today we are justified in hoping that when a physical Goetheanum will again be there, it will be merely the symbol of our spiritual Goetheanum which we will bear with us as idea when we now again go out into the world.

Over the Foundation Stone laid here will be erected the building in which the single stones will be the work achieved in every one of our groups all over the world. We will now turn our thoughts to this work and become conscious of the responsibility of the individuals of today when they are standing before the Guardian of the Threshold, who is obliged to forbid them entrance into the spiritual world.

Quite certainly it will never occur to us to feel anything except the deepest pain and sorrow for what happened to us a year ago. But of one thing we may be sure—everything in the world that has achieved some measure of greatness is born from pain. May our own pain be applied in such a way that a vigorous, light-filled Anthroposophical Society will come into being as the result of your work, my dear friends.

To this end we will ponder deeply on the words with which I began the Christmas Conference and with which I want to end it. May it become for us a festival of consecration not only of a year's beginning but of the beginning of a turning-point of worlds, to which we will dedicate ourselves in selfless cultivation of the spiritual life:

Soul of Man!
Thou livest in the Limbs
Which bear thee through the world of Space
Into the ocean-being of the Spirit.
Practise Spirit-Recollection
In the depths of soul.
Where in the wielding
World-Creator-Life
Thine own I
Comes to being
Within the I of God.
Then in the All-World-Being of Man
Thou wilt truly *live.*

For the Father-Spirit of the Heights holds sway
In Depths of Worlds begetting Life.
Spirits of Strength!
Let this ring out from the Heights
And in the Depths be echoed,
Speaking:
From God, Mankind has Being.
The Spirits hear it in East and West and North and South:
May human beings hear it!

Soul of Man!
Thou livest in the beat of Heart and Lung
Which leads thee through the rhythmic tides of Time

Into the feeling of thine own Soul-being.
Practise Spirit-Mindfulness
In balance of the soul,
Where the surging
Deeds of the World's Becoming
Do thine own I
Unite
Unto the I of the World.
Then 'mid the weaving of the Soul of Man
Thou wilt truly *feel.*
For the Christ-Will in the encircling Round holds sway
the Rhythms of the Worlds, blessing the Soul.
Spirits of Light!
Let this be fired from the East
And through the West be formed,
Speaking:
In Christ, Death becomes Life.
The Spirits hear it in East and West and North and South:
May human beings hear it!

Soul of Man!
Thou livest in the resting Head
Which from the ground of the Eternal
Opens to thee the Thoughts of Worlds.
Practise *Spirit-Vision*
In quietness of thought,
Where the eternal aims of Gods
World-Being's Light
On thine own I
Bestow
For thy free Willing.
Then from the ground of the Spirit in Man
Thou wilt truly *think*.

For the Spirit's Universal Thoughts hold sway
the Beings of all Worlds, craving for Light.
Spirits of Soul!
Let this be prayed in the Depths

And from the Heights be answered,
Speaking:
the Spirit's Universal Thoughts, the Soul awakens.
The Spirits hear it in East and West and North and South:
May human beings hear it!

At the turning-point of Time
The Spirit-Light of the World
Entered the stream of Earthly Being.
Darkness of Night
Had held its sway;
Day-radiant Light
Poured into the souls of men;
Light that gives Warmth
To simple Shepherds' Hearts,
Light that enlightens
The wise Heads of Kings.

O Light Divine,
O Sun of Christ!
Warm Thou
Our Hearts
Enlighten Thou
Our Heads,
That good may become
What from our Hearts we would found
And from our Heads direct
With single purpose.

And so, my dear friends, carry out into the world your warm hearts in which you have laid the Foundation Stone for the Anthroposophical Society, carry out into the world these warm hearts which promote strong, health-giving activity in the world. And help will be vouchsafed to you, enlightening your heads in what you would fain direct with single purpose. We will set about this with all possible strength. And if we prove to be worthy of this aim we shall see that a good star will hold sway over what is willed from here. Follow this good star, my dear friends! We shall see whither the Gods will lead us by the light of this star.

APPENDICES

Appendix 1

THE EVOLUTION OF CONSCIOUSNESS

ONE of Rudolf Steiner's greatest insights was the idea that Owen Barfield has termed 'the evolution of consciousness'. As opposed to conventional intellectual history, in which a succession of different ideas are seen as inhabiting epistemological structures presumed to be constant, Steiner argued forcefully that the structure of human consciousness itself has changed, and that it is the evolution of the structure of consciousness itself that is the main contributor to the succession of different paradigms or mentalities that are the object of intellectual history.

The best single treatment of Steiner's conception of the evolution of consciousness is Owen Barfield's magisterial study *Saving the Appearances: A Study in Idolatry* (1957; most recently rpt. Middletown: Wesleyan University Press, 1988). He sees humanity progressing from 'original participation' through 'onlooker consciousness' (the consciousness that prevails today) toward a 'final participation', of which we are beginning to see the first glimmerings. See especially Ch. VI, 'Original Participation', where Barfield connects Steiner's insights with more familiar anthropological notions such as Émile Durkheim's work on totemism and Levy-Brühl's 'participation mystique'.

Appendix 2

Representation

Translators' introductions or notes invariably comment on the difficulty of translating *vorstellen/Vorstellung* and a few other German philosophical and psychological terms such as *Geist*, *Anschauung*, and *Gemüt*. Tellingly, in the title of Schopenhauer's *magnum opus*, *Die Welt als Wille und Vorstellung*, has been translated three different ways: initially as 'Representation', but then more recently as 'Idea' and finally as 'Presentation'. Both Michael Wilson's translation of Steiner's *Philosophy of Freedom* and Owen Barfield's *The Case for Anthroposophy*[62] begin their discussions by noting that the standard translation of this Kantian philosophical term is 'representation'. But then Wilson goes on to argue (rightly) that this is too technical a term for most contexts, and that 'representation' has other, distracting meanings outside of philosophy, which led him to translate *Vorstellung* and its variants as 'mental picture'. Barfield chooses 'representation', which is understandable given that the context is Steiner's discussion of Brentano's neo-Kantian treatise. The reasons why this term is so very difficult to translate are (1) that it encompasses many different kinds of mental acts; (2) it refuses any sharp distinction between subjective and objective; (3) it can refer to a faculty, the activity of a faculty, or the result of that activity; (4) it often has a distinctly visual quality, but it can also refer to abstract concepts; and (5) it straddles the conventional divide between philosophy and psychology.

Appendix 3

THE HIERARCHIES

STEINER'S complex and highly esoteric ontology affirms the longstanding spiritual teaching that humans occupy a developmental stage between animals 'beneath' and angelic beings 'above' us. ('Beneath' and 'above' are meant to indicate relatively lower and higher levels of consciousness, developmental complexity, and power.) Arthur O. Lovejoy's eponymous study of 1936, which is widely viewed as the founding document of modern intellectual history, called this idea 'The Great Chain of Being', and that is now the conventional term for this set of ideas. This idea is in keeping with a Christian tradition extending back through Thomas Aquinas to Dionysius the Areopagite (late fifth or early sixth century CE; now referred to as 'Pseudo-Dionysius' to distinguish him from his much-earlier namesake), and ultimately to St. Paul. In his treatise *On the Celestial Hierarchy* (Pseudo-Dionysius, *The Complete Works* [Mahwah, NJ: Paulist Press, 1987], pp. 143-192), Pseudo-Dionysius had distinguished nine ranks of beings 'above' humans in the spiritual or intelligible world: in ascending order, he terms them 'Angels', 'Archangels', and 'Principalities' (together the 'Third Hierarchy'); 'Authorities', 'Powers', and 'Dominions' (among other current translations; together the 'Second Hierarchy'); and 'Thrones', 'Cherubim', and 'Seraphim' (together the First Hierarchy). Steiner tends to refer to the Third and Second Hierarchies by their Greek names: 'Angeloi', 'Archangeloi', 'Archai'; 'Exusiai', 'Dynamis', and 'Kyriotetes'. Another set of terms Steiner often employs is 'Spirits of Form' (rather than 'Exusiai'), 'Spirits of Movement' (rather than 'Dynamis'), 'Spirits of Wisdom' (rather than 'Kyriotetes'), and 'Spirits of Will' (rather than Thrones). Among Steiner's many discussions of the hierarchies, the most fundamental are Ch. 4 of CW 13: *An Outline of Esoteric Science*, trans. Catherine E. Creeger (Great Barrington, MA: SteinerBooks, 1997); CW 136: *Spiritual Beings in the Heavenly Bodies and in the Kingdoms of Nature* (Great Barrington, MA: SteinerBooks, 2012); and CW 110: *The Spiritual Hierarchies and the Physical World: Zodiac, Planets and Cosmos*, trans. René M. Querido (Great Barrington, NY: SteinerBooks, 2008).

Appendix 4

COSMIC EVOLUTION

Steiner's account of cosmic evolution is grand beyond all imagining. Steiner affirmed the reality of evolution, but not as Darwin understood it. He honoured Darwin's theory, which was the inspiration and the precondition for Steiner's own research into what one might better term evolutionary cosmology. The same process Darwin describes from an earthly perspective as a gradually *ascending* evolution of increasingly complex biological forms, Steiner describes from a spiritual perspective as a gradual *descent* of spiritual entities into ever more adequate material vessels. In other places, Steiner offers additional perspectives on his cosmology, complementing the 'outer' view of the finished products in *Esoteric Science*, for example, with an especially sublime cycle of five short lectures offering, as it were, an 'Elohim's-eye view' of the same unfolding process.

In Steiner's account, humanity was created from the top down, but it has evolved from the bottom up, over successive 'incarnations' of Earth evolution proper, which was preceded by Saturn, Sun, and Moon. Evolution allows us to approach multiple goals: over many eons, we have been guided from simplicity toward complexity, from unconsciousness toward consciousness, from passivity toward activity, and from necessity toward freedom. Having received the gift of wisdom, our task is now to internalize that wisdom and transform it into active love. The paradox of freedom implies that the further we progress towards these goals, the less certain is the outcome of the process, which will increasingly be placed into our own hands.

The central texts are:

- Chapter 4 of CW 13, *The Secret Science/Esoteric Science*;
- CW 132, *Inner Experiences of Evolution* (Great Barrington, Massachusetts: SteinerBooks, 2009);
- CW 136, *Spiritual Beings in the Heavenly Bodies and in the Kingdoms of Nature* (Great Barrington, Massachusetts: SteinerBooks, 2012);
- CW 110, *The Spiritual Hierarchies and the Physical World: Zodiac, Planets and Cosmos*, trans. René M. Querido (Great Barrington, New York: SteinerBooks, 2008);
- and GA 122, *Genesis: Secrets of Creation* (2002; London: Rudolf Steiner Press, 2012).

APPENDIX 5

THE ETHERIC AND THE ASTRAL BODIES

'ETHERIC body' is Steiner's early, theosophical term for the subtle body of supra-physical forces that sustains life. Later he would also refer to it variously as 'the life body', or the 'formative forces body', or (echoing Spinoza's distinction between *natura naturans* and *natura naturata*) the realm of 'living working' as opposed to the physical realm of 'finished work'.

The etheric body is known through Imaginaton, and first reveals itself to strengthened thinking as supra-sensible pictures. The etheric body consists of centrifugal forces, expresses itself in all aqueous processes, and flows in great currents through the cosmos. The etheric is a 'time body'; here time becomes space. It is a unity that is always there as a temporal totality, right up to the present moment.

The individual etheric body is precipitated out of a vast cosmic ether. It can be subdivided further into warmth ether, light ether, chemical or tone ether, and life ether. Theodor Schwenk's *Sensitive Chaos: The Creation of Flowing Forms in Water and Air* (London: Rudolf Steiner Press, 1996) is a scientifically compelling and aesthetically beautiful exploration of these forces.

'Astral body' is Steiner's early, theosophical term for the subtle body that corresponds generally to 'soul' or 'psyche'. Like Freud and Jung, he sees it as internally differentiated and gradually transformed by the activity of the higher faculty of the 'I' or 'ego'. The astral body reveals itself to Inspiration, and emerges in a sense from behind Imagination. The traditional concept of the Music of the Spheres is an experience of macrocosmic astrality. It consists of centripetal forces, and expresses itself in breathing and in the airy element generally. It also expresses itself as the human nervous system. The astral body has remained behind in time, and casts its beams forward into the present incarnation; it remains in the spiritual world before conception and birth.

The *locus classicus* for both of these bodies among Steiner's introductory works is the uncharacteristically schematic and static description in his early book *Theosophy* (1904; many English editions are available, including now very inexpensive ebook editions). A much more dynamic (but also much more difficult) account is to be found in the middle four lectures of Rudolf Steiner, *A Psychology of Body, Soul, & Spirit* (New York: SteinerBooks, 1999), which includes a valuable introduction by Robert Sardello. See also Lecture 5 (February 2, 1924) of the cycle GA 234; *Anthroposophy: An Introduction*, trans. and intro. Owen Barfield (London: Anthroposophical Publishing Co., 1961). (Reprinted as *Anthroposophy and the Inner Life*, Rudolf Steiner Press, Bristol, 1994.)

Appendix 6

AHRIMAN AND LUCIFER

Rudolf Steiner spoke often about the dual nature of evil, ascribing its source to supersensible beings he calls Lucifer and Ahriman. Lucifer might be termed the 'red devil', who tempts humans to sin on the side of *superbia*: pride, anger, egotism, erotic passions, etc. 'Ahriman' is a traditional name for a black demon, beginning with the Zoroastrian figure Angra Mainyu, opponent of the Sun God Ahura Mazda. Ahriman's temptations are those of *acedia*: laziness, greed, and denial of the Spirit generally.

Lucifer incarnated in the third millennium BCE, in the distant East. Ahriman will incarnate in the twenty-first century, in the West. Lucifer wants us to live in the past, while Ahriman cuts us off from the past. Lucifer wants us to flee the earth; Ahriman wants to bind us to the earth. Lucifer is responsible for the glories of pagan culture, which, however, provided no moral impulses. He longs for his cosmic home, which is the planet Venus. Ahriman seeks to subvert culture by promoting materialism, utility, nationalism, and literalism. He wants to reduce the freedom of the spiritual-cultural sphere to politics and economics. He wants to reduce all qualities to quantities.

Steiner argues that the assaults of these beings are providential: only by overcoming their resistance and holding them in proper balance can humanity become inwardly strong enough to develop genuine freedom, knowledge, and love. Both figures are represented in Steiner's monumental sculpture 'The Group' (from which the photos below have been taken). In 'The Group', Christ as the Representative of Humanity shows us how to hold the balance: he does not vanquish Lucifer and Ahriman, but he keeps each in their place, restricting their activity.

For an excellent discussion of Steiner's ideas as applied to Goethe's *Faust*, see Alan P. Cottrell, *Goethe's View of Evil and the Search for a New Image of Man in our Time* (Edinburgh: Floris Press, 1982). Mephistopheles in Goethe's *Faust* exhibits traits of both beings by turns, and Steiner was critical of Goethe for having conflated them. Lucifer and Ahriman also appear as characters in Steiner's own expressionist *Mystery Dramas* (1910-1913): see GA 14, Rudolf Steiner, *Four Mystery Dramas*, trans. Ruth and Hans Pusch (Great Barrington, MA: SteinerBooks, 2007).

Ahriman

Lucifer

Appendix 7

ITA WEGMAN

ITA Wegman (1876-1943) was a leading anthroposophist, and the co-founder, with Rudolf Steiner, of anthroposophic medicine. Born in Java, she emigrated to Europe around the turn of the century to study therapeutic gymnastics and massage. She first met Rudolf Steiner in 1902; he encouraged her to enter medical school, and in 1911 she was granted the M.D. by the University of Zürich, where the usual discrimination against women was absent.

In 1917, she developed a cancer remedy from an extract of mistletoe, following indications of Steiner. In 1921, Ita Wegman founded the first anthroposophical medical clinic in Arlesheim, Switzerland, the Clinical-Therapeutic Institute. She was a woman of extraordinary energy and initiative, with a great talent for putting theory into practice.

The following year she founded a therapeutic home for mentally handicapped children in Arlesheim as well. Ita Wegman was instrumental in developing therapies involving rhythmic massage. She also co-founded the pharmaceutical company *Weleda*, which thrives today, and is especially known for its healthcare products.

She was invited by Rudolf Steiner to join the Executive Council of the Anthroposophical Society, and she also chaired the Medical Section. Together with Rudolf Steiner, she co-authored GA 27; *Extending Practical Medicine: Fundamental Principles Based on the Science of the Spirit* (London: Rudolf Steiner Press, 1997), which is the main text on the theoretical underpinnings of anthroposophical medicine. During his illness, which turned out to be terminal, Ita Wegman cared for Rudolf Steiner.

In the mid-1930s, tensions developed between Ita Wegman and the rest of the Executive Council, which led to her expulsion from the General Anthroposophical Society, and indeed of the whole Dutch and British national Socities. She died in 1943 at the age of 67.

Notes

[1] The Christmas Conference took place in Dornach from December 24, 1923 to January 1, 1924. It was a refounding of the Society on a more esoteric basis. The central event was Rudolf Steiner's recitation of the Foundation Stone meditation, laying it in the hearts of the membership. Rudolf Steiner also assumed leadership of the Society, which he had studiously avoided up to that point. See CW 260: *The Christmas Conference for the Foundation of the General Anthroposophical Society 1923/1924: The Laying of the Foundation Stone: Lectures and Addresses: Discussion of the Statutes: Dornach, 24 December 1923 to 1 January 1924* (Hudson, NY: Anthroposophic Press, 1990).

[2] 'The Mystery of Golgotha' is Steiner's favoured term for all that is more conventionally referred to as the Incarnation, the Passion, and the Resurrection. One of Steiner's earliest publications, his book *Christianity as Mystical Fact*, situates Christianity squarely within the context of ancient Mystery religions (rather than mysticism, which the title might seem to imply). This important text is now volume 8 of Steiner's *Complete Works* in English, and the latest edition (New York: Anthroposophic Press, 1997) was both translated and introduced by a scholar and anthroposophist of great stature, Andrew Welburn. In the same spirit, Steiner also refers to 'the Easter Mystery'.

[3] See Appendix 1.

[4] See Appendix 2.

[5] 'This part of the brain known as the optic thalamus was later defined as a large mass of grey matter, involved with visual stimuli, and in the processing of all sensory modalities, except olfaction' [*Springer link*]. The *corpora quadrigemina* are 'two pairs of colliculi on the dorsal surface of the midbrain composed of white matter externally and grey matter within, the superior pair containing correlation centres for optic reflexes and the inferior pair containing correlation centres for auditory reflexes' [*Merriam-Webster*].

[6] The *Bhagavad Gita* '(Sanskrit: 'Song of God') is an episode recorded in the great Sanskrit poem of the Hindus, the *Mahabharata.* It occupies chapters 23 to 40 of Book VI of the *Mahabharata* and is composed in the form of a dialogue between

Prince Arjuna and Krishna, an avatar (incarnation) of the god Vishnu. Composed perhaps in the 1st or 2nd century CE, it is commonly known as the *Gita*. [*Britannica*]

7 The Vedas are a collection of hymns written in Vedic Sanskrit as part of the Vedic religion in the Northwest of India sometime during approximately 1,500 and 1,200 BCE. They are the oldest layer of both Sanskrit and the Hindu religion. These hymns formed a liturgical body that in part grew up around the soma ritual and sacrifice, and were recited or chanted during rituals. (Soma seems to have been some kind of hallucinogenic drink.) The most important collection is the Rigveda.

8 John 8:2-11.

9 Steiner's fullest accounts of epochs such as Atlantis in the remote past of human evolution are to be found in Ch. 4 of CW 13, *An Outline of Esoteric Science*, trans. Catherine E. Creeger (Great Barrington, Massachusetts: SteinerBooks, 1997), and in CW 11, *Cosmic Memory: Atlantis and Lemuria* (San Francisco: HarperCollins, 1981). (Unfortunately, an earlier translation of the former bore the mistranslated title *Occult Science*; various other editions of the latter have appeared recently in English.) Because Steiner uses theosophical rather than modern geological terms, it is difficult to date this epoch, but Atlantis seems to correspond to the end of the Pleistocene, when the transition to the much warmer temperatures of the Holocene would have led to the massive flooding of areas that had previously been dry land. The Biblical myth of the Flood may represent an archetypal recollection of this primordial transition.

10 The rise and fall of civilizations in the post-Atlantean world is related by Rudolf Steiner to the cosmic rhythm of the precession of the equinox through the signs of the zodiac in periods of 2,160 years: 7227 BCE for the beginning of a prehistoric high culture in India; 5067 BCE for prehistoric Iran (Persia); 2907 BCE for the beginnings of Egyptian civilization; 747 BCE for Greek culture; 1413 CE for the beginning of the modern ('fifth post-Atlantean') age. The sixth epoch to follow will commence around 3573 CE. Steiner's terminology is idiosyncratic here, but the underlying thoughts are commonplaces of intellectual history.

11 See Appendix 3.

12 See Appendix 4.

13 'The Mysteries' is the Greek term for schools and rites that were esoteric in the strong sense: neophytes were forbidden to divulge their teachings—in some cases (such as the Pythagoreans) on pain of death. The most important Mystery centres were in Eleusis, Samothrace, and Ephesus.

14 CW 8; *Christianity as Mystical Fact and the Mysteries of Antiquity*, trans. Andrew Welburn, ed. Christopher Bamford (Great Barrington: SteinerBooks, 2006).

15 Xerxes I (519–465 BC), 'called Xerxes the Great, was the fourth King of Kings of the Achaemenid dynasty of Persia. Like his father and predecessor Darius I, he ruled the empire at its territorial apex. He ruled from 486 BC until his assassination in 465 BC at the hands of Artabanus, the commander of the royal bodyguard.' [*Wikipedia*]

16 Translated as CW 13; *An Outline of Esoteric Science*, trans. Catherine E. Creeger (Great Barrington, MA: SteinerBooks, 1997). An otherwise excellent earlier translation by George Adams bore the unfortunate title *Occult Science*. At the time of writing, Steiner was the head of the Theosophical Society in Germany, and the word *Geheimwissenschaft* in his title was meant to echo Blavatsky's tome, *The Secret Doctrine*. Thus my alteration of the title. CW 13 is now considered one of the four 'basic books' of anthroposophy.

17 See Appendix 5.

18 The *Epic of Gilgamesh* was woven together from even earlier fragmentary material during the Middle Babylonian Period (c. 1600-c. 1155). It was rediscovered in the form of twelve cuneiform panels in the Library of Ashurbanipal in 1849, and it was not widely known when Steiner spoke of it.

19 GA 126; *Occult History: Historical Personalities and Events in the Light of Spiritual Science* (London: Rudolf Steiner Press, 1982).

20 'Ishtar or Inanna is an ancient Mesopotamian goddess associated with love, beauty, sex, war, justice and political power. She was originally worshiped in Sumer under the name "Inanna", and was later worshipped by the Akkadians, Babylonians, and Assyrians under the name Ishtar. She was known as the "Queen of Heaven" and was the patron goddess of the Eanna temple in the city of Uruk, which was her main cult center.' [*Wikipedia*]

21 Pythagoras of Samos (c. 570 – c. 495 BCE) 'was an ancient Ionian Greek philosopher ... His political and religious teachings were well known in Magna Graecia influenced the philosophies of Plato, Aristotle, and, through them, Western philosophy. ... The teaching most securely identified with Pythagoras is *metempsychosis*, or the transmigration of souls, which holds that every soul is immortal and, upon death, enters into a new body. He may have also devised the doctrine of *musica universalis*, which holds that the planets move according to mathematical equations and thus resonate to produce an inaudible symphony of music'. [*Wikipedia*]

22 *flüchtig-flüssig*, a neologism.

23 Plato (428-347 BCE) was a Greek philosopher. He founded the first public school of Philosophy, the Academy, in Athens, and he introduced into the discipline both dialogue and dialectics. His import is hard to overestimate: indeed, Alfred North Whitehead wrote of the European philosophical tradition that it was nothing but

a succession of footnotes to Plato. He is exceptional in that his full oeuvre seems to have been transmitted intact. His immediate teacher was Socrates, and Aristotle was his student.

24 CW 8; *Christianity as Mystical Fact and the Mysteries of Antiquity*, trans. Andrew Welburn, ed. Christopher Bamford (Great Barrington: SteinerBooks, 2006).

25 The darkly obscure pre-Socratic philosopher Heraclitus was a native of Ephesus (ca. 535-ca. 475 BCE). *Fragments: The Collected Wisdom of Heraclitus* (New York: Viking, 2001) is an excellent English translation. The standard English-language treatment of the pre-Socratics remains G. S. Kirk and J. E. Raven, *The Presocratic Philosophers: A Critical History with a Selection of Texts* (Cambridge: Cambridge UP, 1971).

26 Aristotle (384-322 BCE) was a Greek philosopher, the student of Plato, and one of the greatest philosophers who ever lived. 'A prodigious researcher and writer, Aristotle left a great body of work, perhaps numbering as many as two-hundred treatises, from which approximately thirty-one survive. His extant writings span a wide range of disciplines, from logic, metaphysics and philosophy of mind, through ethics, political theory, aesthetics and rhetoric, and into such primarily non-philosophical fields as empirical biology, where he excelled at detailed plant and animal observation and description.' [*Stanford Encyclopedia of Philosophy*] He was the teacher of Alexander the Great.

27 Alexander III of Macedon, better known by his epithet Alexander the Great (356-323 BCE), son of Philip II and Olympias. A great general who was never defeated in battle, Alexander conducted military campaigns that led to creating one of the largest empires the world has ever known. He was the philosophical student of Aristotle.

28 Steiner's theosophical term for a long epoch he sees as having ended ca. 747 BCE. He also calls it the third post-Atlantean epoch or age. The implication of the term is that the Egyptian, Sumerian and Babylonian cultures were in the vanguard of human cultural evolution during that period—quite a conventional notion after all, despite the idiosyncrasy of the label. Because it has become a standard anthroposophical term, 'Chaldean' stands here rather that Sumerian and/or Babylonian, which would be more conventional in English.

29 See GA 232; *Mystery Knowledge and Mystery Centres*, revised translation Pauline Wehrle, intro. Andrew Welburn (Rudolf Steiner Press, 2012).

30 'Maya' is a theosophical term that Steiner uses frequently. It is a contraction of the Sanskrit terms *maha* [great], *a* [not or non-, like 'alpha privative' in Ancient Greek; cf. 'apolitical'], and *ya* [being]; hence, 'maya' means literally 'the great non-being'. It is illusory because it seems to exist, but ultimately does not.

[31] The easternmost and least populous state of Austria.

[32] Inspired and deeply religious, Aeschylus (c. 525-456 BCE) was the eldest of the great triumvirate of Athenian tragic dramatists; he has been called 'the father of tragedy'.

[33] A group of three enigmatic deities who were worshipped in Samothrace and other places throughout the Eastern Aegean.

[34] Lamprecht the Priest was a German poet of the twelfth century. He followed a French model in composing the *Song of Alexander*.

[35] The term means 'primordial man'. The Gnostics speculated that physical Adam was made from or modelled on a macrocosmic individual, also named Adam. Later the term was assimilated into the Jewish Kaballah.

[36] See Appendix 4.

[37] The Akashic Record is a symbolic, spiritual script in which everything is recorded that has ever happened on Earth. It can be read by an initiate, and this is how the spiritual researcher can speak of things about which no historical records survive. Ervin Lászlo in *Science and the Akashic Field: An Integral Theory of Everything* (2004), based on ideas by Rudolf Steiner, posits 'a field of information' as the substance of the cosmos, which he calls 'Akashic field' or 'A-field'.

[38] Inspired and deeply religious, Aeschylus (c. 525-456 BCE) was the eldest of the great triumvirate of Athenian tragic dramatists; he has been called 'the father of tragedy'.

[39] Sophocles (c. 496-406 BCE) was the most honoured and prolific dramatist of his age, but only seven of his 120-plus tragedies survive complete.

[40] Herodotus (c. 484-c. 425 BCE) was dubbed 'the father of history' by the Roman orator Cicero. His book *The Histories*, an account of the Greco-Persian Wars, is the first known exemplar of a history in the modern sense.

[41] A city in Upper Mesopotamia.

[42] The Academy of Gondishapur was founded in the Iranian city of the same name. It would later achieve high eminence under Islam.

[43] See Appendix 7.

[44] Julian (c. 331-363), best known by his epithet 'the Apostate', ruled as Roman Emperor from 361 to 363. 'Julian was a man of unusually complex character: he was the military commander, the theosophist, the social reformer, and the man of letters. He was the last non-Christian ruler of the Roman Empire, and he believed that it was necessary to restore the Empire's ancient Roman values and traditions in order to save it from dissolution. He purged the top-heavy state bureaucracy, and attempted to revive traditional Roman religious practices at the expense of Christianity. ... His rejection of Christianity, and his promotion of Neoplatonic Hellenism in its place, caused him to be remembered as *Julian the Apostate* by the Church.' [*Wikipedia*]

45 CW 9; *Theosophy* (1904; many English editions are available, including now very inexpensive ebook editions). This early work presents the basics of Steiner's spiritual psychology using the terminology of theosophy. A much more dynamic (but also much more difficult) account is to be found in the middle four lectures of Rudolf Steiner, *A Psychology of Body, Soul, & Spirit* (New York: SteinerBooks, 1999), which includes a valuable Introduction by Robert Sardello.

46 'Devachan' is a theosophical term for the spiritual world.

47 See the eighth and ninth lectures in GA 233a; *Mystery Knowledge and Mystery Centres*.

48 Theophrastus (c. 371-c. 287 BCE) was a successor to Aristotle in the Peripatetic School.

49 Jacob Böhme (1575-1624, also spelled 'Boehme') was a great and prolific Silesian mystic and theologian whose works are however also notoriously obscure. Böhme began writing his most important text, *Aurora*, 12 years after a powerful spiritual experience that befell him in 1600. It is indicative that, although it was his first work, *Aurora* remained unfinished at his death.

50 Phillipus von Hohenheim (1493-1541), better known by his pen-name Paracelsus, the Swiss physician, botanist, and esotericist. Paracelsus is one of the most important and influential thinkers of the early modern period. Goethe knew his writings intimately. Steiner's long, biographical lecture 'From Paracelsus to Goethe' of 16 November, 1911 (collected in GA 61) is sensitive and insightful; unfortunately, it seems not to have been translated into English.

51 Valentin Weigel (1533–1588) was a German theologian, philosopher, and mystic.

52 An Anglicization of Basilius Valentinus [dates uncertain], traditionally identified as a Benedictine monk and alchemist of the fifteenth century. Steiner confirms the traditional interpretation. The works published under this name were undoubtedly very adept, even in terms of modern chemistry, let alone alchemy. The *Twelve Keys* (1602) and *The Triumphant Chariot of Antinomy* (1604) are especially important. According to Steiner, Basil Valentine's works were actually compiled by his students, hidden, and then discovered and published by Johann Thölde.

53 Rudolf Steiner spoke in detail about this for instance in GA 307; *A Modern Art of Education*, trans. Jesse Darrell et al. (Great Barrington, Massachusetts: Anthroposophic Press, 2004) and in *CW 310: Human Values in Education*, Trans. Vera Compton-Burnett and Frederick Amrine, (Online Waldorf Library, 2020).

54 The intellectual soul developed between 747 BCE and 1413 CE. It represents the beginnings of rational thought, and especially of logic. This autonomous form of thinking, which is all about self-consistency and tells us nothing about the world, is both a cognitional loss and a tremendous advance in the evolution toward human freedom.

55 The consciousness soul is evolving during the current historical epoch, which Steiner sees as having begun ca. 1413—i.e., with the Renaissance. The consciousness soul marks the beginnings of self-consciousness, and the focus on the trans-personal in the soul.

[56] See the lecture of December 31, 1922 in GA 219; *Man and the World of the Stars: Spiritual Communion of Humanity* (SteinerBooks, 1982).

[57] Steiner's main introductory treatment of this topic is in Ch. 10 of his basic book CW 10, *How to Know Higher Worlds: A Modern Path of Initiation* (Great Barrington, MA: Anthroposophic Press, 1994). He describes the Guardian as a wise being who blocks our access to the spiritual world until we have achieved an appropriate stage of spiritual and especially moral development.

[58] 'At the heart of the Anthroposophical Society is the School of Spiritual Science, an institution intended to be an esoteric school for spiritual scientific research and study. During the course of 1924 Rudolf Steiner held 19 esoteric lessons in which he introduced his followers to a series of meditations (mantras) along with instructions and guidelines for their use. This set of lessons is known as the First Class and they are made available to those who become members of the School.' (*Anthroposophical Society in America*). They are now also published as *Esoteric Lessons for the First Class of the School of Spiritual Science* (Rudlof Steiner Press, Sussex, 2020).

[59] F. W. Zeylmans van Emmichoven (1893-1961), a Dutch doctor and writer. He was the General Secretary of the Dutch Anthroposophical Society.

[60] See Appendix 8.

[61] The *Vorstand* is the Executive Council of the Society. The original *Vorstand* was appointed by Rudolf Steiner himself at the Foundation Meeting on December 28, 1923, and it was intended above all to provide esoteric guidance for the Anthroposophical Society.

[62] This is an older, partial translation. For a newer translation, see Rudolf Steiner, CW 21; *On The Enigmas of the Soul*, trans. Frederick Amrine and Owen Barfield, commentary by Frederick Amrine, Keryx 2017.

Rudolf Steiner's Collected Works

The German Edition of Rudolf Steiner's Collected Works (the *Gesamtausgabe* [GA] published by Rudolf Steiner Verlag, Dornach, Switzerland) presently runs to 354 titles, organized either by type of work (written or spoken), chronology, audience (public or other), or subject (education, art, etc.). For ease of comparison, the Collected Works in English [CW] follows the German organization exactly. A complete listing of the CWs follows with literal translations of the German titles. Other than in the case of the books published in his lifetime, titles were rarely given by Rudolf Steiner himself, and were often provided by the editors of the German editions. The titles in English are not necessarily the same as the German; and, indeed, over the past seventy-five years have frequently been different, with the same book sometimes appearing under different titles.

For ease of identification and to avoid confusion, we suggest that readers looking for a title should do so by CW number. Because the work of creating the Collected Works of Rudolf Steiner is an ongoing process, with new titles being published every year, we have not indicated in this listing which books are presently available. To find out what titles in the Collected Works are currently in print, please check our website at www.rudolfsteinerpress.com (or www.steinerbooks.org for US readers).

Written Work

CW 1 Goethe: Natural-Scientific Writings, Introduction, with Footnotes and Explanations in the text by Rudolf Steiner
CW 2 Outlines of an Epistemology of the Goethean World View, with Special Consideration of Schiller
CW 3 Truth and Science
CW 4 The Philosophy of Freedom
CW 4a Documents to 'The Philosophy of Freedom'
CW 5 Friedrich Nietzsche, A Fighter against His Time

CW 6 Goethe's Worldview
CW 6a Now in CW 30
CW 7 Mysticism at the Dawn of Modern Spiritual Life and Its Relationship with Modern Worldviews
CW 8 Christianity as Mystical Fact and the Mysteries of Antiquity
CW 9 Theosophy: An Introduction into Supersensible World Knowledge and Human Purpose
CW 10 How Does One Attain Knowledge of Higher Worlds?
CW 11 From the Akasha-Chronicle
CW 12 Levels of Higher Knowledge
CW 13 Occult Science in Outline
CW 14 Four Mystery Dramas
CW 15 The Spiritual Guidance of the Individual and Humanity
CW 16 A Way to Human Self-Knowledge: Eight Meditations
CW 17 The Threshold of the Spiritual World. Aphoristic Comments
CW 18 The Riddles of Philosophy in Their History, Presented as an Outline
CW 19 Contained in CW 24
CW 20 The Riddles of the Human Being: Articulated and Unarticulated in the Thinking, Views and Opinions of a Series of German and Austrian Personalities
CW 21 The Riddles of the Soul
CW 22 Goethe's Spiritual Nature and its Revelation in 'Faust' and through the 'Fairy Tale of the Snake and the Lily'
CW 23 The Central Points of the Social Question in the Necessities of Life in the Present and the Future
CW 24 Essays Concerning the Threefold Division of the Social Organism and the Period 1915-1921
CW 25 Cosmology, Religion and Philosophy
CW 26 Anthroposophical Leading Thoughts
CW 27 Fundamentals for Expansion of the Art of Healing according to Spiritual-Scientific Insights
CW28 The Course of My Life
CW 29 Collected Essays on Dramaturgy, 1889-1900
CW 30 Methodical Foundations of Anthroposophy: Collected Essays on Philosophy, Natural Science, Aesthetics and Psychology, 1884-1901
CW 31 Collected Essays on Culture and Current Events, 1887-1901
CW 32 Collected Essays on Literature, 1884-1902
CW 33 Biographies and Biographical Sketches, 1894-1905
CW 34 Lucifer-Gnosis: Foundational Essays on Anthroposophy and Reports from the Periodicals 'Lucifer' and 'Lucifer-Gnosis', 1903-1908
CW 35 Philosophy and Anthroposophy: Collected Essays, 1904-1923
CW 36 The Goetheanum-Idea in the Middle of the Cultural Crisis of the Present: Collected Essays from the Periodical 'Das Goetheanum', 1921-1925

CW 37 Now in CWs 260a and 251
CW 38 Letters, Vol. 1: 1881-1890
CW 39 Letters, Vol. 2: 1890-1925
CW 40 Truth-Wrought Words
CW 40a Sayings, Poems and Mantras; Supplementary Volume
CW 42 Now in CWs 264-266
CW 43 Stage Adaptations
CW 44 On the Four Mystery Dramas. Sketches, Fragments and Paralipomena on the Four Mystery Dramas
CW 45 Anthroposophy: A Fragment from the Year 1910

Public Lectures

CW 51 On Philosophy, History and Literature
CW 52 Spiritual Teachings Concerning the Soul and Observation of the World
CW 53 The Origin and Goal of the Human Being
CW 54 The Riddles of the World and Anthroposophy
CW 55 Knowledge of the Supersensible in Our Times and Its Meaning for Life Today
CW 56 Knowledge of the Soul and of the Spirit
CW 57 Where and How Does One Find the Spirit?
CW 58 The Metamorphoses of the Soul Life. Paths of Soul Experiences: Part One
CW 59 The Metamorphoses of the Soul Life. Paths of Soul Experiences: Part Two
CW 60 The Answers of Spiritual Science to the Biggest Questions of Existence
CW 61 Human History in the Light of Spiritual Research
CW 62 Results of Spiritual Research
CW 63 Spiritual Science as a Treasure for Life
CW 64 Out of Destiny-Burdened Times
CW 65 Out of Central European Spiritual Life
CW 66 Spirit and Matter, Life and Death
CW 67 The Eternal in the Human Soul. Immortality and Freedom
CW 68 Public lectures in various cities, 1906-1918
CW 69 Public lectures in various cities, 1906-1918
CW 70 Public lectures in various cities, 1906-1918
CW 71 Public lectures in various cities, 1906-1918
CW 72 Freedom—Immortality—Social Life
CW 73 The Supplementing of the Modern Sciences through Anthroposophy
CW 73a Specialized Fields of Knowledge and Anthroposophy
CW 74 The Philosophy of Thomas Aquinas
CW 75 Public lectures in various cities, 1906-1918
CW 76 The Fructifying Effect of Anthroposophy on Specialized Fields
CW 77a The Task of Anthroposophy in Relation to Science and Life: The Darmstadt College Course
CW 77b Art and Anthroposophy. The Goetheanum-Impulse

CW 78 Anthroposophy, Its Roots of Knowledge and Fruits for Life
CW 79 The Reality of the Higher Worlds
CW 80 Public lectures in various cities, 1922
CW 81 Renewal-Impulses for Culture and Science—Berlin College Course
CW 82 So that the Human Being Can Become a Complete Human Being
CW 83 Western and Eastern World-Contrast. Paths to Understanding It through Anthroposophy
CW 84 What Did the Goetheanum Intend and What Should Anthroposophy Do?

Lectures to the Members of the Anthroposophical Society

CW 88 Concerning the Astral World and Devachan
CW 89 Consciousness—Life—Form. Fundamental Principles of a Spiritual-Scientific Cosmology
CW 90 Participant Notes from the Lectures during the Years 1903-1905
CW 91 Participant Notes from the Lectures during the Years 1903-1905
CW 92 The Occult Truths of Ancient Myths and Sagas
CW 93 The Temple Legend and the Golden Legend
CW 93a Fundamentals of Esotericism
CW 94 Cosmogony. Popular Occultism. The Gospel of John. The Theosophy in the Gospel of John
CW 95 At the Gates of Theosophy
CW 96 Origin-Impulses of Spiritual Science. Christian Esotericism in the Light of New Spirit-Knowledge
CW 97 The Christian Mystery
CW 98 Nature Beings and Spirit Beings—Their Effects in Our Visible World
CW 99 The Theosophy of the Rosicrucians
CW 100 Human Development and Christ-Knowledge
CW 101 Myths and Legends. Occult Signs and Symbols
CW 102 The Working into Human Beings by Spiritual Beings
CW 103 The Gospel of John
CW 104 The Apocalypse of John
CW 104a From the Picture-Script of the Apocalypse of John
CW 105 Universe, Earth, the Human Being: Their Being and Development, as well as Their Reflection in the Connection between Egyptian Mythology and Modern Culture
CW 106 Egyptian Myths and Mysteries in Relation to the Active Spiritual Forces of the Present
CW 107 Spiritual-Scientific Knowledge of the Human Being
CW 108 Answering the Questions of Life and the World through Anthroposophy
CW 109 The Principle of Spiritual Economy in Connection with the Question of Reincarnation. An Aspect of the Spiritual Guidance of Humanity
CW 110 The Spiritual Hierarchies and Their Reflection in the Physical World. Zodiac, Planets and Cosmos

CW 111	Contained in CW 109
CW 112	The Gospel of John in Relation to the Three Other Gospels, Especially the Gospel of Luke
CW 113	The Orient in the Light of the Occident. The Children of Lucifer and the Brothers of Christ
CW 114	The Gospel of Luke
CW 115	Anthroposophy—Psychosophy—Pneumatosophy
CW 116	The Christ-Impulse and the Development of I-Consciousness
CW 117	The Deeper Secrets of the Development of Humanity in Light of the Gospels
CW 118	The Event of the Christ-Appearance in the Etheric World
CW 119	Macrocosm and Microcosm. The Large World and the Small World. Soul-Questions, Life-Questions, Spirit-Questions
CW 120	The Revelation of Karma
CW 121	The Mission of Individual Folk-Souls in Connection with Germanic-Nordic Mythology
CW 122	The Secrets of the Biblical Creation-Story. The Six-Day Work in the First Book of Moses
CW 123	The Gospel of Matthew
CW 124	Excursus in the Area of the Gospel of Mark
CW 125	Paths and Goals of the Spiritual Human Being. Life Questions in the Light of Spiritual Science
CW 126	Occult History. Esoteric Observations of the Karmic Relationships of Personalities and Events of World History
CW 127	The Mission of the New Spiritual Revelation. The Christ-Event as the Middle-Point of Earth Evolution
CW 128	An Occult Physiology
CW 129	Wonders of the World, Trials of the Soul, and Revelations of the Spirit
CW 130	Esoteric Christianity and the Spiritual Guidance of Humanity
CW 131	From Jesus to Christ
CW 132	Evolution from the View Point of the Truth
CW 133	The Earthly and the Cosmic Human Being
CW 134	The World of the Senses and the World of the Spirit
CW 135	Reincarnation and Karma and their Meaning for the Culture of the Present
CW 136	The Spiritual Beings in Celestial Bodies and the Realms of Nature
CW 137	The Human Being in the Light of Occultism, Theosophy and Philosophy
CW 138	On Initiation. On Eternity and the Passing Moment. On the Light of the Spirit and the Darkness of Life
CW 139	The Gospel of Mark
CW 140	Occult Investigation into the Life between Death and New Birth. The Living Interaction between Life and Death
CW 141	Life between Death and New Birth in Relationship to Cosmic Facts

CW 142	The Bhagavad Gita and the Letters of Paul
CW 143	Experiences of the Supersensible. Three Paths of the Soul to Christ
CW 144	The Mysteries of the East and of Christianity
CW 145	What Significance Does Occult Development of the Human Being Have for the Sheaths—Physical Body, Etheric Body, Astral Body, and Self?
CW 146	The Occult Foundations of the Bhagavad Gita
CW 147	The Secrets of the Threshold
CW 148	Out of Research in the Akasha: The Fifth Gospel
CW 149	Christ and the Spiritual World. Concerning the Search for the Holy Grail
CW 150	The World of the Spirit and Its Extension into Physical Existence; The Influence of the Dead in the World of the Living
CW 151	Human Thought and Cosmic Thought
CW 152	Preliminary Stages to the Mystery of Golgotha
CW 153	The Inner Being of the Human Being and Life Between Death and New Birth
CW 154	How Does One Gain an Understanding of the Spiritual World? The Flowing in of Spiritual Impulses from out of the World of the Deceased
CW 155	Christ and the Human Soul. Concerning the Meaning of Life. Theosophical Morality. Anthroposophy and Christianity
CW 156	Occult Reading and Occult Hearing
CW 157	Human Destinies and the Destiny of Peoples
CW 157a	The Formation of Destiny and the Life after Death
CW 158	The Connection Between the Human Being and the Elemental World. Kalevala—Olaf Asteson—The Russian People—The World as the Result of the Influences of Equilibrium
CW 159	The Mystery of Death. The Nature and Significance of Middle Europe and the European Folk Spirits
CW 160	In CW 159
CW 161	Paths of Spiritual Knowledge and the Renewal of the Artistic Worldview
CW 162	Questions of Art and Life in Light of Spiritual Science
CW 163	Coincidence, Necessity and Providence. Imaginative Knowledge and the Processes after Death
CW 164	The Value of Thinking for a Knowledge That Satisfies the Human Being. The Relationship of Spiritual Science to Natural Science
CW 165	The Spiritual Unification of Humanity through the Christ-Impulse
CW 166	Necessity and Freedom in the Events of the World and in Human Action
CW 167	The Present and the Past in the Human Spirit
CW 168	The Connection between the Living and the Dead
CW 169	World-being and Selfhood
CW 170	The Riddle of the Human Being. The Spiritual Background of Human History. Cosmic and Human History, Vol. 1

CW 171	Inner Development-Impulses of Humanity. Goethe and the Crisis of the 19th Century. Cosmic and Human History, Vol. 2
CW 172	The Karma of the Vocation of the Human Being in Connection with Goethe's Life. Cosmic and Human History, Vol. 3
CW 173	Contemporary-Historical Considerations: The Karma of Untruthfulness, Part One. Cosmic and Human History, Vol. 4
CW 174	Contemporary-Historical Considerations: The Karma of Untruthfulness, Part Two. Cosmic and Human History, Vol. 5
CW 174a	Middle Europe between East and West. Cosmic and Human History, Vol. 6
CW 174b	The Spiritual Background of the First World War. Cosmic and Human History, Vol. 7
CW 175	Building Stones for an Understanding of the Mystery of Golgotha. Cosmic and Human Metamorphoses
CW 176	Truths of Evolution of the Individual and Humanity. The Karma of Materialism
CW 177	The Spiritual Background of the Outer World. The Fall of the Spirits of Darkness. Spiritual Beings and Their Effects, Vol. 1
CW 178	Individual Spiritual Beings and their Influence in the Soul of the Human Being. Spiritual Beings and their Effects, Vol. 2
CW 179	Spiritual Beings and Their Effects. Historical Necessity and Freedom. The Influences on Destiny from out of the World of the Dead. Spiritual Beings and Their Effects, Vol. 3
CW 180	Mystery Truths and Christmas Impulses. Ancient Myths and their Meaning. Spiritual Beings and Their Effects, Vol. 4
CW 181	Earthly Death and Cosmic Life. Anthroposophical Gifts for Life. Necessities of Consciousness for the Present and the Future.
CW 182	Death as Transformation of Life
CW 183	The Science of the Development of the Human Being
CW 184	The Polarity of Duration and Development in Human Life. The Cosmic Pre-History of Humanity
CW 185	Historical Symptomology
CW 185a	Historical-Developmental Foundations for Forming a Social Judgement
CW 186	The Fundamental Social Demands of Our Time—In Changed Situations
CW 187	How Can Humanity Find the Christ Again? The Threefold Shadow-Existence of our Time and the New Christ-Light
CW 188	Goetheanism, a Transformation-Impulse and Resurrection-Thought. Science of the Human Being and Science of Sociology
CW 189	The Social Question as a Question of Consciousness. The Spiritual Background of the Social Question, Vol. 1
CW 190	Impulses of the Past and the Future in Social Occurrences. The Spiritual Background of the Social Question, Vol. 2

CW 191 Social Understanding from Spiritual-Scientific Cognition. The Spiritual Background of the Social Question, Vol. 3

CW 192 Spiritual-Scientific Treatment of Social and Pedagogical Questions

CW 193 The Inner Aspect of the Social Riddle. Luciferic Past and Ahrimanic Future

CW 194 The Mission of Michael. The Revelation of the Actual Mysteries of the Human Being

CW 195 Cosmic New Year and the New Year Idea

CW 196 Spiritual and Social Transformations in the Development of Humanity

CW 197 Polarities in the Development of Humanity: West and East Materialism and Mysticism Knowledge and Belief

CW 198 Healing Factors for the Social Organism

CW 199 Spiritual Science as Knowledge of the Foundational Impulses of Social Formation

CW 200 The New Spirituality and the Christ-Experience of the 20th Century

CW 201 The Correspondences Between Microcosm and Macrocosm. The Human Being—A Hieroglyph of the Universe. The Human Being in Relationship with the Cosmos: 1

CW 202 The Bridge between the World-Spirituality and the Physical Aspect of the Human Being. The Search for the New Isis, the Divine Sophia. The Human Being in Relationship with the Cosmos: 2

CW 203 The Responsibility of Human Beings for the Development of the World through their Spiritual Connection with the Planet Earth and the World of the Stars. The Human Being in Relationship with the Cosmos: 3

CW 204 Perspectives of the Development of Humanity. The Materialistic Knowledge-Impulse and the Task of Anthroposophy. The Human Being in Relationship with the Cosmos: 4

CW 205 Human Development, World-Soul, and World-Spirit. Part One: The Human Being as a Being of Body and Soul in Relationship to the World. The Human Being in Relationship with the Cosmos: 5

CW 206 Human Development, World-Soul, and World-Spirit. Part Two: The Human Being as a Spiritual Being in the Process of Historical Development. The Human Being in Relationship with the Cosmos: 6

CW 207 Anthroposophy as Cosmosophy. Part One: Characteristic Features of the Human Being in the Earthly and the Cosmic Realms. The Human Being in Relationship with the Cosmos: 7

CW 208 Anthroposophy as Cosmosophy. Part Two: The Forming of the Human Being as the Result of Cosmic Influence. The Human Being in Relationship with the Cosmos: 8

CW 209 Nordic and Central European Spiritual Impulses. The Festival of the Appearance of Christ. The Human Being in Relationship with the Cosmos: 9

CW 210 Old and New Methods of Initiation. Drama and Poetry in the Change of Consciousness in the Modern Age
CW 211 The Sun Mystery and the Mystery of Death and Resurrection. Exoteric and Esoteric Christianity
CW 212 Human Soul Life and Spiritual Striving in Connection with World and Earth Development
CW 213 Human Questions and World Answers
CW 214 The Mystery of the Trinity: The Human Being in Relationship with the Spiritual World in the Course of Time
CW 215 Philosophy, Cosmology, and Religion in Anthroposophy
CW 216 The Fundamental Impulses of the World-Historical Development of Humanity
CW 217 Spiritually Active Forces in the Coexistence of the Older and Younger Generations. Pedagogical Course for Youth
CW 217a Youth's Cognitive Task
CW 218 Spiritual Connections in the Forming of the Human Organism
CW 219 The Relationship of the World of the Stars to the Human Being, and of the Human Being to the World of the Stars. The Spiritual Communion of Humanity
CW 220 Living Knowledge of Nature. Intellectual Fall and Spiritual Redemption
CW 221 Earth-Knowing and Heaven-Insight
CW 222 The Imparting of Impulses to World-Historical Events through Spiritual Powers
CW 223 The Cycle of the Year as Breathing Process of the Earth and the Four Great Festival-Seasons. Anthroposophy and the Human Heart (Gemüt)
CW 224 The Human Soul and its Connection with Divine-Spiritual Individualities. The Internalization of the Festivals of the Year
CW 225 Three Perspectives of Anthroposophy. Cultural Phenomena observed from a Spiritual-Scientific Perspective
CW 226 Human Being, Human Destiny, and World Development
CW 227 Initiation-Knowledge
CW 228 Science of Initiation and Knowledge of the Stars. The Human Being in the Past, the Present, and the Future from the Viewpoint of the Development of Consciousness
CW 229 The Experiencing of the Course of the Year in Four Cosmic Imaginations
CW 230 The Human Being as Harmony of the Creative, Building, and Formative World-Word
CW 231 The Supersensible Human Being, Understood Anthroposophically
CW 232 The Forming of the Mysteries
CW 233 World History Illuminated by Anthroposophy and as the Foundation for Knowledge of the Human Spirit

CW 233a Mystery Sites of the Middle Ages: Rosicrucianism and the Modern Initiation-Principle. The Festival of Easter as Part of the History of the Mysteries of Humanity
CW 234 Anthroposophy. A Summary after 21 Years
CW 235 Esoteric Observations of Karmic Relationships in 6 Volumes, Vol. 1
CW 236 Esoteric Observations of Karmic Relationships in 6 Volumes, Vol. 2
CW 237 Esoteric Observations of Karmic Relationships in 6 Volumes, Vol. 3: The Karmic Relationships of the Anthroposophical Movement
CW 238 Esoteric Observations of Karmic Relationships in 6 Volumes, Vol. 4: The Spiritual Life of the Present in Relationship to the Anthroposophical Movement
CW 239 Esoteric Observations of Karmic Relationships in 6 Volumes, Vol. 5
CW 240 Esoteric Observations of Karmic Relationships in 6 Volumes, Vol. 6
CW 243 The Consciousness of the Initiate
CW 245 Instructions for an Esoteric Schooling
CW 250 The Building-Up of the Anthroposophical Society. From the Beginning to the Outbreak of the First World War
CW 251 The History of the Goetheanum Building-Association
CW 252 Life in the Anthroposophical Society from the First World War to the Burning of the First Goetheanum
CW 253 The Problems of Living Together in the Anthroposophical Society. On the Dornach Crisis of 1915. With Highlights on Swedenborg's Clairvoyance, the Views of Freudian Psychoanalysts, and the Concept of Love in Relation to Mysticism
CW 254 The Occult Movement in the 19th Century and Its Relationship to World Culture. Significant Points from the Exoteric Cultural Life around the Middle of the 19th Century
CW 255 Rudolf Steiner during the First World War
CW 255a Anthroposophy and the Reformation of Society. On the History of the Threefold Movement
CW 255b Anthroposophy and Its Opponents, 1919–1921
CW 256 How Can the Anthroposophical Movement Be Financed?
CW 256a Futurum, Inc. / International Laboratories, Inc.
CW 256b The Coming Day, Inc.
CW 257 Anthroposophical Community-Building
CW 258 The History of and Conditions for the Anthroposophical Movement in Relationship to the Anthroposophical Society. A Stimulus to Self-Contemplation
CW 259 The Year of Destiny 1923 in the History of the Anthroposophical Society. From the Burning of the Goetheanum to the Christmas Conference
CW 260 The Christmas Conference for the Founding of the General Anthroposophical Society

CW 278	Eurythmy as Visible Song
CW 279	Eurythmy as Visible Speech
CW 280	The Method and Nature of Speech Formation
CW 281	The Art of Recitation and Declamation
CW 282	Speech Formation and Dramatic Art
CW 283	The Nature of Things Musical and the Experience of Tone in the Human Being
CW 284/285	Images of Occult Seals and Pillars. The Munich Congress of Whitsun 1907 and Its Consequences
CW 286	Paths to a New Style of Architecture. 'And the Building Becomes Human'
CW 287	The Building at Dornach as a Symbol of Historical Becoming and an Artistic Transformation Impulse
CW 288	Style-Forms in the Living Organic
CW 289	The Building-Idea of the Goetheanum: Lectures with Slides from the Years 1920–1921
CW 290	The Building-Idea of the Goetheanum: Lectures with Slides from the Years 1920–1921
CW 291	The Nature of Colours
CW 291a	Knowledge of Colours. Supplementary Volume to 'The Nature of Colours'
CW 292	Art History as Image of Inner Spiritual Impulses
CW 293	General Knowledge of the Human Being as the Foundation of Pedagogy
CW 294	The Art of Education, Methodology and Didactics
CW 295	The Art of Education: Seminar Discussions and Lectures on Lesson Planning
CW 296	The Question of Education as a Social Question
CW 297	The Idea and Practice of the Waldorf School
CW 297a	Education for Life: Self-Education and the Practice of Pedagogy
CW 298	Rudolf Steiner in the Waldorf School
CW 299	Spiritual-Scientific Observations on Speech
CW 300a	Conferences with the Teachers of the Free Waldorf School in Stuttgart, 1919 to 1924, in 3 Volumes, Vol. 1
CW 300b	Conferences with the Teachers of the Free Waldorf School in Stuttgart, 1919 to 1924, in 3 Volumes, Vol. 2
CW 300c	Conferences with the Teachers of the Free Waldorf School in Stuttgart, 1919 to 1924, in 3 Volumes, Vol. 3
CW 301	The Renewal of Pedagogical-Didactical Art through Spiritual Science
CW 302	Knowledge of the Human Being and the Forming of Class Lessons
CW 302a	Education and Teaching from a Knowledge of the Human Being
CW 303	The Healthy Development of the Human Being
CW 304	Methods of Education and Teaching Based on Anthroposophy
CW 304a	Anthroposophical Knowledge of the Human Being and Pedagogy

CW 305 The Soul-Spiritual Foundational Forces of the Art of Education. Spiritual Values in Education and Social Life
CW 306 Pedagogical Praxis from the Viewpoint of a Spiritual-Scientific Knowledge of the Human Being. The Education of the Child and Young Human Beings
CW 307 The Spiritual Life of the Present and Education
CW 308 The Method of Teaching and the Life-Requirements for Teaching
CW 309 Anthroposophical Pedagogy and Its Prerequisites
CW 310 The Pedagogical Value of a Knowledge of the Human Being and the Cultural Value of Pedagogy
CW 311 The Art of Education from an Understanding of the Being of Humanity
CW 312 Spiritual Science and Medicine
CW 313 Spiritual-Scientific Viewpoints on Therapy
CW 314 Physiology and Therapy Based on Spiritual Science
CW 315 Curative Eurythmy
CW 316 Meditative Observations and Instructions for a Deepening of the Art of Healing
CW 317 The Curative Education Course
CW 318 The Working Together of Doctors and Pastors
CW 319 Anthroposophical Knowledge of the Human Being and Medicine
CW 320 Spiritual-Scientific Impulses for the Development of Physics 1: The First Natural-Scientific Course: Light, Colour, Tone, Mass, Electricity, Magnetism
CW 321 Spiritual-Scientific Impulses for the Development of Physics 2: The Second Natural-Scientific Course: Warmth at the Border of Positive and Negative Materiality
CW 322 The Borders of the Knowledge of Nature
CW 323 The Relationship of the various Natural-Scientific Fields to Astronomy
CW 324 Nature Observation, Mathematics, and Scientific Experimentation and Results from the Viewpoint of Anthroposophy
CW 324a The Fourth Dimension in Mathematics and Reality
CW 325 Natural Science and the World-Historical Development of Humanity since Ancient Times
CW 326 The Moment of the Coming Into Being of Natural Science in World History and Its Development Since Then
CW 327 Spiritual-Scientific Foundations for Success in Farming. The Agricultural Course
CW 328 The Social Question
CW 329 The Liberation of the Human Being as the Foundation for a New Social Form
CW 330 The Renewal of the Social Organism
CW 331 Work-Council and Socialization
CW 332 The Alliance for Threefolding and the Total Reform of Society. The Council on Culture and the Liberation of the Spiritual Life

CW 332a The Social Future
CW 333 Freedom of Thought and Social Forces
CW 334 From the Unified State to the Threefold Social Organism
CW 335 The Crisis of the Present and the Path to Healthy Thinking
CW 336 The Great Questions of the Times and Anthroposophical Spiritual Knowledge
CW 337a Social Ideas, Social Reality, Social Practice, Vol. 1: Question-and-Answer Evenings and Study Evenings of the Alliance for the Threefold Social Organism in Stuttgart, 1919-1920
CW 337b Social Ideas, Social Realities, Social Practice, Vol. 2: Discussion Evenings of the Swiss Alliance for the Threefold Social Organism
CW 338 How Does One Work on Behalf of the Impulse for the Threefold Social Organism?
CW 339 Anthroposophy, Threefold Social Organism, and the Art of Public Speaking
CW 340 The National-Economics Course. The Tasks of a New Science of Economics, Volume 1
CW 341 The National-Economics Seminar. The Tasks of a New Science of Economics, Volume 2
CW 342 Lectures and Courses on Christian Religious Work, Vol. 1: Anthroposophical Foundations for a Renewed Christian Religious Working
CW 343 Lectures and Courses on Christian Religious Work, Vol. 2: Spiritual Knowledge—Religious Feeling—Cultic Doing
CW 344 Lectures and Courses on Christian Religious Work, Vol. 3: Lectures at the Founding of the Christian Community
CW 345 Lectures and Courses on Christian Religious Work, Vol. 4: Concerning the Nature of the Working Word
CW 346 Lectures and Courses on Christian Religious Work, Vol. 5: The Apocalypse and the Work of the Priest
CW 347 The Knowledge of the Nature of the Human Being According to Body, Soul and Spirit. On Earlier Conditions of the Earth
CW 348 On Health and Illness. Foundations of a Spiritual-Scientific Doctrine of the Senses
CW 349 On the Life of the Human Being and of the Earth. On the Nature of Christianity
CW 350 Rhythms in the Cosmos and in the Human Being. How Does One Come To See the Spiritual World?
CW 351 The Human Being and the World. The Influence of the Spirit in Nature. On the Nature of Bees
CW 352 Nature and the Human Being Observed Spiritual-Scientifically
CW 353 The History of Humanity and the World-Views of the Folk Cultures
CW 354 The Creation of the World and the Human Being. Life on Earth and the Influence of the Stars

SIGNIFICANT EVENTS IN THE LIFE OF RUDOLF STEINER

1829: June 23: birth of Johann Steiner (1829–1910)—Rudolf Steiner's father—in Geras, Lower Austria.

1834: May 8: birth of Franciska Blie (1834–1918)—Rudolf Steiner's mother—in Horn, Lower Austria. 'My father and mother were both children of the glorious Lower Austrian forest district north of the Danube.'

1860: May 16: marriage of Johann Steiner and Franciska Blie.

1861: February 25: birth of *Rudolf Joseph Lorenz Steiner* in Kraljevec, Croatia, near the border with Hungary, where Johann Steiner works as a telegrapher for the South Austria Railroad. Rudolf Steiner is baptized two days later, February 27, the date usually given as his birthday.

1862: Summer: the family moves to Modling, Lower Austria.

1863: The family moves to Pottschach, Lower Austria, near the Styrian border, where Johann Steiner becomes station master. 'The view stretched to the mountains . . . majestic peaks in the distance and the sweet charm of nature in the immediate surroundings.'

1864: November 15: birth of Rudolf Steiner's sister, Leopoldine (d. November 1, 1927). She will become a seamstress and live with her parents for the rest of her life.

1866: July 28: birth of Rudolf Steiner's deaf-mute brother, Gustav (d. May 1, 1941).

1867: Rudolf Steiner enters the village school. Following a disagreement between his father and the schoolmaster, whose wife falsely accused the boy of causing a commotion, Rudolf Steiner is taken out of school and taught at home.

1868: A critical experience. Unknown to the family, an aunt dies in a distant town. Sitting in the station waiting room, Rudolf Steiner sees her 'form', which speaks to him, asking for help. 'Beginning with this experience, a new soul life began in the boy, one in which not only the outer trees and mountains spoke to him, but also the worlds that lay behind them. From this moment on, the boy began to live with the spirits of nature . . .'

1869: The family moves to the peaceful, rural village of Neudörfl, near Wiener Neustadt in present-day Austria. Rudolf Steiner attends the village school. Because of the 'unorthodoxy' of his writing and spelling, he has to do 'extra lessons'.

1870: Through a book lent to him by his tutor, he discovers geometry: 'To grasp something purely in the spirit brought me inner happiness. I know that I first learned happiness through geometry.' The same tutor allows him to draw, while other students still struggle with their reading and writing. 'An artistic element' thus enters his education.

1871: Though his parents are not religious, Rudolf Steiner becomes a 'church child', a favourite of the priest, who was 'an exceptional character'. 'Up to the age of ten or eleven, among those I came to know, he was far and away the most significant.' Among other things, he introduces Steiner to Copernican, heliocentric cosmology. As an altar boy, Rudolf Steiner serves at masses, funerals, and Corpus Christi processions. At year's end, after an incident in which he escapes a thrashing, his father forbids him to go to church.

1872: Rudolf Steiner transfers to grammar school in Wiener-Neustadt, a five-mile walk from home, which must be done in all weathers.

1873–75: Through his teachers and on his own, Rudolf Steiner has many wonderful experiences with science and mathematics. Outside school, he teaches himself analytic geometry, trigonometry, differential equations, and calculus.

1876: Rudolf Steiner begins tutoring other students. He learns bookbinding from his father. He also teaches himself stenography.

1877: Rudolf Steiner discovers Kant's *Critique of Pure Reason,* which he reads and rereads. He also discovers and reads von Rotteck's *World History.*

1878: He studies extensively in contemporary psychology and philosophy.

1879: Rudolf Steiner graduates from high school with honours. His father is transferred to Inzersdorf, near Vienna. He uses his first visit to Vienna 'to purchase a great number of philosophy books'—Kant, Fichte, Schelling, and Hegel, as well as numerous histories of philosophy. His aim: to find a path from the 'I' to nature.

October 1879–1883: Rudolf Steiner attends the Technical College in Vienna—to study mathematics, chemistry, physics, mineralogy, botany, zoology, biology, geology, and mechanics—with a scholarship. He also attends lectures in history and literature, while avidly reading philosophy on his own. His two favourite professors are Karl Julius Schröer (German language and literature) and Edmund Reitlinger (physics). He also audits lectures by Robert Zimmermann on aesthetics and Franz Brentano on philosophy. During this year he begins his friendship with Moritz Zitter (1861–1921), who will help support him financially when he is in Berlin.

1880: Rudolf Steiner attends lectures on Schiller and Goethe by Karl Julius Schröer, who becomes his mentor. Also 'through a remarkable combination of circumstances', he meets Felix Koguzki, a 'herb gatherer' and healer, who could 'see deeply into the secrets of nature'. Rudolf Steiner will meet and study with this 'emissary of the Master' throughout his time in Vienna.

1881: January: '... I didn't sleep a wink. I was busy with philosophical problems until about 12:30 a.m. Then, finally, I threw myself down on my couch. All my striving during the previous year had been to research whether the following statement by Schelling was true or not: *Within everyone dwells a secret, marvellous capacity to draw back from the stream of time—out of the self clothed in all that comes to us from outside—into our innermost being and there, in the immutable form of the Eternal, to look into ourselves.* I believe, and I am still quite certain of it, that I discovered this capacity in myself; I had long had an inkling of it. Now the whole of idealist philosophy stood before me in modified form. What's a sleepless night compared to that!'

Rudolf Steiner begins communicating with leading thinkers of the day, who send him books in return, which he reads eagerly.

July: 'I am not one of those who dives into the day like an animal in human form. I pursue a quite specific goal, an idealistic aim—knowledge of the truth! This cannot be done offhandedly. It requires the greatest striving in the world, free of all egotism, and equally of all resignation.'

August: Steiner puts down on paper for the first time thoughts for a 'Philosophy of Freedom'. 'The striving for the absolute: this human yearning is freedom'. He also seeks to outline a 'peasant philosophy,' describing what the worldview of a 'peasant'—one who lives close to the earth and the old ways—really is.

1881–1882: Felix Koguzki, the herb gatherer, reveals himself to be the envoy of another, higher initiatory personality, who instructs Rudolf Steiner to penetrate Fichte's philosophy and to master modern scientific thinking as a preparation for right entry into the spirit. This 'Master' also teaches him the double (evolutionary and involutionary) nature of time.

1882: Through the offices of Karl Julius Schröer, Rudolf Steiner is asked by Joseph Kürschner to edit Goethe's scientific works for the *Deutschen National-Literatur* edition. He writes 'A Possible Critique of Atomistic Concepts' and sends it to Friedrich Theodor Vischer.

1883: Rudolf Steiner completes his college studies and begins work on the Goethe project.

1884: First volume of Goethe's *Scientific Writings* (CW 1) appears (March). He lectures on Goethe and Lessing, and Goethe's approach to science. In July, he enters the household of Ladislaus and Pauline Specht as tutor to the four Specht boys. He will live there until 1890. At this time, he meets Josef Breuer (1842–1925), the co-author with Sigmund Freud of *Studies in Hysteria,* who is the Specht family doctor.

1885: While continuing to edit Goethe's writings, Rudolf Steiner reads deeply in contemporary philosophy (Eduard von Hartmann, Johannes Volkelt, and Richard Wahle, among others).

1886: May: Rudolf Steiner sends Kürschner the manuscript of *Outlines of Goethe's Theory of Knowledge* (CW 2), which appears in October, and which he sends out widely. He also meets the poet Marie Eugenie Delle Grazie and writes 'Nature and Our Ideals' for her. He attends her salon, where he meets many priests, theologians, and philosophers, who will become his friends. Meanwhile, the director of the Goethe Archive in Weimar requests his collaboration with the *Sophien* edition of Goethe's works, particularly the writings on colour.

1887: At the beginning of the year, Rudolf Steiner is very sick. As the year progresses and his health improves, he becomes increasingly 'a man of letters', lecturing, writing essays, and taking part in Austrian cultural life. In August–September, the second volume of Goethe's *Scientific Writings* appears.

1888: January–July: Rudolf Steiner assumes editorship of the 'German Weekly' *(Deutsche Wochenschrift*). He begins lecturing more intensively, giving, for example, a lecture titled 'Goethe as Father of a New Aesthetics'. He meets and becomes soul friends with Friedrich Eckstein (1861–1939), a vegetarian, philosopher of symbolism, alchemist, and musician, who will introduce him to various spiritual currents (including Theosophy) and with whom he will meditate and interpret esoteric and alchemical texts.

1889: Rudolf Steiner first reads Nietzsche *(Beyond Good and Evil).* He encounters Theosophy again and learns of Madame Blavatsky in the theosophical circle around Marie Lang (1858–1934). Here he also meets well-known figures of Austrian life, as well as esoteric figures like the occultist Franz Hartmann and Karl Leinigen-Billigen (translator of C.G. Harrison's *The Transcendental Universe).* During this period, Steiner first reads A.P. Sinnett's *Esoteric Buddhism* and Mabel Collins's *Light on the Path.* He also begins travelling, visiting Budapest, Weimar, and Berlin (where he meets philosopher Eduard von Hartmann).

1890: Rudolf Steiner finishes Volume 3 of Goethe's scientific writings. He begins his doctoral dissertation, which will become *Truth and Science* (CW 3). He also meets the poet and feminist Rosa Mayreder (1858–1938), with whom he can exchange his most intimate thoughts. In September, Rudolf Steiner moves to Weimar to work in the Goethe-Schiller Archive.

1891: Volume 3 of the Kürschner edition of Goethe appears. Meanwhile, Rudolf Steiner edits Goethe's studies in mineralogy and scientific writings for the *Sophien* edition. He meets Ludwig Laistner of the Cotta Publishing Company, who asks for a book on the basic question of metaphysics. From this will result, ultimately, *The Philosophy of Freedom* (CW 4), which will be published not by Cotta but by Emil Felber. In October, Rudolf Steiner takes the oral exam for a doctorate in philosophy, mathematics, and mechanics at Rostock University, receiving his doctorate on the twenty-sixth. In November, he gives his first lecture on Goethe's 'Fairy Tale' in Vienna.

1892: Rudolf Steiner continues work at the Goethe-Schiller Archive and on his *Philosophy of Freedom. Truth and Science,* his doctoral dissertation, is published. Steiner undertakes to write Introductions to books on Schopenhauer and Jean Paul for Cotta. At year's end, he finds lodging with Anna Eunike, née Schulz (1853–1911), a widow with four daughters and a son. He also develops a friendship with Otto Erich Hartleben (1864–1905) with whom he shares literary interests.

1893: Rudolf Steiner begins his habit of producing many reviews and articles. In March, he gives a lecture titled 'Hypnotism, with Reference to Spiritism'. In September, Volume 4 of the Kürschner edition is completed. In November, *The Philosophy of Freedom* appears. This year, too, he meets John Henry Mackay (1864–1933), the anarchist, and Max Stirner, a scholar and biographer.

1894: Rudolf Steiner meets Elisabeth Fürster Nietzsche, the philosopher's sister, and begins to read Nietzsche in earnest, beginning with the as yet unpublished *Antichrist.* He also meets Ernst Haeckel (1834–1919). In the fall, he begins to write *Nietzsche, A Fighter against His Time* (CW 5).

1895: May, *Nietzsche, A Fighter against His Time* appears.

1896: January 22: Rudolf Steiner sees Friedrich Nietzsche for the first and only time. Moves between the Nietzsche and the Goethe-Schiller

Archives, where he completes his work before year's end. He falls out with Elisabeth Förster Nietzsche, thus ending his association with the Nietzsche Archive.

1897: Rudolf Steiner finishes the manuscript of *Goethe's Worldview* (CW 6). He moves to Berlin with Anna Eunike and begins editorship of the *Magazin für Literatur.* From now on, Steiner will write countless reviews, literary and philosophical articles, and so on. He begins lecturing at the 'Free Literary Society'. In September, he attends the Zionist Congress in Basel. He sides with Dreyfus in the Dreyfus affair.

1898: Rudolf Steiner is very active as an editor in the political, artistic, and theatrical life of Berlin. He becomes friendly with John Henry Mackay and poet Ludwig Jacobowski (1868–1900). He joins Jacobowski's circle of writers, artists, and scientists—'The Coming Ones' (*Die Kommenden)*—and contributes lectures to the group until 1903. He also lectures at the 'League for College Pedagogy'. He writes an article for Goethe's sesquicentennial, 'Goethe's Secret Revelation', on the 'Fairy Tale of the Green Snake and the Beautiful Lily'.

1898–99: 'This was a trying time for my soul as I looked at Christianity. . . . I was able to progress only by contemplating, by means of spiritual perception, the evolution of Christianity. . . Conscious knowledge of real Christianity began to dawn in me around the turn of the century. This seed continued to develop. My soul trial occurred shortly before the beginning of the twentieth century. It was decisive for my soul's development that I stood spiritually before the Mystery of Golgotha in a deep and solemn celebration of knowledge.'

1899: Rudolf Steiner begins teaching and giving lectures and lecture cycles at the Workers' College, founded by Wilhelm Liebknecht (1826–1900). He will continue to do so until 1904. Writes: *Literature and Spiritual Life in the Nineteenth Century; Individualism in Philosophy; Haeckel and His Opponents; Poetry in the Present;* and begins what will become (fifteen years later) *The Riddles of Philosophy* (CW 18). He also meets many artists and writers, including Kothe Kollwitz, Stefan Zweig, and Rainer Maria Rilke. On October 31, he marries Anna Eunike.

1900: 'I thought that the turn of the century must bring humanity a new light. It seemed to me that the separation of human thinking and willing from the spirit had peaked. A turn or reversal of direction in human evolution seemed to me a necessity.' Rudolf Steiner finishes *World and Life Views in the Nineteenth Century* (the second part of what will become *The Riddles of Philosophy)* and dedicates it to

Ernst Haeckel. It is published in March. He continues lecturing at *Die Kommenden,* whose leadership he assumes after the death of Jacobowski. Also, he gives the Gutenberg Jubilee lecture before 7,000 typesetters and printers. In September, Rudolf Steiner is invited by Count and Countess Brockdorff to lecture in the Theosophical Library. His first lecture is on Nietzsche. His second lecture is titled 'Goethe's Secret Revelation'. October 6, he begins a lecture cycle on the mystics that will become *Mystics after Modernism* (CW 7). November–December: 'Marie von Sivers appears in the audience. . . .' Also in November, Steiner gives his first lecture at the Giordano Bruno Bund (where he will continue to lecture until May, 1905). He speaks on Bruno and modern Rome, focusing on the importance of the philosophy of Thomas Aquinas as monism.

1901: In continual financial straits, Rudolf Steiner's early friends Moritz Zitter and Rosa Mayreder help support him. In October, he begins the lecture cycle *Christianity as Mystical Fact* (CW 8) at the Theosophical Library. In November, he gives his first 'theosophical lecture' on Goethe's 'Fairy Tale' in Hamburg at the invitation of Wilhelm Hubbe-Schleiden. He also attends a gathering to celebrate the founding of the Theosophical Society at Count and Countess Brockdorff's. He gives a lecture cycle, 'From Buddha to Christ', for the circle of the *Kommenden.* November 17, Marie von Sivers asks Rudolf Steiner if Theosophy needs a Western–Christian spiritual movement (to complement Theosophy's Eastern emphasis). 'The question was posed. Now, following spiritual laws, I could begin to give an answer. . . .' In December, Rudolf Steiner writes his first article for a theosophical publication. At year's end, the Brockdorffs and possibly Wilhelm Hubbe-Schleiden ask Rudolf Steiner to join the Theosophical Society and undertake the leadership of the German section. Rudolf Steiner agrees, on the condition that Marie von Sivers (then in Italy) work with him.

1902: Beginning in January, Rudolf Steiner attends the opening of the Workers' School in Spandau with Rosa Luxemberg (1870–1919). January 17, Rudolf Steiner joins the Theosophical Society. In April, he is asked to become general secretary of the German Section of the theosophical Society, and works on preparations for its founding. In July, he visits London for a theosophical congress. He meets Bertram Keightly, G.R.S. Mead, A.P. Sinnett, and Annie Besant, among others. In September, *Christianity as Mystical Fact* appears. In October, Rudolf Steiner gives his first public lecture on Theosophy ('Monism and Theosophy') to about three hundred people at the Giordano Bruno Bund. On October 19–21, the

German Section of the Theosophical Society has its first meeting; Rudolf Steiner is the general secretary, and Annie Besant attends. Steiner lectures on practical karma studies. On October 23, Annie Besant inducts Rudolf Steiner into the Esoteric School of the Theosophical Society. On October 25, Steiner begins a weekly series of lectures: 'The Field of Theosophy'. During this year, Rudolf Steiner also first meets Ita Wegman (1876–1943), who will become his close collaborator in his final years.

1903: Rudolf Steiner holds about 300 lectures and seminars. In May, the first issue of the periodical *Luzifer* appears. In June, Rudolf Steiner visits London for the first meeting of the Federation of the European Sections of the Theosophical Society, where he meets Colonel Olcott. He begins to write *Theosophy* (CW 9).

1904: Rudolf Steiner continues lecturing at the Workers' College and elsewhere (about 90 lectures), while lecturing intensively all over Germany among theosophists (about 140 lectures). In February, he meets Carl Unger (1878–1929), who will become a member of the board of the Anthroposophical Society (1913). In March, he meets Michael Bauer (1871–1929), a Christian mystic, who will also be on the board. In May, *Theosophy* appears, with the dedication: 'To the spirit of Giordano Bruno'. Rudolf Steiner and Marie von Sivers visit London for meetings with Annie Besant. June: Rudolf Steiner and Marie von Sivers attend the meeting of the Federation of European Sections of the Theosophical Society in Amsterdam. In July, Steiner begins the articles in *Luzifer-Gnosis* that will become *How to Know Higher Worlds* (CW 10) and *Cosmic Memory* (CW 11). In September, Annie Besant visits Germany. In December, Steiner lectures on Freemasonry. He mentions the High Grade Masonry derived from John Yarker and represented by Theodore Reuss and Karl Kellner as a blank slate 'into which a good image could be placed'.

1905: This year, Steiner ends his non-theosophical lecturing activity. Supported by Marie von Sivers, his theosophical lecturing—both in public and in the Theosophical Society—increases significantly: 'The German Theosophical Movement is of exceptional importance.' Steiner recommends reading, among others, Fichte, Jacob Boehme, and Angelus Silesius. He begins to introduce Christian themes into Theosophy. He also begins to work with doctors (Felix Peipers and Ludwig Noll). In July, he is in London for the Federation of European Sections, where he attends a lecture by Annie Besant: 'I have seldom seen Mrs. Besant speak in so inward and heartfelt a manner... Through Mrs. Besant I have found the way to H.P. Blavatsky.' September to October, he gives a course of 31 lectures for a small group of esoteric students. In October, the annual meeting of the German Section of the Theosophical Society, which still remains very small, takes place. Rudolf Steiner reports membership has risen from 121 to 377 members. In November, seeking to establish esoteric 'continuity', Rudolf Steiner and Marie von Sivers participate in a 'Memphis-Misraim' Masonic ceremony. They pay 45 marks for membership. 'Yesterday, you saw how little remains of former esoteric institutions.' 'We are dealing only with a "framework" for the present, nothing lies behind it. The occult powers have completely withdrawn.'

1906: Expansion of theosophical work. Rudolf Steiner gives about 245 lectures, only 44 of which take place in Berlin. Cycles are given in Paris, Leipzig, Stuttgart, and Munich. Esoteric work also intensifies. Rudolf Steiner begins writing *An Outline of Esoteric Science* (CW 13). In January, Rudolf Steiner receives permission (a patent) from the Great Orient of the Scottish A & A Thirty-Three Degree Rite of the Order of the Ancient Freemasons of the Memphis-Misraim Rite to direct a chapter under the name 'Mystica Aeterna'. This will become the 'Cognitive-Ritual Section' (also called 'Misraim Service') of the Esoteric School. (See: *Freemasonry and Ritual Work: The Misraim Service,* CW 265.) During this time, Steiner also meets Albert Schweitzer. In May, he is in Paris, where he visits Édouard Schuré. Many Russians attend his lectures (including Konstantin Balmont, Dimitri Mereszkovski, Zinaida Hippius, and Maximilian Woloshin). He attends the General Meeting of the European Federation of the Theosophical Society, at which Col. Olcott is present for the last time. He spends the year's end in Venice and Rome, where he writes and works on his translation of H.P. Blavatsky's *Key to Theosophy.*

1907: Further expansion of the German Theosophical Movement according to the Rosicrucian directive to 'introduce spirit into the world'—in education, in social questions, in art, and in science. In February, Col. Olcott dies in Adyar. Before he dies, Olcott indicates that 'the Masters' wish Annie Besant to succeed him: much politicking ensues. Rudolf Steiner supports Besant's candidacy. April–May: preparations for the Congress of the Federation of European Sections of the Theosophical Society—the great, watershed Whitsun 'Munich Congress', attended by Annie Besant and others. Steiner decides to separate Eastern and Western (Christian–Rosicrucian) esoteric schools. He takes his esoteric school out of the Theosophical Society (Besant and Rudolf Steiner are 'in harmony' on this). Steiner makes his first lecture tours to Austria and Hungary. That summer, he is in Italy. In September, he visits Édouard Schuré, who will write the Introduction to the French edition of *Christianity as Mystical Fact* in Barr, Alsace. Rudolf Steiner writes the autobiographical statement known as the 'Barr Document'. In *Luzifer-Gnosis*, 'The Education of the Child' appears.

1908: The movement grows (membership: 1,150). Lecturing expands. Steiner makes his first extended lecture tour to Holland and Scandinavia, as well as visits to Naples and Sicily. Themes: St. John's Gospel, the Apocalypse, Egypt, science, philosophy, and logic. *Luzifer-Gnosis* ceases publication. In Berlin, Marie von Sivers (with Johanna Mücke (1864–1949) forms the *Philosophisch-Theosophisch* (after 1915 *Philosophisch-Anthroposophisch) Verlag* to publish Steiner's work. Steiner gives lecture cycles titled *The Gospel of St. John* (CW 103) and *The Apocalypse* (104).

1909: *An Outline of Esoteric Science* appears. Lecturing and travel continues. Rudolf Steiner's spiritual research expands to include the polarity of Lucifer and Ahriman; the work of great individualities in history; the Maitreya Buddha and the Bodhisattvas; spiritual economy (CW 109); the work of the spiritual hierarchies in heaven and on earth (CW 110). He also deepens and intensifies his research into the Gospels, giving lectures on the Gospel of St. Luke (CW 114) with the first mention of two Jesus children. Meets and becomes friends with Christian Morgenstern (1871–1914). In April, he lays the foundation stone for the Malsch model—the building that will lead to the first Goetheanum. In May, the International Congress of the Federation of European Sections of the Theosophical Society takes place in Budapest. Rudolf Steiner receives the Subba Row medal for *How to Know Higher Worlds*. During this time, Charles W. Leadbeater discovers Jiddu Krishnamurti (1895–1986) and proclaims him the future 'world teacher', the bearer of the Maitreya Buddha and the 'reappearing Christ.' In October, Steiner delivers seminal lectures on 'anthroposophy', which he will try, unsuccessfully, to rework over the next years into the unfinished work, *Anthroposophy (A Fragment)* (CW 45).

1910: New themes: *The Reappearance of Christ in the Etheric* (CW 118); *The Fifth Gospel; The Mission of Folk Souls* (CW 121); *Occult History* (CW 126); the evolving development of etheric cognitive capacities. Rudolf Steiner continues his Gospel research with *The Gospel of St. Matthew* (CW 123). In January, his father dies. In April, he takes a month-long trip to Italy, including Rome, Monte Cassino, and Sicily. He also visits Scandinavia again. July–August, he writes the first Mystery Drama, *The Portal of Initiation* (CW 14). In November, he gives 'psychosophy' lectures. In December, he submits 'On the

Psychological Foundations and Epistemological Framework of Theosophy' to the International Philosophical Congress in Bologna.

1911: The crisis in the Theosophical Society deepens. In January, 'The Order of the Rising Sun', which will soon become 'The Order of the Star in the East,' is founded for the coming world teacher, Krishnamurti. At the same time, Marie von Sivers, Rudolf Steiner's co-worker, falls ill. Fewer lectures are given, but important new ground is broken. In Prague, in March, Steiner meets Franz Kafka (1883–1924) and Hugo Bergmann (1883–1975). In April, he delivers his paper to the Philosophical Congress. He writes the second Mystery Drama, *The Soul's Probation* (CW 14). Also, while Marie von Sivers is convalescing, Rudolf Steiner begins work on *Calendar 1912/1913*, which will contain the 'Calendar of the Soul' meditations. On March 19, Anna (Eunike) Steiner dies. In September, Rudolf Steiner visits Einsiedeln, birthplace of Paracelsus. In December, Friedrich Rittelmeyer, future founder of the Christian Community, meets Rudolf Steiner. The *Johannes-Bauverein,* the 'building committee', which would lead to the first Goetheanum (first planned for Munich), is also founded, and a preliminary committee for the founding of an independent association is created that, in the following year, will become the Anthroposophical Society. Important lecture cycles include *Occult Physiology* (CW 128); *Wonders of the World* (CW 129); *From Jesus to Christ* (CW 131). Other themes: esoteric Christianity; Christian Rosenkreutz; the spiritual guidance of humanity; the sense world and the world of the spirit.

1912: Despite the ongoing, now increasing crisis in the Theosophical Society, much is accomplished: *Calendar 1912/1913* is published; eurythmy is created; both the third Mystery Drama, *The Guardian of the Threshold* (CW 14) and *A Way of Self-Knowledge* (CW 16) are written. New (or renewed) themes included life between death and rebirth and karma and reincarnation. Other lecture cycles: *Spiritual Beings in the Heavenly Bodies and in the Kingdoms of Nature* (CW 136); *The Human Being in the Light of Occultism, Theosophy, and Philosophy* (CW 137); *The Gospel of St. Mark* (CW 139); and *The Bhagavad Gita and the Epistles of Paul* (CW 142). On May 8, Rudolf Steiner celebrates White Lotus Day, H.P. Blavatsky's death day, which he had faithfully observed for the past decade, for the last time. In August, Rudolf Steiner suggests the 'independent association' be called the 'Anthroposophical Society'. In September, the first eurythmy course takes place. In October, Rudolf Steiner declines recognition of a Theosophical Society Lodge dedicated to the Star of the East and decides to expel all Theosophical Society members belonging to the Order.

Also, with Marie von Sivers, he first visits Dornach, near Basel, Switzerland, and they stand on the hill where the Goetheanum will be built. In November, a Theosophical Society Lodge is opened by direct mandate from Adyar (Annie Besant). In December, a meeting of the German section occurs at which it is decided that belonging to the Order of the Star of the East is incompatible with membership in the Theosophical Society. December 28: informal founding of the Anthroposophical Society in Berlin.

1913: Expulsion of the German section from the Theosophical Society. February 2–3: Foundation meeting of the Anthroposophical Society. Board members include: Marie von Sivers, Michael Bauer, and Carl Unger. September 20: Laying of the foundation stone for the *Johannes Bau* (Goetheanum) in Dornach. Building begins immediately. The third Mystery Drama, *The Soul's Awakening* (CW 14), is completed. Also: *The Threshold of the Spiritual World* (CW 147). Lecture cycles include: *The Bhagavad Gita and the Epistles of Paul* and *The Esoteric Meaning of the Bhagavad Gita* (CW 146), which the Russian philosopher Nikolai Berdyaev attends; *The Mysteries of the East and of Christianity* (CW 144); *The Effects of Esoteric Development* (CW 145); and *The Fifth Gospel* (CW 148). In May, Rudolf Steiner is in London and Paris, where anthroposophical work continues.

1914: Building continues on the *Johannes Bau* (Goetheanum) in Dornach, with artists and co-workers from 17 nations. The general assembly of the Anthroposophical Society takes place. In May, Rudolf Steiner visits Paris, as well as Chartres Cathedral. June 28: assassination in Sarajevo ('Now the catastrophe has happened!'). August 1: War is declared. Rudolf Steiner returns to Germany from Dornach—he will travel back and forth. He writes the last chapter of *The Riddles of Philosophy*. Lecture cycles include: *Human and Cosmic Thought* (CW 151); *Inner Being of Humanity between Death and a New Birth* (CW 153); *Occult Reading and Occult Hearing* (CW 156). December 24: marriage of Rudolf Steiner and Marie von Sivers.

1915: Building continues. Life after death becomes a major theme, also art. Writes: *Thoughts during a Time of War* (CW 24). Lectures include: *The Secret of Death* (CW 159); *The Uniting of Humanity through the Christ Impulse* (CW 165).

1916: Rudolf Steiner begins work with Edith Maryon (1872–1924) on the sculpture 'The Representative of Humanity' ('The Group'—Christ, Lucifer, and Ahriman). He also works with the alchemist Alexander von Bernus on the quarterly *Das Reich*. He writes *The Riddle of Humanity* (CW 20). Lectures include: *Necessity and Freedom in World History and Human Action* (CW 166); *Past and Present in the*

Human Spirit (CW 167); *The Karma of Vocation* (CW 172); *The Karma of Untruthfulness* (CW 173).

1917: Russian Revolution. The U.S. enters the war. Building continues. Rudolf Steiner delineates the idea of the 'threefold nature of the human being' (in a public lecture March 15) and the 'threefold nature of the social organism' (hammered out in May–June with the help of Otto von Lerchenfeld and Ludwig Polzer-Hoditz in the form of two documents titled *Memoranda,* which were distributed in high places). August–September: Rudolf Steiner writes *The Riddles of the Soul* (CW 20). Also: commentary on 'The Chymical Wedding of Christian Rosenkreutz' for Alexander Bernus (*Das Reich*). Lectures include: *The Karma of Materialism* (CW 176); *The Spiritual Background of the Outer World: The Fall of the Spirits of Darkness* (CW 177).

1918: March 18: peace treaty of Brest-Litovsk—'Now everything will truly enter chaos! What is needed is cultural renewal.' June: Rudolf Steiner visits Karlstein (Grail) Castle outside Prague. Lecture cycle: *From Symptom to Reality in Modern History* (CW 185). In mid-November, Emil Molt, of the Waldorf-Astoria Cigarette Company, has the idea of founding a school for his workers' children.

1919: Focus on the threefold social organism: tireless travel, countless lectures, meetings, and publications. At the same time, a new public stage of Anthroposophy emerges as cultural renewal begins. The coming years will see initiatives in pedagogy, medicine, pharmacology, and agriculture. January 27: threefold meeting: 'We must first of all, with the money we have, found free schools that can bring people what they need.' February: first public eurythmy performance in Zurich. Also: 'Appeal to the German People' (CW 24), circulated March 6 as a newspaper insert. In April, *Towards Social Renewal* (CW 23) appears—'perhaps the most widely read of all books on politics appearing since the war'. Rudolf Steiner is asked to undertake the 'direction and leadership' of the school founded by the Waldorf-Astoria Company. Rudolf Steiner begins to talk about the 'renewal' of education. May 30: a building is selected and purchased for the future Waldorf School. August–September, Rudolf Steiner gives a lecture course for Waldorf teachers, *The Foundations of Human Experience (Study of Man)* (CW 293). September 7: Opening of the first Waldorf School. December (into January): first science course, the *Light Course* (CW 320).

1920: The Waldorf School flourishes. New threefold initiatives. Founding of limited companies *Der Kommende Tag* and *Futurum A.G.* to infuse spiritual values into the economic realm. Rudolf Steiner also focuses on the sciences. Lectures: *Introducing Anthroposophical*

Medicine (CW 312); *The Warmth Course* (CW 321); *The Boundaries of Natural Science* (CW 322); *The Redemption of Thinking* (CW 74). February: Johannes Werner Klein—later a co-founder of the Christian Community—asks Rudolf Steiner about the possibility of a 'religious renewal', a 'Johannine church'. In March, Rudolf Steiner gives the first course for doctors and medical students. In April, a divinity student asks Rudolf Steiner a second time about the possibility of religious renewal. September 27–October 16: anthroposophical 'university course'. December: lectures titled *The Search for the New Isis* (CW 202).

1921: Rudolf Steiner continues his intensive work on cultural renewal, including the uphill battle for the threefold social order. 'University' arts, scientific, theological, and medical courses include: *The Astronomy Course* (CW 323); *Observation, Mathematics, and Scientific Experiment* (CW 324); the *Second Medical Course* (CW 313); *Colour*. In June and September–October, Rudolf Steiner also gives the first two 'priests' courses' (CW 342 and 343). The 'youth movement' gains momentum. Magazines are founded: *Die Drei* (January), and—under the editorship of Albert Steffen (1884–1963)—the weekly, *Das Goetheanum* (August). In February–March, Rudolf Steiner takes his first trip outside Germany since the war (Holland). On April 7, Steiner receives a letter regarding 'religious renewal', and May 22–23, he agrees to address the question in a practical way. In June, the Klinical-Therapeutic Institute opens in Arlesheim under the direction of Dr. Ita Wegman. In August, the Chemical-Pharmaceutical Laboratory opens in Arlesheim (Oskar Schmiedel and Ita Wegman are directors). The Clinical Therapeutic Institute is inaugurated in Stuttgart (Dr. Ludwig Noll is director); also the Research Laboratory in Dornach (Ehrenfried Pfeiffer and Gunther Wachsmuth are directors). In November–December, Rudolf Steiner visits Norway.

1922: The first half of the year involves very active public lecturing (thousands attend); in the second half, Rudolf Steiner begins to withdraw and turn toward the Society—'The Society is asleep.' It is 'too weak' to do what is asked of it. The businesses—*Der Kommende Tag* and *Futurum A.G.*—fail. In January, with the help of an agent, Steiner undertakes a twelve-city German lecture tour, accompanied by eurythmy performances. In two weeks he speaks to more than 2,000 people. In April, he gives a 'university course' in The Hague. He also visits England. In June, he is in Vienna for the East–West Congress. In August–September, he is back in England for the Oxford Conference on Education. Returning to Dornach, he gives the lectures *Philosophy, Cosmology, and Religion*

(CW 215), and gives the third priests' course (CW 344). On September 16, The Christian Community is founded. In October–November, Steiner is in Holland and England. He also speaks to the youth: *The Youth Course* (CW 217). In December, Steiner gives lectures titled *The Origins of Natural Science* (CW 326), and *Humanity and the World of Stars: The Spiritual Communion of Humanity* (CW 219). December 31: Fire at the Goetheanum, which is destroyed.

1923: Despite the fire, Rudolf Steiner continues his work unabated. A very hard year. Internal dispersion, dissension, and apathy abound. There is conflict—between old and new visions—within the Society. A wake-up call is needed, and Rudolf Steiner responds with renewed lecturing vitality. His focus: the spiritual context of human life; initiation science; the course of the year; and community building. As a foundation for an artistic school, he creates a series of pastel sketches. Lecture cycles: *The Anthroposophical Movement; Initiation Science* (CW 227) (in Wales at the Penmaenmawr Summer School); *The Four Seasons and the Archangels* (CW 229); *Harmony of the Creative Word* (CW 230); *The Supersensible Human* (CW 231), given in Holland for the founding of the Dutch society. On November 10, in response to the failed Hitler-Ludendorff putsch in Munich, Steiner closes his Berlin residence and moves the *Philosophisch-Anthroposophisch Verlag* (Press) to Dornach. On December 9, Steiner begins the serialization of his *Autobiography: The Course of My Life* (CW 28) in *Das Goetheanum*. It will continue to appear weekly, without a break, until his death. Late December–early January: Rudolf Steiner re-founds the Anthroposophical Society (about 12,000 members internationally) and takes over its leadership. The new board members are: Marie Steiner, Ita Wegman, Albert Steffen, Elisabeth Vreede, and Gunther Wachsmuth. (See *The Christmas Meeting for the Founding of the General Anthroposophical Society*, CW 260.) Accompanying lectures: *Mystery Knowledge and Mystery Centres* (CW 232); *World History in the Light of Anthroposophy* (CW 233). December 25: the Foundation Stone is laid (in the hearts of members) in the form of the 'Foundation Stone Meditation'.

1924: January 1: having founded the Anthroposophical Society and taken over its leadership, Rudolf Steiner has the task of 'reforming' it. The process begins with a weekly newssheet ('What's Happening in the Anthroposophical Society') in which Rudolf Steiner's 'Letters to Members' and 'Anthroposophical Leading Thoughts' appear (CW 26). The next step is the creation of a new esoteric class, the 'first class' of the 'University of Spiritual Science' (which was to have been followed, had Rudolf Steiner lived longer, by two more advanced classes). Then comes a new language for

Anthroposophy—practical, phenomenological, and direct; and Rudolf Steiner creates the model for the second Goetheanum. He begins the series of extensive 'karma' lectures (CW 235–40); and finally, responding to needs, he creates two new initiatives: biodynamic agriculture and curative education. After the middle of the year, rumours begin to circulate regarding Steiner's health. Lectures: January–February, *Anthroposophy* (CW 234); February: *Tone Eurythmy* (CW 278); June: *The Agriculture Course* (CW 327); June–July: *Speech Eurythmy* (CW 279); *Curative Education* (CW 317); August: (England, 'Second International Summer School'), *Initiation Consciousness: True and False Paths in Spiritual Investigation* (CW 243); September: *Pastoral Medicine* (CW 318). On September 26, for the first time, Rudolf Steiner cancels a lecture. On September 28, he gives his last lecture. On September 29, he withdraws to his studio in the carpenter's shop; now he is definitively ill. Cared for by Ita Wegman, he continues working, however, and writing the weekly installments of his *Autobiography* and *Letters to the Members/Leading Thoughts* (CW 26).

1925: Rudolf Steiner, while continuing to work, continues to weaken. He finishes *Extending Practical Medicine* (CW 27) with Ita Wegman. On March 30, around ten in the morning, Rudolf Steiner dies.

Index

Steiner

A NOTE FROM RUDOLF STEINER PRESS

We are an independent publisher and registered charity (non-profit organisation) dedicated to making available the work of Rudolf Steiner in English translation. We care a great deal about the content of our books and have hundreds of titles available – as printed books, ebooks and in audio formats.

As a publisher devoted to anthroposophy...

- We continually commission translations of previously unpublished works by Rudolf Steiner and invest in re-translating, editing and improving our editions.
- We are committed to making anthroposophy available to all by publishing introductory books as well as contemporary research.
- Our new print editions and ebooks are carefully checked and proofread for accuracy, and converted into all formats for all platforms.
- Our translations are officially authorised by Rudolf Steiner's estate in Dornach, Switzerland, to whom we pay royalties on sales, thus assisting their critical work.

So, look out for Rudolf Steiner Press as a mark of quality and support us today by buying our books, or contact us should you wish to sponsor specific titles or to support the charity with a gift or legacy.